THE SOVEREIGNTY OF JOY:
NIETZSCHE'S VISION OF GRAND POLITICS

ALEX McINTYRE

# The Sovereignty of Joy: Nietzsche's Vision of Grand Politics

UNIVERSITY OF TORONTO PRESS
Toronto Buffalo London

© University of Toronto Press Incorporated 1997
Toronto Buffalo London
Printed in Canada

ISBN 0-8020-4110-8

Printed on acid-free paper

Toronto Studies in Philosophy
Edited by James R. Brown and Calvin Normore

**Canadian Cataloguing in Publication Data**

McIntyre, Alex, 1950–
    The sovereignty of joy : Nietzsche's Vision of Grand Politics

(Toronto studies in philosophy)
Includes bibliographical references and index.
ISBN 0-8020-4110-8

    1. Nietzsche, Friedrich Wilhelm, 1844–1900 –
Contributions in political science.
2. Sovereignty.   3. Joy.   I. Title.   II. Series.

JC233.N52M24 1997      3209.092      C97-930847-X

University of Toronto Press acknowledges the financial assistance of the Canada
Council for the Arts and the Ontario Arts Council to its publishing program.

This book has been published with the help of a grant from the Humanities
and Social Sciences Federation of Canada, using funds provided by the Social
Sciences and Humanities Research Council of Canada

# Contents

For my parents

'What from your forebears you received as heir
Acquire, if you would  possess it!'

Goethe

# Acknowledgments

I would like to express my thanks to Jacques Chevalier who read an earlier version of the manuscript and offered many suggestions that helped me to revise and clarify the argument. I am especially grateful for the support and friendship that both he and his wife, Michelle Bourassa, have so generously offered me over the years. I am also deeply indebted to Laurence Lampert for his encouragement and critical support of my research into Nietzsche's vision of grand politics. And for her patience and encouragement, I owe a great debt of gratitude to Gemma Rose Brown-McIntyre.

It is a daunting task to write in the shadow of Nietzsche, but the support of the editors of the University of Toronto Press has made this much easier. Editor-in-Chief Ron Schoeffel was a constant source of enthusiasm. Linda Biesenthal and Anne Forte offered many editorial suggestions that significantly improved the clarity and flow of the text. I'm especially grateful for A. Lynne's imagination and insight.

The community of these friends and colleagues has made it much easier to understand and elaborate the sense of Dionysian joy as genuine communion in Nietzsche's grand politics.

# Abbreviations

Quotations from Nietzsche's works are cited in the text using the following abbreviations:

AC  *The Anti-Christ.* Translated by R.J. Hollingdale. Harmondsworth: Penguin Books, 1986.

BGE  *Beyond Good and Evil.* Translated by Walter Kaufmann. New York: Vintage Books, 1966.

BT  *The Birth of Tragedy.* Translated by Walter Kaufmann. New York: Vintage Books, 1967.

CW  *The Case of Wagner.* Translated by Walter Kaufmann. New York: Vintage Books, 1967.

D  *Daybreak.* Translated by R.J. Hollingdale. Cambridge: Cambridge University Press, 1982.

GM  *On the Genealogy of Morals.* Translated by Walter Kaufmann. New York: Vintage Books, 1969.

EH  *Ecce Homo.* Translated by Walter Kaufmann. New York: Vintage Books, 1969.

GS  *The Gay Science.* Translated by Walter Kaufmann. New York: Vintage Books, 1974.

H  *Human, All Too Human.* Translated by R.J. Hollingdale, 2 volumes. Cambridge: Cambridge University Press, 1984.

KGW  *Werke. Kritische Gesamtausgabe.* Edited by Giorgi Colli and Mazzino Montinari. Berlin: Walter de Gruyter, 1967–.

PT  *Philosophy and Truth: Selections from Nietzsche's Notebooks from the Early 1870s.* Edited and translated by Daniel Breazeale. Atlantic Highlands: Humanities Press, 1979.

TI    *Twilight of the Idols.* Translated by R.J. Hollingdale. Harmonds-
      worth: Penguin Books, 1986.

TL    *On the Truth and Lies in a Nonmoral Sense.* In *Philosophy and
      Truth: Selections from Nietzsche's Notebooks from the Early 1870s.*

SE    *Schopenhauer as Educator.* In *Untimely Meditations.* Translated
      by R.J. Hollingdale. Cambridge: Cambridge University Press,
      1983.

UDH   *On the Uses and Disadvantages of History for Life.* In *Untimely
      Meditations.*

WP    *Will to Power.* Translated by Walter Kaufmann and R.J. Holling-
      dale. New York: Vintage Books, 1968.

WS    *The Wanderer and His Shadow.* In *Human, All Too Human,* vol-
      ume 2.

Z     *Thus Spoke Zarathustra: A Book for Everyone and No One.* Trans-
      lated by R.J. Hollingdale. Harmondsworth: Penguin Books, 1969.

# THE SOVEREIGNTY OF JOY:
# NIETZSCHE'S VISION OF GRAND POLITICS

# 1

# Joy, Sovereignty, and Atopia

Only the curious blending and duality in the emotions of the Dionysian revelers reminds us – as medicines remind us of deadly poisons – of the phenomenon that pain begets joy, that ecstasy may wring sounds of agony from us. At the very climax of joy there sounds a cry of horror or a yearning lamentation for an irretrievable loss. (*BT*, 2)

There are many ways of finding and losing our way in the labyrinth of Nietzsche's thought, and perhaps we can never become sufficiently lost before finally experiencing the joy of his writing as labyrinthine. Loss, tragedy, suffering, meaninglessness, evil, absurdity, and death – all these 'negativities' characterize Nietzsche's conception of life and especially his understanding of joy. Perhaps the most labyrinthine and enigmatic feature of Nietzsche's philosophy is his insistence upon this: that joy (*Lust*) is inseparable from loss (*Verlust*) and suffering, that joy is loss and fulfils itself precisely by encompassing its own negation, by longing for itself through its other. 'For all joy wants itself, therefore it also wants heart's agony! O happiness! O pain! Oh break, heart! You Higher Men, learn this, learn that joy wants eternity, joy wants the eternity of all things, *wants deep, deep, deep eternity*!' (Z, 'The Intoxicated Song,' 11). Dionysian joy affirms itself in and through the otherness of loss, as the will to lose itself, to squander and overflow itself; and therefore joy is not unlike *eros* that realizes itself through *thanatos*, a 'going-over' that is necessarily a 'going-under' (Z, Prologue, 4), an 'annihilation in victory' (Z, 'Of Old and New Law-Tables,' 30). For me, tragic joy is the poetic dissonance that stands at the heart of Nietzsche's philosophy and animates all of his central ideas – will to power, self-mastery, the Overman, *amor fati*, eternal return – and especially his 'grand politics' inasmuch as grand politics is the political philosophy of the sovereignty of joy.[1]

Perhaps the most labyrinthine of all the enigmas of Nietzsche's work concerns his status as a political philosopher, for it is all too easy and, at the same time, extremely difficult to read and interpret Nietzsche as a political thinker. After all, he himself did not expound any systematic political theory, and what observations and arguments he does express concerning traditional political categories (the state, authority, freedom, equality, etc.) are fragmentary and seem to be peripheral and even contradictory to his philosophical thought. And yet ideologues of both the right and the left have attempted to appropriate Nietzsche in order to maintain their traditional positions in relationship to these traditional political categories.

However, it seems to me that if tragic joy is fundamental to Nietzsche's philosophy as a theory of culture, then 'grand politics' (*die grosse Politik*), as the political elaboration of the sovereignty of joy, is necessarily intrinsic to Nietzsche's whole enterprise. This involves the obligation not only to expose it as being antithetical to traditional political theory and ideology, but also to show that his 'grand politics' attempts to redefine politics itself for the epoch following the death of God. We could even say that Nietzsche's entire philosophic effort begins and ends with the question of sovereignty and whether it will be determined by the spirit of revenge or joy towards life. Indeed, Nietzsche confronts humanity with a loss of sovereignty so profound that it defines its fundamental dilemma – the fact that 'God is dead' and nihilism is the inexorable reality facing humanity. This by itself poses the question: What, if anything, can now be sovereign?

Whether we experience Nietzsche's writing through his aesthetics, his critique of metaphysics, his psychology, his ambivalence around 'the feminine,' or his politics, sooner or later we are confronted with the relationship between joy and sovereignty in his philosophy. I have chosen to concentrate on Nietzsche's grand politics because, with few exceptions in the existing literature, it has been either ignored or misunderstood, and also because it highlights this fundamental relationship between joy and sovereignty. Moreover, although he is far from being a political theorist in the traditional sense, the pivotal metaphors of Nietzsche's thought – will to power, *amor fati*, eternal return, and the *Übermensch* or Overman – are best illuminated through his conception of sovereignty as joy and thus in the context of his grand politics.

The basic features of Nietzsche's grand politics as the sovereignty of joy will be outlined following a summary of the critical aspects of joy and their place in his philosophy.

## Tragic Joy and Dionysus

How little you know of human *happiness*, you comfortable and benevolent people, for happiness and unhappiness are sisters and even twins that either grow up together or, as in your case, *remain small* together. (*GS*, 338)

Throughout his work, Nietzsche contrasts two conceptions of joy: one is linear, idealistic, and optimistic; the other, tragic, Dionysian, and pessimistic. More precisely, he counterposes two conceptions of the relationship between joy and pain, or joy (*Lust*) and loss (*Verlust*). Underlying this relationship is the question of one's strength in the face of the tragic nature of life, the question of one's sovereignty. The idealistic view holds a negative conception of joy that places it against the primacy of pain as its end or conclusion in a linear process. Schopenhauer, for example, asserts the positivity of pain as the intrinsic quality of the will to live and characterizes happiness as purely negative inasmuch as it entails the temporary or permanent cessation of desire or the will. What is most significant about the negative conception of happiness, for Nietzsche, is its equation of joy with the negation and even the annihilation of reality/pain (hence, its idealism): here, the will to joy comes at the expense of life as the will to nothingness and nihilism.

Against this, Nietzsche puts forward a positive conception of joy which is also and necessarily tragic and pessimistic. For me, all the generosity and passion of Nietzsche's thought resides in the phrase: 'joy in the actual and active *of every kind* [Lust am Wirklichen, Wirkenden *jeder Art*]' (*H* 2:220; *KGW* 4.3:110). Where the idealistic and negative view of happiness expresses a profound rejection of actual life because it is painful (a rejection that arises from an equally profound lack of sovereignty in the face of reality), Nietzsche's work teaches the primacy of joy in and through the affirmation of the fullness of reality not inspite of, but because of the necessity of pain. 'Joy in the actual' is the affirmative *ethos* that Nietzsche tries to express in his later work through the Stoic concept of *amor fati* (love of fate) and, finally, in the eternal return of the same.

This is the affirmative teaching of Nietzsche's philosophy: joy encompasses and transforms suffering as a part of the fullness of becoming. His positive conception of joy is therefore tragic because it affirms the necessity of joy fulfilling itself through pain and pessimistic because this identity of joy and pain is also eternal. Furthermore, Nietzsche's paradoxical conception of joy as encompassing pain implies a radical critique of being and identity.

Given that Nietzsche's understanding of joy is positive, tragic, and pessimistic, what role does it play in his philosophy as a whole? If the affirmative *ethos* is central to his work, it should provide the basis for his avowed task: the critique of morality and the revaluation of all values. In the following propositions, I shall briefly summarize my argument that 'joy in the actual and active *of every kind*' (*H* 2:220) constitutes the fundamental *ethos* from which Nietzsche develops his critique of morality and his cultural revaluation.

Nietzsche's critique of morality is really a critique of the denaturalization of morality – the abstraction of morality from the actual, from nature, and its perversion into revenge or *ressentiment* against nature. This analysis may be simplified into the following points: first, the critique of morality as anti-nature is fundamentally the critique of the idea of responsibility; second, it entails the critique of the subject presupposed by the idea of responsibility; third, the critique of the moral subject engenders a radical critique of being as such through Nietzsche's concept of will to power; and fourth, these three critiques of free will, the subject, and being lead to the revaluation of valuation itself so that it is seen as a consequence of physiology, as the semiotics of the body.

First, at the centre of denaturalized morality lies the attempt to make individuals responsible (*verantwortlich*) for their actions and even their nature, according to Nietzsche. Morality is the belief that individuals are the free cause, the free will, that precedes and determines action. For only in this way can they be held accountable for their behaviour. Responsibility presupposes free will which, in turn, requires the transformation of every action into a deed and a doer who is the free author of the deed. Hence, the second point in Nietzsche's analysis of morality: the critique of responsibility or free will requires the critique of the subject. The thesis of responsibility implies that all the antecedents of human actions can be found in the individual's consciousness, in her or his 'motives' for acting. There must, therefore, be an 'I,' an 'ego,' that is the responsible subject of human actions. Third, the critique of the subject calls forth a radical critique of identity as such, of being, substance, or presence as the reality of realities.

These three critiques (of free will, the subject, and identity) constitute the fundamental matrix of Nietzsche's analysis of morality. In opposition to morality as free cause, Nietzsche argues that morality is a necessary consequence of actuality and its value is therefore entirely dependent upon the health of that actuality. More precisely, against the thesis of responsibility, he insists upon complete unaccountability (*Unverantwortlichkeit*) and thereby the unconditional unfreedom of the will:

'Everything is necessity – thus says the new knowledge; and this knowledge itself is necessity. Everything is innocence: and knowledge is the
path to insight into this innocence' (*H* 1:107). Morality versus necessity
or fate – that is the fundamental struggle and those are the alternatives.
To restore innocence, joy, and reality to human life, one must take the
doer back into the deed (*WP*, 675), one must '*"naturalize"* humanity in
terms of a pure, newly discovered, newly redeemed nature' (*GS*, 109), and
thus affirm necessity and the innocence of becoming (cf. *TI*, 'The Four
Great Errors,' 8).

In this way, 'joy in the actual' does indeed constitute the foundation of
Nietzsche's revaluation of values: if morality possesses value solely as a
consequence of reality (one only becomes what one is), then the affirmation
of the necessity and innocence of becoming is not only the basis for a critique of morality as anti-nature, but the precondition of a natural morality.
This 'decentred' naturalism is implicit in Nietzsche's critique of responsibility and free will; for in taking the doer back into the deed, he also
engages in a critique of the subject. The conscious ego, with its reason and
intelligence, is no longer the sovereign author and free cause of human
action. According to Nietzsche, the ego is a little intelligence and instrument of the body and its greater intelligence. Behind the conscious self,
there is the higher sovereignty of the unconscious self, the body (*Z*, 'Of the
Despisers of the Body'). Moreover, in taking the ego back into the body
and the body into 'a pure, newly discovered, newly redeemed nature' (*GS*,
109), Nietzsche's critique of the subject is also a critique of being or God.
In asserting that 'one is necessary, one is a piece of fate, one belongs to the
whole, one *is* in the whole' (*TI*, 'The Four Great Errors,' 8), Nietzsche
begins a critique of being as identity through a 'newly redeemed nature' –
through the will to power. For the attack on the subject is precisely an
attack on the abstraction of the subject from nature or the ego from the
body: 'we find ourselves in the midst of a rude fetishism when we call to
mind the basic presuppositions of the metaphysics of language – which is to
say, of *reason*' (*TI*, '"Reason" in Philosophy,' 5). It is this 'rude fetishism'
that creates an imaginary subject and an equally fictitious and abstract
object through the separation of doer and deed.

It is *this* which sees everywhere deed and doer; this which believes in will as cause in
general; this which believes in the 'ego', in the ego as being, in the ego as substance,
and which *projects* its belief in the ego – substance onto all things – only thus does it
*create* the concept 'thing' ... Being is everywhere thought in, *foisted on*, as cause; it is
only from the conception 'ego' that there follows, derivatively, the concept 'being'

... At the beginning stands the great fateful error that the will is something which *produces an effect* – that will is a *faculty*. (*TI*, '"Reason" in Philosophy,' 5)

In taking the doer back into the deed, Nietzsche is actually conducting a radical attack on both the 'subject' and 'being' whose enormous implications make themselves felt in the concept of will to power. Here is announced the 'newly redeemed nature' that is no longer outside and apart from humanity, but encompasses and redeems it in the innocence of becoming. Newly redeemed – wholly decentred, absolute difference – this is the revolution announced in the concept of 'will to power.' If will to power is reality, for Nietzsche, then 'joy in the actual' is the celebration of one's self-overcoming, one's self-mastery or sovereignty – one's becoming what one is.

Will to power also implies *amor fati* and the eternal return. If Nietzsche's will to power does away with the concepts of 'subject' and 'being,' with the whole 'rude fetishism' of predicative consciousness, then it already contains within itself the assertion that 'one is necessary, one is a piece of fate, one belongs to the whole, one *is* in the whole' (*TI*, 'The Four Great Errors,' 8). That is to say, it already contains in itself the overcoming of the error of 'setting man and fate over against one another as two separate things' (*WS*, 61). And, in overcoming this error, will to power becomes not a pacifying, but an activating and empowering, identification of humanity and fate. In this sense, *amor fati* belongs to will to power and teaches one not resignation to an external force, but an active love and celebration of who one is now, a 'joy in the actual and active' that teaches one to make one's actuality itself into an activating source of joy.

Similarly, will to power is the eternal return of the same – the highest teaching that Nietzsche wished to embody in his philosophy. Through the concept of will to power, Nietzsche denies the legitimacy of the 'subject' and its correlate, 'being,' and, as a result, the foundations and ontological preconditions of judgment are also undermined. Thus, because one belongs to fate, it is no longer possible to step outside of the whole and judge or evaluate it – '*nothing exists apart from the whole!*' (*TI*, 'The Four Great Errors,' 8). Here again, the newly redeemed nature is announced: the pre-predicative nature of the will to power means that judgments can never be true and therefore '*the value of life cannot be estimated*' (*TI*, 'The Problem of Socrates,' 2). Because one belongs to fate, because nothing exists outside of the whole, becoming cannot be judged or evaluated; or, what amounts to the same thing, 'becoming must appear justified at every moment' (*WP*, 708). Insofar as humanity and fate cannot be set against one another as two separate things in the will to power, becoming has the same value at every moment; it remains eternally the same at each moment in its coming and going and returning. In this way, to say yes to one moment is to say yes to all moments, and the affirmation of one joy is also the affirmation of all suffering: 'All things are chained and entwined together, all things are in love; if ever you wanted one moment twice ... then you wanted *everything* to return!' (Z, 'The Intoxicated Song,' 10). To will the eternal return of the same is therefore to affirm the identity of humanity and nature or fate, to say yes to the immanence of this moment in the whole and the whole in each and every moment. The will to power, *amor fati*, and the eternal return of the same announce the fullness, the perfection, of becoming at each moment. In the same way, will to power, *amor fati*, and eternal return all express 'joy in the actual' – in the wholeness of the actual, a fullness that precludes the linear conception of becoming that reduces the present moment to a mere stage on the way to a final state of absolute being. In one form or another, this identification of joy and wholeness makes its presence felt in everything Nietzsche writes – and particularly in his understanding of sovereignty and grand politics.

## Joy and Sovereignty

*At the sea.* – I would not build a house for myself, and I count it part of my good fortune that I do not own a house. But if I had to, then I should build it as some of the Romans did – right into the sea. I should not mind sharing a few secrets with this beautiful monster. (*GS*, 240)

Nietzsche's grand politics (indeed, his whole philosophy) is a process of building a new cultural edifice, a new style of human dwelling, whose foundations will no longer be solid earth because he is building it 'right into the sea.' The new, higher history that begins with the death of God (death of the 'rude fetishism' of 'the subject' and 'being') demands that the human things be built upon or into a fluid sovereignty, a newly redeemed nature without substance and being, that the human dwelling be built right into 'this beautiful monster,' 'the necessary wave-play of becoming' (*H* 2:33), and that the human tragedy give way and return 'into the eternal comedy of existence; ... [into] "the waves of uncountable laughter"' (*GS*, 1). For there is something playful, albeit monstrously playful, about this new sovereignty for human dwelling, something placeless, groundless, fluid, and infinite. This sovereignty, this foundation, is itself without foundation.

The intertwining of joy and sovereignty constitutes the matrix of

Nietzsche's grand politics, which itself occupies the centre of his philosophy as a whole. The thesis elaborated and defended in this book is that 'joy in the actual' (*amor fati* and eternal return) is the sovereign and legislating experience from which arise the basic categories of Nietzsche's politics: the Overman (*Übermensch*), the natural morality of breeding or cultivation (*Züchtung*) of higher types, hierarchy or order of rank (*Rangordnung*), and communion in joy (*Mitfreude*).

The nature of this sovereign joy and the manner in which it reigns constitute the fundamental dilemmas of finding our way through Nietzsche's grand politics. In order to clarify both the meaning of these categories of his political thought and my method of interpretation, I shall briefly summarize my seven fundamental theses concerning grand politics.

First, at the centre of grand politics stands the sovereignty of joy. Inasmuch as tragic or Dionysian joy constitutes the idiom within which will to power, *amor fati*, and eternal recurrence take shape and flourish, it also becomes the measure and substance of the self-mastery or sovereignty that is embodied in the Overman. And as the sovereign experience, 'joy in the actual' also becomes, must become, the legislating experience, the source and standard of strength, courage, creativity, and greatness in the revaluation of all values. Joy in the actual is both the way in which morality is overcome and the new, redeemed form of existence: by overcoming the radical subjectivity of the moral experience of the world (its abstraction of the doer from the deed), joy takes the subject back into the deed and releases the subject into pure becoming. In particular, through eternal return, one learns how to free oneself from the past by releasing the past into becoming – by affirming the 'It was' as an 'I wanted it thus!' In this way, joy in becoming releases one into the whole and, thereby, makes one a part of the encompassing power that underlies culture.

For Nietzsche, therefore, the sovereignty of joy is not an arbitrary moral ideal – it belongs to necessity, to 'the necessary wave-play of becoming' – and yet it also represents the natural source for morality, for the practice of revaluation and grand politics.

Second, Nietzsche's grand politics is grand because it is 'atopian.' Nietzsche takes up and ironically employs Bismarck's term, 'grand politics' (*die grosse Politik*), not only to emphasize how antagonistic the power politics of the state is to matters of culture (*TI*, 'What the Germans Lack,' 4; *H* 1:465, 474), but also to describe the cultural task of the philosopher as legislator and cultivator of higher types of human beings. In this way, 'politics,' insofar as it revolves around the exercise of, or struggle for, power in the state and its bureaucracies, is demoted to 'petty politics' (*kleine Politik*), while 'great or grand politics' concerns itself with the encompassing cultural order within which 'power or petty politics' takes place.

In order to clarify this, I employ a distinction, used by Paul Ricoeur, between *le politique* or polity and *la politique* or politics.[2] For Ricoeur, 'polity' refers to the 'ideal' sphere of political rationality within which 'politics' can take place; this 'ideality' is composed of the forms and modes of discourse, the meanings and customs that order and structure concrete political behaviour and speech. Thus, 'politics,' the empirical realities of political rule and the struggle to capture, maintain, or redefine its power, functions within this 'ideality' which is irreducible to the category of 'ideology' because it cannot be an instrument of particular or class interests; it is not a passive 'super-structure' at the service of a determinant 'infra-structure,' even though certain terms from the realm of polity can be and are used 'ideologically' in the practice of 'power politics' without vitiating their reality. In this sense, Ricoeur's distinction between polity and politics parallels Nietzsche's differentiation of grand politics and petty politics.

The significance of this distinction for understanding Nietzsche's grand politics cannot be minimized because it makes it possible to formulate what I call the 'atopian' character of grand politics. By differentiating between grand politics and petty politics, Nietzsche achieves not only a demotion of the latter to an instrument of polity, not only a relativization of the state to a higher sphere of philosophical statesmanship, but he also reveals the paradoxical position of the philosopher to politics and the state. The term 'atopia' has been used to describe the position of the Socratic philosopher as at the centre of the political world and yet outside of it[3] – above the rulers, outside politics, and beyond man. The genuine philosopher in Nietzsche's grand politics is neither utopian nor fully political but atopian because, instead of addressing itself to 'politics,' the sovereignty of joy rebuilds 'polity,' not on solid ground, but right into placelessness (a-topia), into the monstrous playfulness of the necessary wave-play of becoming.

Third, sovereignty is 'something one has and does not have.' For Nietzsche, sovereignty is defined by one's generosity, courage, and strength for 'joy in the actual' and therefore by the power one has to build oneself right into the sea, the courage to overcome the subjectivity of morality and release oneself into becoming. Far from being a struggle to possess and preserve (oneself through) power, sovereignty involves a squandering and giving away of (oneself) power. Like the tragic joy that constitutes it, sovereignty realizes itself in an overflowing loss of itself, in an exuberance that does not preserve itself. And this further implies that interpretations of Nietzsche's grand politics that reduce sovereignty to 'domination' ignore both its atopian character and this quality of giving. Nietzsche's sovereignty of joy is a power and freedom that 'one has and does *not* have' (*TI*, 'Expeditions of an Untimely Man,' 38), a foundation that builds itself right into the sea.

Fourth, by keeping the atopian character of Nietzsche's grand politics in mind, one avoids the common mistake of reducing his political categories to those of power politics, and this is particularly true of Nietzsche's notion of hierarchy or order of rank (*Rangordnung*). It should not, as it often is, be reduced to a class structure or any sort of social stratification. He describes his order of rank as division of noble and base types which is radically distinct from a social structure of power between ruler and ruled. Nietzsche emphasizes this in two ways. He characterizes this hierarchy as a differentiation of three 'physiological types,' not social classes. In contrast to class structure, hierarchy is not a relation of economic or political power, but a relation between that which encompasses and that which is encompassed. Far from being the fossilization of class differences, this hierarchical structure precedes and underlies all social relations just as polity precedes and encompasses politics. For Nietzsche, culture is merely the sanctioning in law of this encompassing order. He also emphasizes its distance from a class structure of power by placing the spiritual types above and outside the 'guardians' of state power (*AC*, 57; *BGE*, 61; *WP*, 998, 999, 1057), thereby subordinating the state and its power holders to the status of the spiritual élite. Here again the joy in the actual constitutes the idiom of Nietzsche's grand politics: the 'physiology'; that is, the strength and joy of the will to power that is able to actualize itself in *amor fati* and eternal return is what really distinguishes the highest type as the embodiment of the sovereignty of joy. For this reason, the most spiritual reign over this order of rank 'not because they want to but because they *are*; they are not free to be second in rank' (*AC*, 57).

Similarly, it follows that Nietzsche's hierarchy is not a moral ideal, something that he believes ought to be. His 'aristocratic radicalism'[4] is much more radical than that: he argues that culture is always hierarchical by its very nature, whether it wishes to be or not, and therefore it is a culture to the extent that it is an order of rank and disintegrates to the extent that it is no longer hierarchical. The order of rank is a natural order 'over which no arbitrary caprice, no "modern idea" has any power' (*AC*, 57). Finally, since Nietzsche's well-known criticisms of egalitarianism, democracy, and liberal optimism flow from his 'aristocratic radicalism,' I shall treat them as Nietzsche does – as negative expositions of his positive views.

Fifth, if culture, as the order of rank, is one of the pillars of grand politics, then cultivation or 'breeding' (*Züchtung*) is another, equally important pillar. Here again, 'nature' constitutes the point of departure of culture or, more precisely, cultivation, in Nietzsche's eyes: actualization follows from the actual.

To the anti-natural morality, Nietzsche counterposes a natural morality of cultivation – nature cultivating itself, 'a *going-up* – up into a high, free, even frightful nature and naturalness' (*TI*, 'Expeditions of an Untimely Man,' 48). In brief, grand politics is an education of the 'spirit' understood as beginning with the cultivation of the body. 'It is decisive ... that one should inaugurate culture in the *right place* – *not* in the "soul" ... the right place is the body, demeanour, diet, physiology: the *rest* follows' (*TI*, 'Expeditions of an Untimely Man,' 47). Thus, Nietzsche's genuine philosopher/ statesman is certainly a legislator and commander but he legislates not through abstract ideals and new 'oughts,' but through an education that is the cultivation and celebration of the actual, of the body, through a 'going-up' into nature and naturalness, through the discipline of *amor fati* and eternal return.

In this way, grand politics transforms morality into 'spiritual discipline and cultivation [geistigen Zucht und Züchtung]' (*BGE*, 188; *KGW* 6.2:111), into a 'project of cultivation and education [Züchtungs – und Erziehungs-swerke]' (*BGE*, 61; *KGW* 6.2:77). However, the corollary of this natural morality in which one becomes or cultivates what one is presupposes the following: 'to *make* morality one must have the unconditional will to the contrary' (*TI*, 'The "Improvers" of Mankind,' 5); the unconditional will to immorality or the extra-moral (joy in the actual) is the condition for making morality or cultivation; or, put more provocatively, '"Man is evil" – all the wisest men have told me that to comfort me ... "Man must grow better and more evil" – thus do *I* teach' (*Z*, 'Of the Higher Man,' 5). Morality as cultivation begins with the body, with the natural and therefore the extra-moral, and it educates not through repression, but through joy in the actual, *amor fati*.

As a corollary of his conception of morality as a *'semeiotics'* (*TI*, 'The "Improvers" of Mankind,' 1), Nietzsche examines and criticizes the moral will from Plato to Kant via Christianity (and particularly Schopenhauer's morality of pity) as 'denaturalized morality,' as revenge or *ressentiment* against the actual. Nietzsche's genealogy of morals interprets the 'ascetic ideal,' the denial of the body as sinful, as arising from a revengeful spirit which, in turn, is symptomatic of a declining or exhausted physiology; and this morality of revenge underlies the linear and idealistic conception of joy as the negation of pain and life – as nihilism.

Sixth, Nietzsche's much misunderstood concept of the Overman (*Übermensch*) should be placed in the context of his natural morality of cultivation, in the idiom of becoming 'better and more evil,' in order to give it its full Dionysian sense. However, insofar as Nietzsche's 'immoralism' is synonymous with his critique of the subject, the Overman should be interpreted as a metaphor for newly redeemed nature (the innocence of becoming) embodied in the most spiritual type. As the embodiment of joy in the actual, the Overman releases himself from the tyranny of the past by releasing the past into becoming through the affirmation of eternal return; he is therefore described by Nietzsche as the most comprehensive and encompassing spirit whose breadth forms a new horizon of culture.

Seventh, by its very nature, joy is, for Nietzsche, a sharing or communion in joy (*Mitfreude*) because it necessarily overflows itself. Moreover, it is not simply one virtue among others but, through its opposition to pity or the sharing of suffering (*Mitleid*), it represents the source of natural or masterly morality. Virtue is no longer the cause but the consequence of the joy that one cultivates through *amor fati* and eternal return. Here joy in the actual becomes the activating and empowering source of action as well as the foundation of community through 'communion in joy.'

In these seven points, I have attempted to summarize the fundamental character of Nietzsche's grand politics in light of its conception of sovereignty as joy in the actual as well as its atopia. I believe that Nietzsche's understanding of culture as an order of rank and of morality as the cultivation of culture in the higher types flows from the atopian nature of the sovereignty of joy. Built upon this conception of joy and sovereignty, grand politics culminates in a rejuvenation of culture through this communion in joy.

## The Problem of Interpretation

Why is it so difficult to bring Nietzsche's politics into view in a way that is both clear and faithful to his vision? There are a number of reasons which have often led to distortions and misunderstandings of his political philosophy. I shall identify and, I hope, rectify these by focusing on his novel and paradoxical relationship to politics. The most fundamental reason is that Nietzsche defines a sovereign type of being who is entrusted with a spiritual-political statesmanship but, at the same time, he insists upon the radical heterogeneity of this sovereign spirit with respect to society as a whole: sovereignty can never be assimilated into common life and vice versa. It is, and must always be, radically other, the exception to the rule of homogeneity, and as such, it will always be foreign and even dangerous to it. At the centre of Nietzsche's political vision lies this conception of sovereignty: the sovereign's heterogeneity is irreducible to any social or political homogeneity just as grand politics is distinct from power politics.

In this way, a fundamental atopia characterizes the peculiar political position of Nietzsche's sovereign Overman. At the same time, it reveals the difficulty in interpreting his political philosophy. The philosopher/statesman occupies no stable, historical place (*topos*) within the polis, nor can he ever, and he remains therefore irredeemably nomadic: 'untimely' and atopian without thereby becoming utopian. Moreover, this atopia renders the philosopher remote, elusive, and yet fundamental to the establishment of polity and culture understood as an order of rank.

As the fate of Nietzsche at the hands of ideologues and scholars alike demonstrates, this ambivalence in his relation to the state leaves the concept of the legislating philosopher vulnerable to fundamental distortions that either ignore or abolish his atopia. In addition, Nietzsche's explicit discussion of political issues is fragmentary and generally derogatory. Given the unsystematic and elusive character of his political philosophy, it is not surprising that there has arisen so much debate about its significance. In fact, a very influential reading of Nietzsche by Walter Kaufmann argues that Nietzsche is best understood as antipolitical.[5] Since so much of the current debate has arisen in response to this reading, it seems appropriate to begin with Kaufmann's interpretation. In an attempt to redress the crude misappropriation of Nietzsche by the ideologues of fascism, Kaufmann emphasizes the spiritual and ethical task of self-mastery to the exclusion of any sort of political inclination in his work. Far from being 'the prophet of great wars and power politics,' Nietzsche denounced 'both the idolatry of the state and political liberalism because he was basically "*antipolitical*" (*EH* 1 3),' wholly concerned with 'the antipolitical individual who seeks self-perfection far from the modern world.'[6] While Kaufmann's attempt to reappropriate the spiritual content of Nietzsche's philosophy from the political misinterpretations of both fascism and liberalism is understandable and fully justified, it has also come at the cost of Nietzsche's genuine political thought and the integral role it plays in his philosophy as a whole.

However, even within his own terms of reference, does Kaufmann's conclusion follow from his thesis: is Nietzsche antipolitical because will to power is a spiritual self-overcoming embodied in the self-mastery of the Overman? For the implication of this formulation is that, for Nietzsche, the concept of politics is exhausted by the struggle for domination and, furthermore, that the only options available are between apolitical self-overcoming (the autonomous free spirit) and the power politics of domination. More important, however, is the absence of any adequate account of Nietzsche's conception of the philosopher as legislator within an order of rank that would cultivate higher, spiritual types.

A more satisfying interpretation has arisen that attempts to recognize Nietzsche's political aspirations as integral to his philosophy without reducing will to power, the Overman, and the order of rank to crude social and historical categories. While the advantage of this reading lies in its demonstration that Nietzsche's political philosophy is not historicist, this important insight is partially vitiated by reading Nietzsche as a utopian political philosopher. Thus Jean Granier elaborates on his interpretation of the will to power with explicit reference to Kaufmann in a similar attempt to show that Nietzsche's conception should not be confused with a will to domination.[7] Yet, in contrast to Kaufmann, Granier argues that, through the Overman, order of rank, and master morality, Nietzsche does elaborate a vision of grand politics which should not be confused with a power or class structure: 'Nietzsche ... ne visait pas à identifier le Surhumain avec quelque catégorie sociologique.'[8] In fact, Granier insists that the concepts of Nietzsche's grand politics are socially indeterminate and acquire a content only in the context of his philosophy as a whole and especially through the affirmation of the eternal return of the same.[9] This power to overcome oneself is, at the same time, the power to overcome one's time in oneself, and as such, this immanent transcendence is precisely what constitues both the utopian position of the Overman and the radical spiritual transformation that animates grand politics.[10] Most important, however, this interpretation of Nietzsche's political thought and particularly his grand politics preserves the spiritual vision that Kaufmann emphasizes, but it also demonstrates that, for Nietzsche, this necessarily entails a spiritual order of rank and morality of cultivation – that is, grand politics represents a philosophic turn away from historical power politics towards a 'Platonic' political and ethical utopia. As Raymond Polin argues, while grand politics represents the cultivation of an élitist order of rank, Nietzsche, like Plato, understands this political action to be the education of a new nobility through the creation of new values.[11] Similarly, Henning Ottmann maintains that the Overman is a Platonic teacher whose higher politics of cultivation and hierarchy fulfils itself, not through historical power politics, but in a Platonic utopia.[12]

While it would be inaccurate to characterize Tracy Strong's seminal work, *Friedrich Nietzsche and the Politics of Transfiguration*, as wholly consistent with a 'utopian' interpretation, his reading does share some fundamental similarities. For example, like Simone Goyard-Fabre, Strong argues that Nietzsche's political thought attempts to fulfil itself in an unprecedented metamorphosis, a 'transfiguration' of previous cultural forms of life that will be so radical that it cannot be reduced to traditional social and historical categories, in particular, the tendency to identify Nietzsche's 'masters' with a dominant class. 'Such a judgment neglects the fact that the activity of Nietzsche's masters is *not just the converse of that of slaves* (oppressing rather than oppressed), but is in fact a *different* form of activity.'[13] Moreover, the truly unprecedented nature of Nietzsche's politics of transfiguration is manifested in the eternal return, the transvaluation of values through the cultivation of affirmative human types who can overcome nihilism. However, in dissociating eternal return from will to power, Strong divorces the practice of affirmation – and thereby the politics of transfiguration – from the intrinsic nature of becoming as a whole, which for Nietzsche completes itself at every moment and therefore implies an affirmation that flows from a plenitude or power that is always already present in life as will to power.[14]

If the difficulty of interpreting Nietzsche's philosophy resides in the obligation to comprehend the immanence of being outside of any historicism,[15] then the problem of understanding his political philosophy must be considered equally demanding and perhaps even more elusive. For one must confront this immanent transcendence as the sovereignty of joy, as an affirmation that is already immanent in will to power and yet somehow still underway.

In this regard, Michel Haar offers a subtle and rich interpretation of grand politics which emphasizes the heterogeneity of the Overman as the embodiment of the power of affirmation, while avoiding the temptation to characterize it as a utopia. For Haar, the Overman is not the fulfilment of humanity, and must be distinguished from any form of 'higher man.' Radically different from any human type, the Overman embodies Nietzsche's vision of the 'more-than-human' which will nevertheless exist alongside the all-too-human. The political implications of this heterogeneity manifest themselves in terms of 'a *reign* that is not at all a *domination*,' in which the noble type possesses neither political power nor wealth nor any effective governing force. As the embodiment of a supra-human affirmation, grand politics can be called a nonviolent 'Caesarism of the Overman.'[16]

It is tempting to dismiss this characterization of grand politics as utopian in effect, if not in intention. When augmented with Gilles Deleuze's notion of the nomad, however, Michel Haar's interpretation lays the groundwork for a fully atopian appreciation of Nietzsche's vision of politics as the sovereignty of joy. In his essay, 'Nomad Thought,' Deleuze insists that Nietzsche announces an unprecedented task that is also 'the advent of a new politics.' In contrast to the concerns of previous political philosophers who seek to recodify the foundation of society, Nietzsche's concern lies 'beyond all the codes of past, present, and future, to transmit something that does not and will not allow itself to be codified.'[17] Grand politics signals the advent of a nomadic adventure, a migration to the periphery of all settled and established states. The insatiable, Faustian motion towards the horizon is primarily a voyage in intensity rather than a geographic dislocation but, unlike Faust, the nomad is an uncodifiable yes that underlies all codes, an affirmative pathos of distance that celebrates the plenitude of becoming. The nomadic intensity of this unprecedented and over-abundant affirmation marks the heterogeneity of Nietzsche's Overman and the atopian sovereignty of joy. In this way, Deleuze and Haar have propelled the interpretation of grand politics far beyond the settled and established terrain and almost made audible the stillest words of a still secret reign. They have almost made perceptible the atopian and nomadic sovereignty of a concealed yes as the 'element of affirmation [that] is the superhuman element.'[18]

In contrast to the preceding interpretations, another reading views Nietzsche as fundamentally nihilistic inasmuch as he contributed to a radical historicist destruction of political philosophy. Leo Strauss, for example, argues that, while Nietzsche 'decisively prepared' the advent of radical historicism and its total rejection of any trans-historical or theoretical stance, he himself did not succumb to it.[19] Moreover, in one of his last and most important essays, 'Note on the Plan of Nietzsche's *Beyond Good and Evil*,' Strauss seems to suggest that, for Nietzsche, the historical sense may offer more than nihilist scepticism in the wake of the complete dissolution of all nature: 'It would seem that this defect, the reverse side of our great virtue, points to a way of thinking and living that transcends historicism, to a peak higher than all earlier peaks.' Through the philosopher of the future, the 'complementary man,' 'history can be said to be integrated into nature.' Yet nature as well as history remain highly problematic in Nietzsche's will to power and eternal return: humanity only becomes natural through history and especially through the transcendence of historicism and nihilism in the affirmation of eternal return; but this 'nature' is no longer divine but 'noble' – indeed, Nietzsche's noble nature replaces divine nature.[20]

The significance of this conclusion and Strauss's general assessment of Nietzsche seems largely negative but also somewhat ambiguous. On the one hand, Strauss seems to suggest that, although he was not a radical historicist, Nietzsche nevertheless remains caught in the contradictions of historicism even while attempting to transcend them. This seems to be the prevailing interpretation of Nietzsche by those who subscribe to Strauss's understanding of political philosophy. For example, Werner Dannhauser argues that Nietzsche agrees with the historicist argument and merely wants to 'transcend the apparent deadliness of the historicist insight by interpreting it nobly.' However, a noble interpretation of the death of divine nature – nihilism – leads Nietzsche to celebrate indiscriminately the creativity of the will to power in the noble nature of the Overman. Unrestrained creativity without any eternal measure leaves this noble nature devoid of virtue and vulnerable to the confusion of barbarism with nature. In short, Dannhauser seems to conclude that Nietzsche's replacement of divine nature with noble nature entails a profound collapse of Platonic political philosophy into a nihilistic 'atheism of the political right.'[21]

On the other hand, Strauss may be interpreted as viewing Nietzsche as overcoming Platonic political philosophy – platonically – just as Plato overcame his Socrates. For example, Laurence Lampert argues that 'Strauss's whole study indicates that noble nature as Nietzsche presents it – no, *embodies* it – replaces divine nature as Plato presents it.' Lampert's wording suggests that there is a more positive relationship between nobility and divinity in Nietzsche's transformation of nature than Strauss is willing to explicitly affirm. While the historical sense undermines divine nature 'as Plato presents it,' it opens the way beyond historicism towards a rediscovery of divine nature as Dionysus embodies it. Nietzsche is carried beyond historicism towards a tragic sense of nature, as the innocence of becoming, by the same force that leads him beyond Platonic political philosophy. Lampert shows that the historical sense allows Nietzsche to abandon the esoteric moderation of Platonic philosophy – especially the noble lie or the pious fraud as Nietzsche describes it – and create a tragic polity based on the 'deadly truths.' 'Strauss's Nietzsche essay shows that Nietzsche as a philosopher of the future breaks with the fundamental stratagem of past philosophers of the future: Nietzsche has no use for the pious fraud. He abandons classical philosophy's virtue of temperance or moderation, its manner of speaking and acting.' Yet Nietzsche overcomes Plato platonically by revealing the beauty and plenitude of becoming, by transforming the deadly truth into the joyful science and making this communion in joy the foundation of grand politics. 'If in the portrayal of these deadly truths Nietzsche platonizes, his beautification is not a cosmetic smeared over the deadly or ugly, for ... Nietzsche's gaze into the deadly led him to see its beauty and to glimpse a new ideal.'[22] This is the significance of Lampert's reading of Strauss and Nietzsche: he reveals how grand politics creates a new sense of community on the deadly truths of pure becoming, immanence, an tragic nature.

Thus, even within Strauss's interpretation of Nietzsche, there remains a basic uncertainty about whether he ultimately transcended historicism and rejuvenated Platonic political philosophy by integrating history and nature through the eternal return (Lampert) or succumbed to a complete nihilism that vitiated his political thought (Dannhauser). The former interpretation seems to me much closer to Nietzsche's grand politics as the sovereignty of an unprecedented nobility that is born of a newly redeemed nature (will to power) through the historical affirmation of the eternal return.

Finally, there is a recent, more nuanced version of the argument that Nietzsche's politics explicitly celebrates a radically aristocratic power politics of the most repressive and even fascist sort. Within this interpretation, however, there remains a great deal of disagreement about the relationship between Nietzsche's philosophy and his politics. For example, Bruce Detwiler argues that there is a continuity between the philosophy of power and the illiberal and inegalitarian politics of domination. On the one hand, Detwiler agrees with Kaufmann that 'Nietzsche's thought is a far cry from fascism in that his interests are overwhelmingly spiritual, with politics intruding only at the periphery.' On the other hand, he writes: 'Politically as well as spiritually, Nietzsche inhabits a realm that is beyond good and evil, beyond any conventional notion of justice, beyond the sanctity of the typical individual, and beyond all conventional notions of compassion.'[23] In the end, Detwiler argues, the spiritual concerns of cultivating a higher type through a hierarchical order of rank suggest an extremely repressive regime, however disinterested in the state Nietzsche may have been. But Detwiler remains within Kaufmann's terms of reference rather than within Nietzsche's in supposing that 'politics' implies a power politics that is exhausted in the struggle to control the state.

Ofelia Schutte perceives a discontinuity between two models of power within Nietzsche's philosophy: the recurrence of energy states and the domination of some energy states by others.[24] While the first model implies a liberating conception of the continuity of life, the second leads to an authoritarian conception of power as domination. With this distinction, Schutte embraces the 'liberating' aspects of Nietzsche's philosophy while deploring his 'authoritarian' conception of power as 'domination.' Mark Warren shares the thesis that 'there are really two Nietzsches, a "gentle" Nietzsche and a "bloody" one,' but argues, against Schutte, that 'Nietzsche's own politics ... violates the intellectual integrity of his philosophical project.' More precisely, Nietzsche's politics – the order of rank, cultivation of higher types, and the Overman – are rejected by Warren not because they fail to conform to a moral standard external to Nietzsche's philosophy, but for reasons that are immanent to his own thought: 'Insofar as Nietzsche's politics are underdetermined by his philosophy of power, and insofar as they require unfounded assumptions to be added to his philosophy, one is justified in distinguishing the *political implications of his philosophy of power* from his *political philosophy*, and treating them as radically different things.'[25]

While both Warren and Schutte characterize Nietzsche's political thought as authoritarian and repressive, they differ in their assessment of the relationship between his politics and his philosophy. I would argue that their difficulty in locating the source for Nietzsche's politics, given their positive assessment of his philosophy (albeit ambivalent in Schutte's case), lies in their reduction of Nietzsche's political thought to historical and social categories that are foreign to his political vision. They are able to characterize his political philosophy as repressive only by ignoring the atopian character of his grand politics. However, it is important to emphasize that there is undoubtedly a dual nature to Nietzsche's project, a disturbing dissonance that is intrinsic to the tragic harmony at the centre of his political philosophy. While it is essential that the dark and troubling side of Nietzsche's political philosophy not be ignored, it should be equally important not to caricature it as 'bloody' or 'fascist.' As Nietzsche himself emphasizes, this 'horrible "witches' brew"' is part of the Dionysian character of life itself (*BT*, 3, 10). In short, his postmodern philosophy is intimately bound up with and rooted in his Dionysian exhortation to become 'better and more evil,' and this 'cruel' proposition characterizes not just Nietzsche's grand politics, but also his 'gentle, liberating' philosophy.

The atopian vision of grand politics and the sovereignty of joy that informs Nietzsche's work is clearly difficult to recognize and express in a form that measures up to its originality and depth. By addressing grand politics in the context of his philosophy as a whole, and by interpreting the former through the concept of atopia, I hope to present a reading of Nietzsche as a political philosopher that is both insightful and faithful to his thought.

# 2

# Joy in the Actual

*The real paganism.* – Perhaps nothing astonishes the observer of the Greek world more than when he discovers that from time to time the Greeks made ... a festival of all their passions and evil natural inclinations ...: this constitutes the real paganism of their world ... Where did the Greeks acquire this freedom, this sense for the actual? Perhaps from Homer and the poets before him; for it is precisely the poets ... who possess ... a joy in the actual and active *of every kind* and have no desire to deny even evil altogether ... (*H* 2:220)

At the heart of Nietzsche's philosophy and grand politics, there is a vision of freedom or sovereignty that is based on 'joy in the actual and active *of every kind* [Lust am Wirklichen, Wirkenden *jeder Art*]' (*H* 2:220; *KGW* 4.3:110), a vision of the sovereignty of joy that entails a profound transformation of the notion of 'reality.' At the same time, he seems to understand humanity as an incorrigible concealer of reality: 'Why does man not see things? He is himself standing in the way: he conceals things' (*D*, 438). Is humanity an obstacle to its own liberation and sovereignty? Is 'joy in the actual' even possible for human beings, for born concealers and illusion creators? Is actuality even accessible to cultural beings?

In order to approach the central concepts of *amor fati*, will to power, eternal return, and the Overman, we must first come to terms with the notions of reality and culture underlying Nietzsche's vision of sovereignty and joy. There are two aspects to his conception of joy in the actual that are relevant here. First, Nietzsche effects a radical philosophical transformation of the idea of the actual: he destroys the idea of 'being' as 'substance' through a critique of the 'subject,' through a fundamental undermining of the predicative dichotomy of doer and deed; in short, Nietzsche's conception of actuality is pre-predicative or pre-objective. Second, this vision of reality has certain 'physiological' and political preconditions. Nietzsche does not simply offer a new theoretical conception of reality, but he wishes instead to cultivate a joy in reality that will embody freedom or sovereignty. Joy in the actual presupposes the cultivation of individuals strong enough to practise this freedom – it presupposes 'grand politics.'

With regard to the first point, Nietzsche insists that joy is inseparable from building oneself into reality or nature – 'a pure, newly discovered, newly redeemed nature' (GS, 109) – building into a reality without substance, into an abyss, a sea. Indeed, for Nietzsche, nature is an undivided and indivisible fluidity: 'a continuous flux ... a continuous, homogeneous, undivided, indivisible flowing' (WS, 11). Reduced to its most abstract elements, Nietzsche's understanding of nature/reality derives from a critique of atomism and a vision of the dissonant unity – humanity and nature, language and (silent) things, freedom and necessity.

Nietzsche's joy in the actual is, then, a 'build[ing] ... into the sea' (GS, 240), into a totally new understanding of nature. With regard to the second point, Nietzsche's joy in the actual does not imply a return to nature, a going-back to some primeval origin; for Nietzsche, it is instead 'a *going-up* [ein *Hinaufkommen*] – up into a high, free, even frightful nature and naturalness' (TI, 'Expeditions of an Untimely Man,' 48; KGW 6.3:144), an ascent of culture to nature. It is only by way of the obstacle (humanity/language), the veil that stands in the way – that leads astray – that humanity arrives at things, the actual. One 'goes up' to nature only by means of that which veils, conceals, and obstructs it. And, in this way, joy in the actual is, for Nietzsche, a thoroughly cultural achievement, perhaps, the cultural achievement of sovereignty and freedom through grand politics.

Finally, implicit in this going-up to nature is one of the most central and controversial themes of Nietzsche's thought. For he consistently characterizes the freedom and sovereignty that is attained through the ascent to nature as 'evil,' 'immoral,' or 'beyond good and evil.' This provocative and much misunderstood aspect of Nietzsche's thought is especially important to his grand politics because to ascend to nature and become sovereign is at the same time to become 'better and more evil' (Z, 'The Convalescent,' 2). Going-up to nature is therefore a going-across, a transgression, a trespassing of the veils, weights, and measures that constitute culture and man – a self-overcoming of culture (WS, 21). But insofar as man transgresses culture, he thereby transcends himself: his going-up (to nature) is also a 'going-under,' a dissolution, 'an annihilation in victory' (Z, 'Of Old and New Law-Tables,' 30).

Instead of plunging into the bricks and mortar of Nietzsche's philosophy (will to power, Overman, eternal return), I shall try first to characterize the passion of this strange new architect who wants to build humanity's future dwelling right into the sea (GS, 240). I hope that Nietzsche's vision of grand politics – of sovereignty through joy in the actual and active of every kind – will be illuminated by this re-imagining of his thought, an image that is itself built right into the sea.

## Forgotten Nature/Forgotten Culture

*Forgotten nature.* We speak of nature and forget to include ourselves: we ourselves are nature, *quand même –*. It follows that nature is something quite different from what we think of when speak its name. (*WS*, 327)

In various ways, Nietzsche thinks and writes about nothing else in his work but this 'forgotten nature' and that which makes it 'something quite different.' For those of us who wish to interpret his work, this imposes the obligation to attend carefully to how Nietzsche thinks about this different nature, this 'pure, newly discovered, newly redeemed nature' by which one may '"*naturalize*" humanity' (GS, 109). For Nietzsche's 'forgotten nature' is neither a golden age of goodness and innocence à la Rousseau nor 'the war of all against all' à la Hobbes or Darwin. Indeed, for Nietzsche, nature is not an origin 'back there' to which one 'returns,' but an indeterminate, cultural sovereignty to which one aspires and ascends: his 'forgotten nature' is, in this way, also a 'forgotten culture' precisely because humanity itself always stands in the way. To remember nature means to recall the manner in which it was and perhaps must be forgotten; it means to recall the manner in which we must forget ourselves as nature 'quand même' and as the concealers of nature, as forgotten culture – as nature's self-concealment.

In *The Birth of Tragedy*, Nietzsche broaches this question of the (necessary) forgetfulness of nature when he writes: 'Dionysus speaks the language of Apollo; and Apollo, finally the language of Dionysus' (*BT*, 21). One of the primary themes of this work is the relationship between nature and art, life and concealment/illusion. Dionysus must always wear the mask, indeed, he is the mask, the illusion, and the appearance. However, he is not the appearance of something else, the exteriority of some essence; Dionysus is pure appearance without any essence or reality. In his mature works, Nietzsche articulates this 'ex-centricity' of nature in less mythic but still poetic terms: 'I suddenly woke up in the midst of this dream, but only to the consciousness that I am dreaming and that I must go on dreaming lest I perish ... What is "appearance" for me now? Certainly not the opposite of some essence' (GS, 54).

But what is 'appearance' now if it is not 'the opposite of some essence'? This is the Nietzschean experience itself: the overcoming of the thing-in-itself, of the opposition of appearance and reality, of exterior otherness and interior identity. Man always stands in the way – of himself, of his view of reality. His concealment of things is not, however, a simple veneer or decorative extravagance that can be removed from perception; it is not even subjective – while veiling things, it belongs to nature. A certain artistry, a peculiar intoxication, indeed, a perverse exteriority, belongs not only to humanity but to nature itself: 'what could I say about any essence except to name the attributes of its appearance! Certainly not a dead mask that one could place on an unknown x or remove from it!' (GS, 54).

Nietzsche emphasizes the role that man plays in this concealment of reality, but he also insists that this concealment, this game of appearance, is reality itself or nature. First, he confronts the 'realists' with the assertion that man is an artist by nature: 'You sober people who feel well armed against passion and fantasies and would like to turn your emptiness into a matter of pride and an ornament: you call yourselves realists and hint that the world really is the way it appears to you' (GS, 57). But what can 'joy in the actual' mean if Nietzsche rejects 'realism'? The transformation of the traditional conception of reality as a thing-in-itself is fundamental to Nietzsche's philosophical and political project. What he goes on to say about these 'sober' realists reveals a concealed intoxication. 'But in your unveiled state are not even you still very passionate and dark creatures compared to fish, and still far too similar to an artist in love? And what is "reality" for an artist in love?' (GS, 57). Here Nietzsche poses the question that must be addressed in order to comprehend his 'grand politics' as 'joy in the actual.' And to answer this question, he explores this artistic love as a form of Dionysian intoxication: 'You are still burdened with those estimates of things that have their origin in the passions and loves of former centuries. Your sobriety still contains a secret and inextinguishable drunkenness. Your love of "reality," for example – oh, that is a primeval "love" [eine alte, uralte "Liebe"]' (GS, 57; KGW 5.2:97).

There is, then, a past that is not really past but continues to flow in the present; in fact, 'we ourselves are ... nothing but that which at every moment we experience of this continued flowing' (H 2:223). The 'continued flowing' of the past in the present maintains this 'secret and inextinguishable drunkenness,' sustains this old, primeval love of reality. More than this, however, the inexorable and continuing past shapes and intoxicates reality in the present, a reality that is therefore not simply external extension placed over against us.

Every feeling and sensation contains a piece of this old love; and some fantasy, some prejudice, some unreason, some ignorance, some fear, and ever so much else has contributed to it and worked on it. That mountain there! That cloud there! What is 'real' in that? Subtract the phantasm and every human *contribution* from it, my sober friends! If you *can*! If you can forget your descent, your past, your training – all of your humanity and animality. There is no 'reality' for us – not for you either, my sober friends. (*GS*, 57)

Thus, humanity stands in its own way and conceals things from itself; it forgets nature because it forgets that it stands in the way and conceals things. It does not see itself (culture) and, failing to recognize this, it cannot see nature or the actual: by forgetting culture, it forgets itself. But this is getting too far ahead because I have yet to explicate Nietzsche's conception or demolition of 'reality.' How does Nietzsche view 'the actual'? How does he relate to these confident realists? Surprisingly, he finds a deep continuity with them: 'We are not nearly as different as you think, and perhaps our good will to transcend [*hinauszukommen*] intoxication is as respectable as your faith that you are altogether incapable of intoxication' (*GS*, 57; *KGW* 5.2:98).

There is a common desire to transcend intoxication and approximate 'reality.' But Nietzsche has already warned that the opposition of appearance and reality is itself unreal (*GS*, 54), and therefore his 'realism' is not a 'sobriety' uncorrupted by 'intoxication.' Put differently, 'second nature' (culture) and 'first nature' not only overlap, but are identical; 'reality' is always drunk, however much it may speak the language of sober Apollo. It seems that, for Nietzsche, it is necessary to overcome the dichotomy of appearance/reality (second/first nature) before one transcends intoxication and ascends to sober reality.

That which stands in the way (humanity/culture) seems to be a part of the substance of reality; and even to be the way towards reality and sobriety. This strange conception of actuality needs a little more explication; even Nietzsche confesses to finding it troublesome: 'This has given me the greatest trouble and still does: to realize that what things *are called* is incomparably more important than what they are' (*GS*, 58). What things are called, the language of Apollo (measure, weight, definition), the whole realm of culture, is more important than what they are – because they determine what things are?

The reputation [*Ruf*], name, and appearance, the usual measure and weight of a thing, what it counts for – originally almost always wrong and arbitrary, thrown over things like a dress and altogether foreign to their nature and even to their skin – all this grows from generation unto generation, merely because people believe in it, until it gradually grows to be part of the thing and turns into its very body. What at first was appearance [*Schein*] becomes in the end, almost invariably, the essence [*Wesen*] and is effective as such [*wirkt als Wesen*]. (*GS*, 58; *KGW* 5.2:98)

For Nietzsche, what things are called enters into their very being, what they are; their appearance becomes their essence; the dress becomes the body. What follows from this? After a long history, second nature becomes first nature (what is first thereby comes second) and, therefore, a necessary forgetfulness of nature because appearance cannot become essence/reality or first nature without forgetfulness: the veil must not be seen, it must be transparent – history, culture must be forgotten. Nature, as 'essence,' is therefore not originary, but comes at the end; the first comes second. And yet Nietzsche says it is possible to transcend 'intoxication,' to overcome culture and history, not to see 'naked' and 'sober reality,' but to see how nature comes into being – how the dress becomes a part of the body, and thus return to the dress. How reality is the appearance of appearance through forgotten culture. To see how the past continues to flow in us, to see ourselves as 'continuous, homogeneous, undivided, indivisible flowing' (*WS*, 11), as indivisible and therefore unknowable, and to see and love our necesssary belonging to this fate, *amor fati*.

Through the critique of atomism, history and science take us back to nature naturing even in the dress become body, in the *natura naturans* become *natura naturata*. Nietzsche criticizes two fundamental forms of atomism that bring into being the illusion of reified things or the 'rude fetishism' (*TI*, '"Reason" in Philosophy,' 5) that separates doer and deed, or really one process with two parts. First, through the distinction between doer and deed, there arises the belief in the will as cause and the ego as permanent house or substance of the will, and second, the projection of this ego-substance onto all things whereby the concept 'thing' comes into being. 'Being is everywhere thought in, *foisted on*, as cause [*Ursache*]; it is only from the conception "ego" [*"Ich"*] that there follows, derivatively, the concept "being" [*"Sein"*] ... At the beginning stands the great fateful error that the will is something which *produces an effect* [*wirkt*] – that will is a *faculty* [*Vermögen*]' (*TI*, '"Reason" in Philosophy,' 5; *KGW* 6.3:71). But this 'rude fetishism,' this abstract atomism, is in no way an arbitrary mode of thinking, but a structure embedded in the nature of language itself. The metaphysical substantialization of becoming is intrinsic to the nature of language.

## The Language of Apollo

A philosophical mythology lies concealed in *language* which breaks out again every moment, however careful one may be otherwise. Belief in freedom of will – that is to say in *identical* facts and in *isolated* facts – has in language its constant evangelist and advocate. (*WS*, 11)

The forgetting of nature through the concealment of things comes about because man stands in the way – of himself. He divides himself from himself and conceals this division as individuum; or, he conceals through division. Moreover, the human or the cultural is elucidated, by Nietzsche, as an 'inextinguishable drunkenness' (*GS*, 57), an inexorable mythology that is 'concealed in *language*' (*WS*, 11). That is to say, language structures culture (the human) such that it conceals the 'continuous ... indivisible flowing' (*WS*, 11) of becoming and breaks it up into isolated and self-identical beings, into substantialized atoms. For Nietzsche, language creates this complex and illusory dichotomy between appearance and the thing-in-itself, even before conceptual thought, by throwing a veil of metaphors over the undivided and indivisible flowing. 'The significance of language for the evolution of culture lies in this, that mankind set up in language a separate world beside the other world, a place it took to be so firmly set that, standing upon it, it could lift the rest of the world off its hinges and make itself master of it' (*H* 1:11). Language legislates what Apollo decrees: it divides the indivisible.

As Nietzsche argues in *The Birth of Tragedy*, Apollo is the god of measure, limitation, boundaries, and individuation, the god of appearance and illusion that makes intelligibility and knowledge possible: knowing as measuring. Apollo conceals 'the other world' and at the same time, by creating an unreal world of logic, he makes it intelligible and knowable: his science is concealment through individuation and measure. In short, Apollo's language brings into being the appearance or illusion of the thing-in-itself. He weaves the veil of individuation: the illusion of metaphysics, the dream of unconditioned, disconnected, self-sufficient being.

At the basis of the Apollonian operation lies the poetic and rhetorical creativity of the metaphor and the forgetting of this creativity. From the original nerve stimulus to the abstract concept, language stretches out a series of more or less conscious metaphors. In his early essay 'On Truth and Lies in a Nonmoral Sense,' Nietzsche argues that all human thought, however rational, is embedded in the dissimulative art of metaphor, an equating of the unequal: 'To begin with, a nerve stimulus is transferred into an image: first metaphor. The image, in turn, is imitated in a sound: second metaphor' (82). Moreover, the abstract concept, far from pre-existing and determining language as its instrument, is itself merely a metaphor of a metaphor two or three times removed from the nerve stimulus. Already in this early work, Nietzsche has freed himself of the correspondence theory of truth and transformed the conception of language from a passive medium of rational thought and truth into the poetic creator of thought itself; the signified is constituted by the signifier and does not exist outside of the linguistic play of signifiers. 'It is this way with all of us concerning language: we believe that we know something about the things themselves when we speak of trees, colours, snow, and flowers; and yet we possess nothing but metaphors for things – metaphors which correspond in no way to the original entities' (82–3).

Language, and therefore thought itself, never touches on a pre-existing thing-in-itself or truth because truth only arises within the metaphorical operation of language itself. 'What then is truth? A movable host of metaphors, metonymies, and anthropomorphisms: ... Truths are illusions which we have forgotten are illusions; ... to be truthful means to employ the usual metaphors' (84). Metaphor and forgetfulness: through the latter, the former becomes fixed and binding; illusions are no longer illusions but truths.

The language of Apollo allows Dionysus to speak and thereby conceal himself. At this point, the consequence of Nietzsche's theory of language for his critique of metaphysics and morality may be briefly summarized. 'Perspectivism' is not a 'subjectivism' anymore than a perspective is the interpretation of an interpreter, an originary subject; but the subject is itself an interpretation (cf. WP, 481). Further, appearance is no longer the appearance of an objective thing-in-itself, but the formation of things themselves. The twin foundations of metaphysics go down together: 'substance' and 'subject' are fictions of an atomistic mythology. 'At last, the "thing-in-itself" also disappears, because this is fundamentally the conception of a "subject-in-itself." But we have grasped that the subject is a fiction. The antithesis "thing-in-itself" and "appearance" is untenable; with that, however, the concept "appearance" also disappears' (WP, 552). With the critique of the abstract subject, Nietzsche also undermines the idea of truth as the correspondence of subject and object and transforms it into a 'will to truth,' 'an active determining – not a becoming-conscious of something that is in itself firm and determined' (WP, 552).

Language creates a simplified and false world, a crude atomism, a 'rude fetishism' out of the continuous flowing of nature. 'Through words and concepts we are still continually misled into imagining things as being simpler than they are, separate from one another, indivisible, each existing in and for itself' (WS, 11). Hence, from language, there arises the metaphysical world: substance, being, truth, reality – the unconditioned being in itself.

The belief in unconditioned substance derives from the prior belief in the unconditioned subject, the ego or free will, in 'soul atomism' (BGE, 12). For Nietzsche, this is the moral foundation of the metaphysical panoply of reified identities. And the foundation of the morality of free will lies in the separation of the doer from the deed. Finally, in his attack on morality as this opposition of subject and activity, Nietzsche must base his argument upon a new foundation with new concepts that affirm the identity of the human and the natural in a pre-objective form, in a kind of 'being in the world,' a belonging to the earth that embodies a joy in the actual.

**The Critique of Free Will**

Now, belief in freedom of will is incompatible precisely with the idea of a continuous, homogeneous, undivided, indivisible flowing: it presupposes that *every individual action is isolate and indivisible*; it is an *atomism* in the domain of willing and knowing ... Belief in freedom of will – that is to say in *identical* facts and in *isolated* facts – has in language its constant evangelist and advocate. (WS, 11)

If, as I argue, Nietzsche's philosophy grows out of the joy in the actual, then I must show how his basic concepts (will to power, *amor fati*, and eternal return) emerge from his critique of morality as the negation of reality and attempt to ascend to a new affirmation of the real in its totality. Insofar as joy in the actual entails the rejection of the metaphysical (and moral) distinctions between appearance and reality and between substance and subject, then it is also necessary to show how *amor fati* and eternal return embody a joy in a 'newly discovered, newly redeemed nature' (GS, 109).

An exorbitant pride attaches to the metaphysical mythology of belief in unconditioned substance and free will, a pride that Nietzsche demolishes not by returning to a humility that preceded this pride, but by advancing through it to a higher modesty – a true modesty that is built upon the recognition that we are not the work of ourselves (H 1:588), that the world of the subject is fundamentally an unknowable world (D, 116; GS, 335).

Language, isolated and identical beings, separation of doer and deed:

these are the legacies and laws of Apollo. For Nietzsche, the 'soul atomism' of free will underlies and structures the metaphysics of the unconditioned substance (the thing-in-itself) by separating doer and deed, by abstracting a subject of action from activity and hypostatizing it as its antecedent. The subject as free and unconditioned cause of behaviour underlies the 'rude fetishism' of isolated and identical things; the concept of the unconditioned subject is, for Nietzsche, the ground of metaphysics and its idealism.

It is *this* which sees everywhere deed and doer; this which believes in will as cause in general; this which believes in the 'ego', in the ego as being, in the ego as substance, and which *projects* its belief in the ego-substance on to all things – only thus does it *create* the concept 'thing' ... it is only from the conception 'ego' that there follows, derivatively, the concept 'being'. (*TI*, '"Reason" in Philosophy,' 5)

We misread ourselves and it is necessarily so; language and the metaphysical atomism of language lead us to 'misread ourselves in this apparently most intelligible of handwriting on the nature of our self' (*D*, 115). For language fosters the pride that the doer of the deed, the subject, is isolated, free, unconditioned, and totally responsible for his actions; that the conscious ego and its rationality precede, not only behaviour, but the thoughts that subsequently fill the box of the mind; that reason precedes its own content, its thoughts. In short, the separation of the doer from the deed (whether the deed be a thought or an action) requires the substantialization of the subject. 'At the beginning stands the great fateful error that the will is something [some-*thing*] which *produces an effect* – that will is a *faculty* [*Vermögen*]' (*TI*, '"Reason" in Philosophy,' 5; *KGW* 6.3:71).

For Nietzsche, to believe in free will is to accept a metaphysical conception of the self as a entity, a faculty, and an unconditioned substance. Its very unconditioned nature makes it free, responsible, and self-knowing; it makes of humanity a *causa sui*, a self-caused being that is able 'to pull [itself] up into existence by the hair, out of the swamps of nothingness' (*BGE*, 21). Hence, morality and the metaphysics of substance coincide; responsibility, guilt, and free will become synonymous through the separation of doer and deed.

Through the metaphysics of the unconditioned free will, morality justifies and presupposes a conception of freedom that Nietzsche sees as oppressive in a number of respects. By viewing himself as free in the sense of being defined by free will, 'man becomes that which he *wills* to become, his willing precedes his existence' (*H* 1:39). Through this metaphysical freedom, humanity is made responsible for its being as well as its actions:

accountability becomes absolute, and thereby guilt and oppression become synonymous with existence. Free will (in the metaphysical sense of unconditioned self-determination) implies complete self-responsibility which, in turn, culminates in endless guilt and oppression or depression. The 'soul atomism' that underlies the morality of responsibility – the unconditioned subject that is presupposed by this metaphysics of total freedom – is, for Nietzsche, a debilitating and erroneous mythology. In opposition to this, Nietzsche argues 'that man can be made accountable for nothing, not for his nature, nor for his motives, nor for his actions, nor for the effects he produces. One has thereby attained to the knowledge that the history of the moral sensations is the history of an error, the error of accountability, which rests on the error of freedom of will' (*H* 1:39).

Thus, Nietzsche's attack on the concepts of substance, the thing-in-itself, reality, etc., is the consequence of his critique of the unconditioned subject or the idea of free will. Since much of his work seems to consist in the destruction of moral idealism, one might be tempted to reduce Nietzsche's philosophy to his critique of morality and especially the metaphysical underpinnings of the morality of free will and complete responsibility of the subject. However, his relentless warfare against this conception of freedom grows out of his attempt to envision a new conception of freedom or sovereignty that is situated within nature or the actual. 'No one is accountable for his deeds, no one for his nature; to judge is the same thing as to be unjust' (*H* 1:39). In fact, far from being merely destructive, the critical aspect of Nietzsche's philosophy originates in an unprecedented and unlimited affirmation of life, in a joy in the actual that constitutes the basis of his critique of morality and the overcoming of metaphysics.

Before we examine the positive nature of this overcoming, it is important to confront interpretations that read Nietzsche's philosophy as purely negative and therefore still entangled in the assumptions of metaphysics. Two figures have been especially influential in asserting this view of Nietzsche: Eugen Fink and Martin Heidegger. For Fink, Nietzsche's relationship to metaphysics is somewhat ambiguous. On the one hand, Nietzsche seems to invert the traditional values of Western culture and philosophy, but because he does so in terms of those values, he remains imprisoned by them. In particular, although he negates the idea of God and the suprasensible world in general as the ground of value, he retains the notions of essence or substance and value as being: he simply conceives this essence as subjectivity and rethinks the value-giving action of human subjectivity as the will to power, that is, the Being of beings is value.[1] On the other hand, Fink suggests that, in his notion of creation as play (*Spiel*), Nietzsche has already transcended Western metaphysics. More precisely, the metaphor of Dionysus as the god of creative play and the innocence of becoming presents a post-metaphysical manner of understanding the world, one that transcends the predicative determinations of subjective will and objective beings.[2] The endless play of appearance never surrenders to the thing-in-itself; the innocence of becoming never culminates in a being, but simply maintains its Dionysian creativity of veiling and unveiling.

For Heidegger, things are much less ambiguous than they are for Fink: Nietzsche is viewed as the consummation of modern nihilism and metaphysical subjectivism. In two areas, Heidegger interprets Nietzsche as the culmination of modern nihilism: in his concept of the Being of beings and in his conception of truth. On the first point: Nietzsche continues and radicalizes the scientific and technological relationship to nature that characterizes the modern spirit. What is peculiar to the spirit of modernity, the scientific spirit, lies in its objectivity, the objectification of beings by placing (*stellen*) them before (*vor*) the subject in a 'representation [*Vorstellen*].' Through representations, the subject reduces beings to objects in order to render them calculable and controllable for the technological domination of nature and humanity. Similarly, through the representation of objects, science transforms the conception of truth into the certitude of representations.

This objectifying of whatever is, is accomplished in a setting-before, a representing, that aims at bringing each particular being before it in such a way that man who calculates can be sure, and that means be certain, of that being. We first arrive at science as research when and only when truth has been transformed into the certainty of representation. What it is to be is for the first time defined as the objectiveness of representing, and truth is first defined as the certainty of representing, in the metaphysics of Descartes.[3]

In this way, Heidegger characterizes the spiritual peculiarity of modernity as the reduction of beings to objects or representations. What is especially relevant to our investigation of Nietzsche is that, in the modern era, morality is also transformed by the objectification of things, and this change manifests itself in the notion of value. Something can become a value only after it has been reduced to a representation, established, employed, and assessed by human beings; this is the pride of humanism. For Heidegger, however, this humanistic transformation of morality through the concept of value is symptomatic of the loss of being – symptomatic of nihilism.

> The representation of value is just as essential to the modern interpretation of that which is, as is the system. Where anything that is has become the object of representing, it first incurs in a certain manner a loss of Being. This loss is adequately perceived, if but vaguely and unclearly, and is compensated for with corresponding swiftness through the fact that we impart value to the object and to that which is, interpreted as object, and that we take the measure of whatever is, solely in keeping with the criterion of value, and make of values themselves the goal of all activity.[4]

However, the irony of the morality of values is that it is through the bestowal of value upon a thing that it 'is robbed of its worth.'[5] By transforming a being into a value, it must first be objectified, represented as an object, and thereby robbed of its real being. Moreover, the other presupposition of value and objectifying representation is the radical subjectification of being-human: 'Every valuing, even where it values positively, is a subjectivizing. It does not let beings: be. Rather, valuing lets beings: be valid – solely as the objects of its doing.'[6] The concepts of value and subjectification are critical to Heidegger's characterization of Nietzsche as a nihilist. The corollary of the transformation of the Being of beings into representations is that human being becomes a subject, the ground of representing and the certainty of representations. Whereas for Plato and ancient philosophy, the subject was the Idea, for modernity, the subject becomes the human: 'However, when man becomes the primary and only real *subjectum*, that means: Man becomes that being upon which all that is, is grounded as regards the manner of its Being and its truth. Man becomes the relational centre of that which is as such.'[7] Even more significant for the interpretation of Nietzsche, however, is the fact that the subjectivity of the subject becomes the will: will is the Being of beings. 'In the subjectness of the subject, will comes to appearance as the essence of subjectness. Modern metaphysics, as the metaphysics of subjectness, thinks the Being of that which is in the sense of will.'[8]

The interplay between objectivism and subjectivism that distinguishes the modern age is grounded, for Heidegger, in two interwoven events: the transformation of the object into a representation and being-human into the 'subjectum,' a subject that grounds and certifies these representations. The will of the human being, as an individual or as a collective entity, is the locus of these two events. For this reason, modernity finds its apex in Nietzsche's philosophy of the will to power. When humanity becomes 'subjectum' or foundation and origin for the things that are, it thereby sets itself free from obligation to other foundations or authorities, particularly, Christian revelational truth. Thus, the human being comes to legislate for itself a new truth as certainty by willing its own conditions of existence, its own obligations, in the certainty of its representations. But since representing or willing is also an objectification that seeks to secure and control the object, this liberation fulfils itself in domination and mastery of nature and humanity through technology. 'Representing is making-stand-over-against, an objectifying that goes forward and masters.'[9]

How does Nietzsche's philosophy of will to power realize and complete modern nihilism, according to Heidegger? In other words, why does Heidegger say that, in Nietzsche's 'revaluation of all values,' in will to power and the eternal return, 'in what Nietzsche calls the pessimism of strength there is accomplished the rising up of modern humanity into the unconditional dominion of subjectivity within the subjectness of what is'?[10] First and foremost, the answer is because the will to power is 'the value-positing will' and, as such, it fulfils the liberation of man as the foundation of all things in technological mastery and domination of beings of all kinds. More precisely, power in the will to power is not something other than the will itself; rather, it is 'the overpowering of itself.' Will and power are not two different things but essentially the same, and therefore the will to power is really 'the will to will.'[11] And because values are the conditions and means by which the will realizes itself, Nietzsche's will to power must be intrinsically a value-positing will, according to Heidegger.

From this basic interpretation of will to power, Heidegger simply elaborates the implications of this thesis in his reading of the Overman and eternal return. In particular, it follows from his reduction of will to power to a value-positing will that it is also a will to mastery and domination of nature through technology. Since the elevation of the human will to the 'subjectum' arises from the degradation of beings into representations for human use, and since values are simply moral representations of man as unconditional will, it follows that the will to power as a value-positing will is a will to technological mastery of nature. Moreover, as the complete 'loss of being,' the will to power is the highest expression of nihilism. Indeed, far from signifying the overcoming of subjectivism and nihilism, for Heidegger the Overman (Übermensch), as the new man of the liberated 'subjectum,' embodies the complete nihilism of the modern age and its will to power. As the realization of the value-positing will, the Overman is the technological dominator of nature through the subjectivism of value. In the will to power of the Overman, fulfilled in willing the eternal return of all things, there is accomplished the going-up into the unconditional domination of nature by modern subjectivity as the subjectness of all things: in and through the subjective nihilism of his revolutionary objectification of beings, the Overman makes nature itself into 'the object of assault ... the object of technology.'[12]

This up-rising into subjectivity does away with the Being of beings, according to Heidegger, and thereby constitutes the heights and depths of nihilism. In modernity's insurrection against being, humanity loses itself in losing being, in the loss of the world and nature: nihilism represents nothing less than the destruction of joy in the actual. However, the irony of Heidegger's interpretation of Nietzsche is that he completely overlooks the fundamental continuity of his own thought with that of Nietzsche. In fact, I have elaborated Heidegger's reading of Nietzsche at some length precisely because it illustrates a common misunderstanding of his philosophy as a humanist subjectivism that has the benefit of accentuating exactly what Nietzsche himself criticized: subjective morality – and the basis of his criticism: a deeper *ethos*.

## The Joy of Becoming as *Ethos*

Despite the fact that the term 'value' figures so prominently in his work and that, through it, he appears to espouse a moral subjectivism that preserves the opposition of fact and value, Nietzsche not only rejects subjectivism, but does so on the basis of a transcendence of the metaphysics of essence. More specifically, in his critique of the abstraction of the doer from the deed, Nietzsche attacks the predicative structure of metaphysics that places an object over against a representing subject. Thus, the same pride and arrogance of anthropocentrism that Heidegger rejects in the notion of value, Nietzsche already confronts in his genealogy of morals. In this sense, Nietzsche 'was the great, fateful figure who fundamentally altered the task of the critique of subjective spirit for our century.'[13]

Is joy in the actual a definitive overcoming of metaphysics, or is Fink more correct when he says that Nietzsche is both a prisoner and a liberator? Put in a way that is more relevant to grand politics, does Nietzsche's confrontation with the metaphysical *logos* grow out of an *ethos* of joy and creation, out of an ethical communion quite different from our modern morality of values? It seems to me that Nietzsche's entire philosophical enterprise – his critique of morality as well as his own philosophical vision – arises from an awareness of culture as a pre-cognitive horizon (the pre-conceptual play of metaphor) within which the *logos* of reason occurs.

Moreover, far from constituting a value system fashioned and manipulated by calculating subjects, culture is an *ethos*, the pre-objective spirit of a people with a particular political and historical reality. Like Hegel, Nietzsche situates the 'I' within a 'we,' an intersubjective spirit that constitutes the individual as a particular cultural subject; therefore, the cultural historicity of the subject determines his concrete philosophical issues: *logos* is the historical product of a particular cultural *ethos*.

If Nietzsche is indeed the fateful figure who transforms the task of the critique of subjective spirit, then it is surely in his attack on morality as the abstraction of the doer from the deed that this task is realized. Moreover, if the conceptual life of reason (*logos*) is dependent upon the pre-conceptual perspective of a culture (*ethos*), then the question of the relationship of doer and deed is not an abstract problem but a lived cultural reality; and the overcoming of metaphysics is, therefore, not an individual event but a cultural one. Joy in the actual, the critique of morality, and his vision of *amor fati* and eternal return may point the way towards the end of metaphysics, but only the full realization of grand politics in a new cultural *ethos* can bring this about. To presume that an individual philosopher can extract himself from metaphysics is itself a metaphysical position that prefaces the deed with an independent doer. In this sense, Nietzsche must remain a prisoner of metaphysical thought.

However, a new culture that takes the doer back into the deed manifests itself, not in a static conception of *ethos* as 'ethical substance,' but only in a new form of action. Since the doer is no longer separated from his deed, action cannot be understood as the consequence of a free and independent subject. The culture of joy in the actual must embody, therefore, an entirely unprecedented conception of activity. Some commentators have identified Nietzsche's notion of activity without a subject as 'play' or 'creation' or 'affirmation' in *amor fati* and eternal return.[14] If this is the real significance of *amor fati* and eternal return, then it is necessary to examine how this action embodies joy in the actual and what the implications are for grand politics.

Nietzsche transforms the critique of subjective spirit through his attempt to think of activity as pure becoming. Given the predicative structure of language, the difficulty of thinking about a form of activity that takes the doer back into the deed is especially daunting. On the conceptual level, Nietzsche deals with it negatively through his philosophical critique of the ideas of responsibility and free will as a critique of language; on the pre-conceptual level, he attempts to articulate it through the metaphors of pregnancy and birth: we let that which is coming to be within us grow, by waiting and watching, until it is ready to be brought forth. In the modesty of this waiting and watching, we overcome 'all presumptuous talk of "willing" and "creating"' (*D*, 552). For, in the state of 'pregnancy,' one is not the subject but an intermediary through which what is coming into being may bring itself forth.

> Is there a more holy condition than that of pregnancy? To do all we do in the unspoken belief that it has somehow to benefit that which is coming to be within us [*Werdenden*]! ... Everything is veiled, ominous, we know nothing of what is taking place, we wait and try to be *ready*. At the same time, a pure and purifying feeling of profound irresponsibility reigns in us ... *it* is growing, *it* is coming to light: *we* have no right to determine either its value or the hour of its coming. All the influence we can exert lies in keeping it safe. (*D*, 552; *KGW* 5.1:326)

Earlier Nietzsche described this 'pure and purifying feeling of profound irresponsibility' as modesty, as 'the recognition that we are not the work of ourselves' (*H* 1:588). This means that we do not 'make' our actions and ideas, let alone ourselves, if, by 'making,' one implies a notion of action as the means of realizing the purposes of an already given subject. On the contrary, far from representing the uprising of modern humanity into the unconditional dominion of subjectivity as free will, action is, for Nietzsche, a 'bringing forth [*Vollbringen*]' of 'that which is coming to be [*Werdenden*] within us'; fundamentally, then, *ethos* is *poiesis*, a bringing to completion of that which is already coming to be. 'And if what is expected is an idea, a deed – towards every bringing forth [*Vollbringen*] we have essentially no other relationship than that of pregnancy and ought to blow to the winds all presumptuous talk of "willing" and "creating"' (*D*, 552; *KGW* 5.1:326–7).

Towards every bringing forth, whether it is an idea or a deed, we have no other relationship than that of pregnancy; we are simply 'intermediaries' (*D*, 552) of becoming, of nature as *natura*: that which is about to be born. However, Nietzsche expresses this immanence in the event of nature not as a passive resignation, but as an active ethical call through his appropriation of Pindar's dictum: '*What does your conscience say?* – "You shall become the person you are [*Du sollst der werden, der du bist*]"' (*GS*, 270; *KGW* 5.2: 197). One becomes only what one is; this is '*ideal selfishness* [*Selbstsucht*]' (*D*, 552; *KGW* 5.1:326), and for Nietzsche, it is also the task and passion of culture to cultivate 'a new and improved *physis*' (*UDH*, 10). It is this sense of nature as becoming, as the event of coming into being, to which man always belongs as intermediary that Nietzsche symbolizes in the phrase 'will to power [*der Wille zur Macht*].'

Nietzsche's critique of moral idealism becomes more understandable in this context because, if the doer is always a part of the deed, then he cannot be the cause of behaviour nor can his will or values precede and determine his actions; if one belongs to the event of nature as becoming, then every 'ought' that presumes to step out of nature and postulate itself as an independent cause appears as an empty and idealistic voluntarism. The 'ought' has meaning to the extent that it is embedded in and affirms what is, to the extent that the ideal is not a cause but a consequence of reality (cf. *TI*, 'The Four Great Errors,' 1, 2, 3; *WP*, 330ff.). Thus, the critique of morality and subjective spirit expressed in taking the doer back into the deed entails the new ethical task of 'ideal selfishness': to become what one is. This presupposes the critique of essentialism and the idealism of the free will: that is, freedom can no longer place itself over against nature as free will, but must embrace reality as joy in the actual.

In order to free culture of moral idealism and prepare the ground for joy in the actual, the moral taste must be overcome and a new taste based in the physics of *physis* inaugurated:

Let us therefore *limit* ourselves to the purification of our opinions and valuations and to the *creation of our own new tables of what is good*, and let us stop brooding about the 'moral value of our actions'! Yes, my friends, regarding all the moral chatter of some about others it is time to feel nauseous. Sitting in moral judgement should offend our taste. Let us leave such chatter and such bad taste to those who have nothing else to do but drag the past a few steps further through time and who never live in the present – which is to say the many, the great majority. We, however, *want to become those we are* – human beings who are new, unique, incomparable, who give themselves laws, who create themselves. To that end we must become the best learners and discoverers of everything that is lawful and necessary in the world: we must become *physicists* in order to be able to be *creators* in this sense ... (*GS*, 335)

In order to 'be able to be *creators* in this sense,' it is first necessary to become physicists. But in what sense? It cannot be in the objectifying sense that Heidegger attributes to modern science as research because this objectification of beings as representations and values involves the 'rude fetishism' that Nietzsche criticizes as 'atomism.' It would be more accurate to argue that Nietzsche's 'physics' refers, in this context, to a nature that is 'newly discovered, [and] newly redeemed' (*GS*, 109). In this sense, nature as *physis* is 'the innocence of becoming'; therefore, to be a creator 'in this sense' means to bring forth to fullness (*Voll-bringen*) that which is coming to be. To be able to be a creator, according to Nietzsche, involves first overcoming all presumptuous talk of 'creating' and 'willing,' and thus presupposes that one belongs to nature in this newly discovered and newly redeemed sense of 'will to power'; to be a 'physicist' presupposes that one is 'the meaning of the earth,' the Overman: that is, the one who is able to *'remain true to the earth'* (Z, Prologue, 3).

## Becoming What One Is: The Historicity of Culture

To liberate culture from moral idealism implies that one must overcome 'the bad taste' of moral judgment. Does this not suggest that one can simply step out of one's past, out of one's becoming, and start anew from point zero? And is this not simply another form of idealism? This is a critical point in Nietzsche's cultural critique and grand politics: How does one become what one is and, at the same time, overcome what has been? Is there a form of becoming that overcomes what is and has been in an affirmative rather than a negative manner?

In taking the doer back into the deed, Nietzsche places man into the continuous flow of becoming in which there is no absolute subject, but only intermediaries of nature who bring forth what is coming to be. This pure becoming is the antithesis of atomism inasmuch as it presupposes 'a continuous, homogeneous, undivided, indivisible flowing' (WS, 11). In this continuous and indivisible flow of becoming, everything is 'chained and entwined together, all things are in love' (Z, 'The Intoxicated Song,' 10). To become what one is, therefore, is not an individualistic enterprise but a taking oneself back into the deed, a bringing forth of what is coming to be in pure becoming.

According to Nietzsche, this is true in an especially temporal sense because becoming implies historicity, a historicity of plenitude: becoming is a historical coming to be of what already fully is. The temporality of becoming involves two points: first, the relationship of what is coming to be, the future, with what has been and continues to be, the past and present; and second, as the relationship between past and future, becoming is not a becoming-other, but an encompassing of the otherness that is intrinsic to what is, a yes-saying to all suffering as part of joy in the actual. These two points bring out the essential identity of Nietzsche's principal concepts: the will to power and the eternal return of the same.

On the first point: that which is coming to be can only grow out of what has been and continues to be, the past and present. There is no present that is not already pregnant with the future because there is no present that is not child of the past. The present moment is not an atom separate from past and future, but a contemporaneous entwining of past and future in the chain of becoming. Nietzsche recognizes this contemporaneity in one of his early essays on history and culture: 'For since we are the outcome of earlier generations, we are also the outcome of their aberrations, passions and errors, and indeed of their crimes; it is not possible wholly to free one-self from this chain. If we condemn these aberrations and regard ourselves as free of them, this does not alter the fact that we originate in them' (*UDH*, 3). Becoming is not becoming other than what has been because it is impossible to free oneself completely from this chain of aberrations and crimes; indeed, we originate from these 'injustices' as their outcome, and to condemn them would mean to condemn ourselves as well as our condemnation. Here again, Nietzsche makes the familiar yet fundamental observation that we cannot step out of our historicity and make ourselves abstract subjects without a past.

Nietzsche envisions a relationship between past and future that is both a 'continuous ... indivisible flowing' and a 'self-overcoming,' a way of taking oneself back into the innocence of becoming and, at the same time, embracing what is passing away in coming into being: a way of releasing oneself from the past by releasing the past into becoming. He conceives of a becoming in which the future both affirms and re-writes the past; by affirming what is and has been as its origin, the future frees itself for its own becoming and brings itself forth from this past, as a passing over itself, forward towards itself. 'It is an attempt to give oneself, as it were *a posteriori*, a past in which one would like to originate in opposition to that in which one did originate' (*UDH*, 3).

In particular, one is called upon to become a 'retroactive force [*rückwirkende Kraft*]' (*GS*, 34; *KGW* 5.2:78) by redeeming and transforming the past from its pastness, and thereby releasing it (and oneself) into becoming. Indeed, this is the task of culture in Nietzsche's grand politics. This implies that the will can learn to will backwards as a retroactive power. 'To redeem the past and to transform every "It was" into an "I wanted it thus!" – that alone do I call redemption! ... All "It was" is a fragment, a riddle, a dreadful chance – until the creative will says to it: "But I willed it thus!"' (*Z*, 'Of Redemption'). This is precisely what is demanded and accomplished in the eternal return of the same: the transformation of the past into a contemporary passing that one must bring forth and release into the fullness of becoming. The task of becoming what one is involves a transformation of one's experience of time and history; and it entails that 'the will become its own redeemer and bringer of joy [*Freudebringer*]' by bringing forth (*Voll-*

*bringen*) the continuous flowing together of past and future (Z, 'Of Redemption'; *KGW* 6.1:175). 'There is no way of telling what may yet become part of history. Perhaps the past is still essentially undiscovered! So many retroactive forces are still needed!' (*GS*, 34).

On the second point: as the flowing together of past and future, becoming is not a becoming-other, born of dissatisfaction with what is, but an affirmative encompassing of the otherness that already belongs to what is; it is a yes-saying to all suffering as a necessary part of the joy of becoming and the historicity of plenitude. Far from being a going-towards or receding-from completion, becoming is always, at every moment, the bringing forth of complete fullness. Its longing is not the longing for joy at the end of history but the longing of joy in becoming.[15] There are two aspects of this fullness of becoming: a completeness that includes the otherness of longing for itself – the feeling of incompleteness; and the plenitude of becoming – the fact that it is justified at every moment – presupposes that becoming is incapable of being evaluated; it presupposes that God (Being) is dead.

Taking the doer back into the deed implies that one releases oneself into becoming, that one releases the past into pure becoming by affirming it as the medium of one's present. Thus, to become what one is means that one must become a retroactive force that transforms every 'It was' into an 'I wanted it thus!' In this way, joy in becoming entails, not a rejection, but a redemption of the past in its passing over itself into a future, a coming to be that re-wills and re-writes the past as a still coming to pass. Nietzsche formulates this redemption as eternal return, as a joy in the actual that realizes itself in an insatiable longing for even the most terrible aspects of one's past: 'For joy wants itself, therefore it also wants heart's agony!' (Z, 'The Intoxicated Song,' 11). In longing for itself, joy wants to become what it is, and therefore, it also wants the suffering of the heart that belongs to what it is as joy in becoming. In affirming any single joy, one already re-wills all the sufferings, aberrations, errors, and even crimes of the past. 'Did you ever say Yes to one joy? O my friends, then you said Yes to *all* woe as well. All things are chained and entwined together; all things are in love; if ever you wanted one moment twice, if ever you said: "You please me, happiness, instant, moment!" then you wanted *everything* to return!' (10).

Redemption is the retroactive transformation of the past that releases the 'It was' into becoming. By re-willing the past, one does not thereby become the 'subjectum' of pure willing, as Heidegger argues; rather, through this affirmation, one is placed back into becoming as an intermediary that releases itself by releasing the past into becoming. This redemption involves an affirmation so total that one wants everything to return, even the most profound sufferings of the heart. The continuous and indivisible nature of becoming underlies the identity of joy and heart's agony: 'for happiness and unhappiness are sisters and even twins that either grow up together or ... *remain small* together' (*GS*, 338). Nietzsche's pursuit of the meaning of joy in the actual through his elaboration of all the consequences of taking the doer back into the deed culminates in the affirmation embodied in eternal return.

The fullness of becoming presupposes that God is dead (*GS*, 125), that there is no transcendent measure, beyond becoming, by which it could be evaluated. Nietzsche insists that these two propositions – the completeness of becoming at every moment and the impossibility of evaluating becoming – amount to the same thing (*WP*, 708). If, as Nietzsche argues, becoming is absolute, then there is no being (God) or standard by which becoming can be judged or evaluated. 'One must reach out and try to grasp this astonishing *finesse, that the value of life cannot be estimated*' (*TI*, 'The Problem of Socrates,' 2). This 'finesse' is, in fact, the great liberation: the restoration of the innocence of becoming.

One is necessary, one is a piece of fate, one belongs to the whole, one *is* in the whole – there exists nothing which could judge, measure, compare, condemn our being, for that would be to judge, measure, compare, condemn the whole ... *But nothing exists apart from the whole!* – That no one is any longer made accountable, that the kind of being manifested cannot be traced back to a *causa prima*, that the world is a unity neither as sensorium nor as 'spirit', *this alone is the great liberation* – thus alone is the *innocence* of becoming restored ... The concept 'God' has hitherto been the greatest *objection* to existence ... We deny God; in denying God, we deny accountability: only by doing *that* do we redeem the world. (*TI*, 'The Four Great Errors,' 8)

Nietzsche takes the impossibility of stepping outside of becoming as the ground of the fullness or eternity of becoming at every moment. In short, becoming is not a linear progression in which the present is justified by reference to a future or the past by reference to the present; on the contrary, becoming is fully justified at every moment. 'Becoming is of equivalent value at every moment; the sum of its values always remains the same; in other words: it has no value at all, for anything against which to measure it, and in relation to which the word "value" would have meaning, is lacking. *The total value of the world cannot be evaluated*' (*WP*, 708).

By restoring the innocence of becoming, Nietzsche unfolds a pure, newly discovered, newly redeemed nature. This restoration and redemption demands an agonizing modesty: a releasing of oneself into the joy of becoming that longs for itself; a releasing into the joy that longs to become itself by belonging to heart's agony. Nietzsche envisions and accomplishes this releasing in the eternal return – the practice of joy in the actual. Thus, in the *ethos* of joy in becoming, Nietzsche sketches the historicity of culture and grand politics.

## Grand Politics: The Historicity of Joy

For Nietzsche, the historicity of culture demands a way of transfiguring and redeeming the past through joy and affirmation rather than suffering reactively from it through the spirit of revenge. It requires a historicity of joy in which one becomes what one is while one overcomes and affirms what one was. In this way, it presupposes retroactive forces of joy, and this is precisely the task of Nietzsche's grand politics.

The cultural past that Nietzsche's grand politics seeks to overcome is nihilism: that is, morality and the whole metaphysics of idealism that abstracts the subject from becoming. Fink believes that Nietzsche is both a prisoner and a liberator of metaphysics, while Heidegger sees him as the consummation of nihilism. Nietzsche's relationship to nihilism is ambiguous, precisely because, for him, overcoming the past necessarily entails one's immersion in it: one can only transfigure nihilism by willing it as 'active nihilism' (*WP*, 14ff.), by going deeper into it (cf. *TI*, 'Expeditions of an Untimely Man,' 43). Nietzsche states his personal dilemma in the following note:

1. My endeavour to oppose decay and increasing weakness of personality. I sought a new *centre*.
2. Impossibility of this endeavour recognized.
3. Thereupon I advanced further down the road of disintegration – where I found new sources of strength for individuals. We have to be destroyers! – I perceived that the state of disintegration, in which individual natures can perfect themselves as never before – is an image and isolated example of existence in general. To the paralyzing sense of general disintegration and incompleteness I opposed the *eternal recurrence*. (*WP*, 417)

Nietzsche overcomes nihilism not by opposing it, but by advancing further down the road of disintegration; thus, 'nihilism, as the denial of a truthful world, of being, might be *a divine way of thinking*' (*WP*, 15).

While 'we have to be destroyers,' it is also true that one destroys only as a creator (*GS*, 58) and, therefore, only as a physicist (*GS*, 335), as one who remains true to becoming. To overcome nihilism, one must first live it and release oneself into its becoming and thereby bring it forth in its own coming to be.

Nietzsche emphasizes this immersion in nihilism especially when it comes to Christianity, which he identifies as the fundamental dynamic of decay and disintegration: 'One must have seen the fatality from close up, better still one must have experienced it in oneself, one must have almost perished by it' (*AC*, 8). He seems to suggest that the fatality must be one's fate before one can overcome it: all redemption is a self-overcoming.

If one cannot step out of history and condemn nihilism, then redemption (*Erlösung*) necessitates a release into the historicity of nihilism, into disintegration (*Auflösung*). Indeed, only one who has 'experienced it in oneself' is really able to overcome it by a retroactive affirmation, an 'I wanted it thus,' through the eternal return.

The Overman, the one who releases himself into the joy of becoming, is not the dominant one, the strongest who steps outside of becoming and rules over it. Through eternal return, he is the one who 'encompasses' the historicity of joy, the eternal dissonance of happiness and unhappiness as twins. As the embodiment of joy in the actual, the Overman is the one who longs for heart's agony, who encompasses the dissonance of joy and suffering in himself. He can say to himself, 'O my soul, now there is nowhere a soul more loving and encompassing [*umfangender*] and spacious [*umfänglicher*]! Where could future and past be closer together than with you?' (*Z*, 'Of the Great Longing'; *KGW* 6.1:275). Thus, the sovereign or noble type is the great soul, the most comprehensive, complete, and encompassing through his joy in the actual, through *amor fati* and eternal return. For Nietzsche, greatness of soul is the spacious and complete encompassing of its own antithesis, of its most extreme other. The really great soul is not stronger and more powerful in the narrow sense, but wider and more open. It embodies 'the greater, more manifold, more comprehensive [*umfänglichere*] life' (*BGE*, 262; *KGW* 6.2:226). It entails a 'more mysterious pathos ... the craving for an ever new widening of distances within the soul itself, the development of ever higher, rarer, more remote, further-stretching, more comprehensive [*umfänglicherer*] states' (*BGE*, 257; *KGW* 6.2:215). Thus, the most noble souls, according to Nietzsche, are not better or more moral, but embrace and contain more life, more tragic dissonances than others: 'In the beginning, the noble caste was always the barbarian caste: their predominance did not lie mainly in physical strength but in strength of the soul – they were more *whole* human beings (which also means, at every level, "more whole beasts")' (*BGE*, 257). The higher type is 'better and more evil' in the sense of being 'a synthetic, summarizing, justi- fying man' (*WP*, 866); what distinguishes the great man from the good man is his wholeness in dissonance, both the presence of the most varied and terrible passions as well as the power to control and sublimate 'these mag- nificent monsters' (*WP*, 933). In short, for Nietzsche greatness of soul arises from the necessity of accommodating two or more heterogeneous powers: 'the only thing for him to do is to turn himself into so large a hall of culture that both powers can be accommodated within it, even if at opposite ends, while between them there reside mediating powers with the strength and authority to settle any contention that might break out' (*H*, 276). The 'grand architecture of culture' seeks to establish a synthesis and harmony between contending powers rather than a monopoly of power by one or the other: a harmony in dissonance rather than a homogeneity devoid of tension.

This encompassing of the heterogeneous illustrates the affirmative prac- tice of the historicity of joy. The Overman summarizes and justifies the historical becoming of his people and culture by releasing himself into its past and releasing this past into becoming through his encompassing affir- mation – through eternal return. This is the cultural bringing forth to full- ness (*Vollbringen*) that Nietzsche assigns to the Overman in his grand politics: to redeem and transfigure our cultural past through the historicity of joy – eternal return.

Anyone who manages to experience the history of humanity as a whole as *his own history* will feel in an enormously generalized way all the grief of an invalid who thinks of health ... But if one endured, if one *could* endure this immense sum of grief of all kinds ... being a person whose horizon encompasses thousands of years past and future, being the heir of all the nobility of all past spirit ... if one could finally contain all this in one soul and crowd it into a single feeling – this would surely have to result in a happiness that humanity has not known so far: the happiness of a god full of power and love, full of tears and laughter, a happiness that, like the sun in the evening continually bestows its inexhaustible riches, pouring them into the sea, feeling richest, as the sun does, only when even the poorest fisherman is still rowing with golden oars! This godlike feeling would then be called – humaneness. (*GS*, 337)

To take in and metabolize the history of humanity as one's 'own history' necessarily means making oneself sick not only with its immense grief and suffering but also with its revenge against life because it includes so much suffering – a spirit of revenge that Nietzsche calls 'nihilism.' Through eternal return, the highest types of humanity are asked to endure this suffering and disgust and, beyond mere endurance, to release this history of suffering and nihilism into becoming so that a new happiness may eventually overcome and embrace this history – indeed, so that a new humaneness (an over-humanness) may finally come to pass through the historicity of joy in the actual.

Through the innocence of becoming and eternal return, Nietzsche moves us constantly and inexorably away from the mythology of the centre towards the reality of the periphery, the encompassing horizon; for the centre never holds, but is held because it is encompassed within affirmative encompassing. Traditionally, the centre was viewed as the essential, and what was peripheral was insignificant. For Nietzsche, the boundary at the far limit of our horizon is central and fundamental: as the grand architecture of culture, the encompassing is both the horizon and, at the same time, the intimate but oblique middle that harmonizes the heterogeneity of what is encompassed; it is the distant horizon that is also our nearest ground and intimate world. That is to say, as the joy in the actual, the encompassing is sovereign because it forms the *ethos* of culture, and it is atopian because it is both the periphery and the centre of human community. As such, it is the sovereignty of joy.

# 3

# The Seasons of a People: Community and Individuality in the Cycle of Natural Morality

Morality [*Sittlichkeit*] is nothing other (therefore *no more!*) than obedience to customs [*Sitten*] ... customs, however, are the *traditional* way of behaving and evaluating ... The free human being is immoral [*unsittlich*] because in all things he is *determined* to depend upon himself and not upon a tradition. (*D*, 9; *KGW* 5.1:17–18)

When 'morals decay [*Sitten verfallen*]' those men emerge whom one calls tyrants: they are the precursors and ... the precocious harbingers of *individuals*. Only a little while later this fruit of fruits hangs yellow and mellow from the tree of a people – and the tree existed only for the sake of these fruits ... The times of corruption are those when the apples fall [*fallen*] from the tree: I mean the individuals ... Corruption is merely a nasty word for the autumn of a people. (*GS*, 23; *KGW* 5.2:70–2)

Much of Nietzsche's work appears to be a relentless and unadulterated attack on morality. He argues, for example, that morality is 'the danger of dangers' (*GM*, Preface, 6), that 'the harm the good do is the most harmful harm' (*Z*, 'Of Old and New Law-Tables,' 26), and that it is 'not the corruption of man but the extent to which he has become tender and moralized [that] is his curse' (*WP*, 98). Given this, one may well ask whether Nietzsche has a positive concept of morality, a concept of a truly natural morality.

It is precisely this perspective, critical of 'moralization,' that reveals Nietzsche's concept of natural morality; for 'moralization' means the 'denaturalization' of 'real morality':

Strong ages and peoples do not reflect on their rights, on the principles on which they act, on their instincts and reasons. Becoming-conscious is a sign that real morality, i.e., instinctive certainty in actions, is going to the devil ... Thesis: the appearance of moralists belongs to an age in which [real] morality is coming to an end. (*WP*, 423)

Moral idealism belongs to a time and a people suffering from the denaturalization of morality, the fatal abstraction of virtue from nature – the denial of the homogeneity of the moral and the immoral.

If moral idealism, or 'moralization,' is symptomatic of the decline and denaturalization of 'real morality,' it follows that Nietzsche has a concept of positive or natural morality. In particular, it is well known that he conceives and promotes 'noble morality' and criticizes only 'slave morality' (*BGE*, 260; *GM* 1:10). This distinction of two general types of morality tends to obscure another form of morality which is fundamental to both his philosophy and his grand politics. This is what Nietzsche calls 'the morality of custom [die Sittlichkeit der Sitte]' or 'herd morality.' It would be a gross misinterpretation to assimilate 'herd morality' to the more critical concept of 'slave morality,' and yet it remains unclear how it relates to 'noble morality.'

My argument in this chapter is that natural morality encompasses both 'the morality of custom' and 'noble morality' within the grand architecture and history of 'a people.' This means that noble morality is not simply a subjective or existential adventure of the Overman as an isolated individual divorced from a social or political culture. For Nietzsche, culture is always the primary concern, and the cultivation of a sovereign individual, a masterly or noble type, is the only cultural activity. In this sense, natural morality is the means of realizing this cultural goal, and this entails a morality that not only would promote 'a living sense of community' and its 'subordination of the individual' (*H* 1:224), but would also accommodate partial weakenings of the sense of community that erupt in individuality and free spiritedness.

For Nietzsche, natural morality contains both elements, community and individuality, in successive phases or seasons of a people. Indeed, Nietzsche's sovereign, autonomous individual is not a subjective reality at all but belongs to and grows out of a people, 'the fruit of fruits ... from the tree of a people' (*GS*, 23). Similarly, 'noble morality' is not a subjective morality, despite its radical individuality; it also grows out of 'the morality of custom' of a people and, as such, remains a phenomenon of a people and thus a phenomenon of politics – grand politics.

In developing his concept of natural morality, Nietzsche uses the term 'morality' in a number of very different senses. Here one encounters a problem in translation because Nietzsche uses two German words that are both translated into English as 'morality': *Sittlichkeit* and *Moralität*. Like Hegel, although far less systematically, Nietzsche uses the word *Sittlichkeit* when referring to the morality of custom (*Sittlichkeit der Sitte*) of a people self-absorbed in its own traditions and the word *Moralität* when referring to the subjective morality of the 'heart' (Rousseau) or the unconditionally free will (Kant). And, again like Hegel, he tends to identify the former with the moral realism of the ancient cultures of early Israel, India, Greece, and Rome and the latter with the moral idealism of Christianity and modern moral-political ideologies.[1]

For Nietzsche, natural morality would be much closer to the moral realism of 'customary morality' (*Sittlichkeit*), although it is by no means identical with it because he wants to incorporate the 'historical sense' and the 'subjectivity' of modernity. Given the predominance of the 'living sense of community' in customary morality, it follows that individuality, freedom, and change are rejected as categorically evil and a corruption of the community. However, it is precisely this evil and corruption that Nietzsche wants to revalue positively as 'the autumn of a people' (*GS*, 23). But through the revaluation of evil, Nietzsche wants to reveal the homogeneity of the moral and the immoral: by showing and affirming the continuity between good and evil, man goes up to nature, humanity naturalizes itself in a newly discovered nature. To use Nietzsche's provocative expression: one only becomes better when one grows more evil (*Z*, 'The Convalescent'; 'Of the Higher Man,' 5; *BGE*, 116, 295).

This conception of nature as the 'homogeneity of all things' (*WP*, 120, 272, 299, 308) also reveals Nietzsche's conception of the highest type of human being: the sovereign individual who is able to practice *amor fati* and joy in the actual. Nietzsche calls this type 'noble' and characterizes him as 'a law-giver.' The noble type is genuinely autonomous because he is able to make laws for himself, and this he can do only because he is free of morality – of tradition. Thus Nietzsche contrasts the noble with the good by characterizing the former as the creator of new laws and a new people and the latter as wanting to preserve the old ways and customs (*H* 1:224; *D*, 9; *GS*, 4, 24; *Z*, 'Of the Tree on the Mountainside').

In this chapter, I shall argue that Nietzsche does have a positive conception of morality as natural morality that goes beyond both *Sittlichkeit* and *Moralität* but also presupposes and grows out of a people and its morality of custom, and that the cultivation of the noble type as 'the fruit of fruits ... from the tree of a people' lies at the centre of his grand politics.

## A Living Sense of Community

Nietzsche's analysis of morality (be it 'noble' or 'slave') is essentially social and political because it reflects the coherence of a people and its 'herd morality.' Thus, all forms of morality derive from either the integration or the disintegration of a people or community. Moreover, morality in its most rudimentary form as the *'prehistoric* labour' (*GM* 2:2) of the human race emerges from custom as the morality of custom (*Sittlichkeit der Sitte*), as the 'living sense of community'; the priority of the collectivity over the individual and his subjective desires underlies the emergence of custom and the morality of custom.

The origin of custom lies in two ideas: 'the community [*Gemeinde*] is worth more than the individual' and 'an enduring advantage is to be preferred to a transient one'; from which it follows that the enduring advantage of the community is to take unconditional precedence over the advantage of the individual, especially over his momentary wellbeing but also over his enduring advantage and even over his survival. (*H* 2:89; *KGW* 4.3:48)

From this priority of the community over the individual intrinsic to custom (*Sitte*), there follows the emergence of morality (*Sittlichkeit*): 'which ... is nothing other than simply a feeling for the whole content of those customs under which we live and have been raised – and raised, indeed, not as an individual, but as a member of the whole, as a cipher in a majority. – So it comes about that through his morality the individual *outvotes* [*majorisiert*] himself' (*H* 2:89; *KGW* 4.3:48).

For Nietzsche, there is a clear and fundamental continuity between custom and original morality inasmuch as morality is simply obedience to custom and its subordination of the individual to the whole: 'To be moral, to act in accordance with custom, to be ethical means to practice obedience towards a law or tradition established from of old ... He is called "good" who does what is customary as if by nature, as a result of a long inheritance, that is to say easily and gladly ...' (*H* 1:96). Nietzsche further emphasizes the social character of morality by dismissing the attempt to make moral categories into the motivation of moral practice: '"Egoistic" and "unegoistic" is not the fundamental antithesis which has led men to make the distinction between "in accordance with custom" and "in defiance of custom", between good and evil, but adherence to a tradition, law, and severance from it' (*H* 1:96).

It would seem, then, that custom and morality are virtually synonymous at this period of human evolution. Nietzsche does appear to identify 'custom' and 'morality' when discussing early cultures: 'morality [*Sittlichkeit*] is nothing other (therefore *no more!*) than obedience to customs [*Sitten*], of whatever kind they may be; customs, however, are the *traditional* ways of behaving and evaluating. In things in which no tradition commands there is no morality; and the less life is determined by tradition, the smaller the circle of morality' (*D*, 9; *KGW* 5.1:17–18). However, it would be a mistake to interpret Nietzsche as attempting to identify morality with custom in this way. I would argue instead that, although he certainly sees a continuity between the two, Nietzsche distinguishes morality from custom by characterizing the former as 'obedience to custom' – and even more precisely, as obedience that comes from a '*sense for custom* (morality)' (*D*, 19) that is so profound that one acts 'as if by nature, as a result of a long inheritance, that is to say easily and gladly' (*H* 1:96). In this way, morality would be obedience to the laws and traditions of one's people that expresses a '*sense for custom.*' Moreover, since custom and tradition are 'directed at the preservation of a *community*, a people' (*H* 1:96), morality as the sense for custom is above all the 'living sense of community' (*H* 1:224).

Furthermore, the sense of community entails a particular self-relation and social concept of the self by which 'the individual *outvotes* [*majorisiert*] himself' (*H* 2:89; *KGW* 4.3:48). Nietzsche emphasizes here the sacrifice that is demanded and extracted by the morality of custom: 'the individual is to sacrifice himself – that is the commandment of morality of custom' (*D*, 9).

*Herd instinct.* – Wherever we encounter a morality, we also encounter valuations and an order of rank of human impulses and actions. These valuations and orders of rank are always expressions of the needs of a community and herd: whatever benefits it most ... that is also considered the first standard for the value of all individuals. Morality trains the individual to be a function of the herd and to ascribe value to himself only as a function ... Morality is herd instinct in the individual. (*GS*, 116; cf. *WP*, 730)

The sense of community is thereby synonymous with the training of the individual to be a function of the community, a sacrifice to the customs of the people. Morality is always a de-personalization of individuals because it expresses the needs of a community and a people. Education serves morality by treating each person as though 'he ought to become ... a *repetition*' (*H* 1:228); and as he repeats the familiar, he himself becomes familiar, and as he 'is visibly narrowly determined by what is already existent ... the child first proclaims its awakening sense of community' (*H* 1:228). The sense of community depends, therefore, upon the cultivation of a relation to the past that is not simply a respectful glance backwards, but a living repetition of the old as the present – and even as a ritual return to the beginning.

There is a palpable ambivalence in Nietzsche's delineation of the sacrifice extracted by morality; on the one hand, morality, as the sense of community, demands the sacrifice of the individual and his freedom through severe limitations and onesidedness, and on the other hand, Nietzsche also characterizes this limitation as the condition of true freedom and self-mastery. Indeed, the constraint and discipline (*Zucht*) of morality are the only means for the cultivation (*Züchtung*) of the noble type (*BGE*, 188; *KGW* 6.2:110–12).

There is a tension in Nietzsche's analysis of morality between measure and measurelessness: it is both a constraint and long unfreedom of the spirit, and it is the condition of real freedom, sovereignty, and autonomy of the individual. But before addressing the latter aspect of natural morality, we need to complete the elaboration of Nietzsche's conception of morality as the 'living sense of community.' And this involves our considering four points: first, customary morality as the subordination of the individual to the community; second, the priority of the past over the present through tradition; third, morality as civil religion; and, fourth, the naturalization of values through a 'going-*up* to nature and naturalness.'

As the living sense of community and the sacrifice of the individual, real morality is the formation of a people, and thus is strongly resistant to and intolerant of 'subjectivity' and 'individuality,' as Nietzsche understands these terms. However, this sense of the community can be realized only to the extent that the individual is cultivated as a 'cipher in a majority ... [and thereby] *outvotes* himself' (*H* 2:89). Nietzsche calls this 'the strong type' or 'the good man': he is characterized by 'narrowness of views,' 'strength of character,' 'a few but always the same motives' (*H* 1:228), as 'the strong or masculine type ... [who] has a sensitivity for making life better and safer' (*GS*, 24), as 'a type with few but very strong traits, a species of severe, war-like, prudently taciturn men, close-mouthed and closely linked ... [and] fixed beyond the changing generations' (*BGE*, 262). In short, the strong and good type is the embodiment of the 'firm-charactered' and similarly bred individual with a 'living sense of community'; and the advantage is that 'the strongest natures *preserve* the type' (*H* 1:224), and thereby preserve the community and the morality of custom. Such an individual embodies the stabilizing element of a people, the traditional type that is limited but strong, conservative but active. Nietzsche sums up 'the strong type' in this way:

History teaches that the branch of a nation that preserves itself best is the one in which most men have, as a consequence of sharing habitual and undiscussable principles, that is to say as a consequence of their common belief, a living sense of community. Here good, sound custom grows strong, here the subordination of the individual is learned and firmness imparted to character as a gift at birth and subsequently augmented. The danger facing these strong communities founded on similarly constituted, firm-charactered individuals is that of the gradually increasing inherited stupidity such as haunts all stability like its shadow. (*H* 1:224)

The second assumption underlying the morality of custom is that the enduring advantage is preferable to the temporary, that the conservation of the past in the present through tradition is essential to morality and therefore to civil society. The good, strong type conserves the past as a repetition, and this is ensured through tradition. Indeed, Nietzsche goes further and says that only the old is good (*GS*, 4) insofar as it is a living past that has become instinct and second nature. Two aspects stand out here: the good is the old; and the old becomes instinct insofar as it is preserved through tradition. Thus, as the embodiment of custom and tradition, morality is necessarily pre-reflective and even unconscious; it is the predominance of the past over the present in all actions: 'What is new, however, is always *evil*, being that which wants to conquer and overthrow the old boundary markers and the old pieties; and only what is old is good. The good men are in all ages those who dig the old thoughts, digging deep and getting them to bear fruit – the farmers of the spirit' (*GS*, 4).

Since custom is the traditional way of behaving and evaluating, it virtually defines the morality of custom and the identification of the good with the old (*D*, 9). Here one should recall Nietzsche's understanding of morality as the means of cultivating 'the certainty of an instinct' (*WP*, 430), 'instinctive certainty in actions' (*WP*, 423) – that is, the means of making second nature into a first nature. Tradition is the means by which custom is transformed into morality, the sense for custom and community by rendering custom unconscious, sacred and undiscussable. 'Custom represents the experiences of men of earlier times as to what they supposed useful and harmful – but the *sense for custom* (morality) applies, not to these experiences as such, but to the age, the sanctity, the indiscussability of the custom' (*D*, 19).

Tradition and sanctity or authority transform custom into morality by declaring certain experiences or customs to be fixed and settled, as eternal or supra-historical.

At a certain point in the evolution of a people its most enlightened, that is to say most reflective and far-sighted, class declares the experience in accordance with which the people is to live – that is, *can* live – to be fixed and settled. Their objective is to bring home the richest and completest harvest from the ages of experimentation and *bad* experience. What, consequently, is to be prevented above all is the continuation of experimenting, the perpetuation *in infinitum* of the fluid condition of values, tests, choices, criticizing of values. (*AC*, 57)

The purpose underlying this harvest of experience that puts an end to experimentation and fixes a people's morality is to generate an instinctive certainty in behaviour and evaluations: 'The higher rationale of such a procedure lies in the intention of gradually making the way of life recognized as correct ... unconscious: so that a complete automatism of instinct is achieved – the precondition for any kind of mastery, any kind of perfection in the art of living' (*AC*, 57).

The significance of tradition as the fundamental cultural authority lies in its ability to make a way of life unconscious and instinctive – that is, to naturalize cultural practices. Nietzsche describes that critical point in the evolution of a people when it declares certain experiences as 'fixed and settled,' when custom becomes morality through the establishment of a sacred tradition, as the crystallization of a social role into character – art into nature (*GS*, 356). In other words, the morality of custom (*Sittlichkeit*) creates the cultural foundation for a people by naturalizing its unique way of life as instinct, character, certainty, unconsciousness. Culture is, therefore, a '*going-up*' (*TI*, 'Expeditions,' 48) to nature and naturalness through morality. And tradition accomplishes this because it is a pre-rational imperative, an authority one obeys without reason or reflection of any kind. 'What is tradition? A higher authority which one obeys, not because it commands what is *useful* to us, but because it *commands*' (*D*, 9). The strength of ages and peoples corresponds to their instinctive certainty in behaviour, to their unreflective, traditional style of evaluating life. Every form of becoming conscious of morality betrays decay and is a symptom that real, natural morality is already undermined. Hence, the appearance of philosophers and the compulsion to resort to reason is an indication that tradition and true morality no longer command.

With Socrates Greek taste undergoes a change in favour of dialectics: what is really happening when that happens? It is above all the defeat of a *nobler* taste; ... What has first to have itself proved is of little value. Wherever authority is still part of accepted usage and one does not 'give reasons' but commands, the dialectician is a kind of buffoon: he is laughed at, he is not taken seriously. (*TI*, 'The Problem of Socrates,' 5; cf. *WP*, 427ff.)

The certainty of instinct emerges from tradition precisely because it is pre-rational, because it commands and thereby provides the imperative tone necessary to institutionalize habits and customs. A people is defined by its morality of custom, and every people speaks its own unique moral language which is enshrined in custom and law (cf. *Z*, 'Of the New Idol'); similarly, every culture is characterized by the authority of tradition, by a pre-rational imperative (rather than a rational contract). 'For institutions to exist there must exist the kind of will, instinct, imperative which is anti-liberal to the point of malice: the will to tradition, to authority, to centuries-long responsibility, to *solidarity* between succeeding generations backwards and forwards *in infinitum*' (*TI*, 'Expeditions,' 39; cf. *GS*, 356).

Therefore, the good is the conservative, he who preserves the traditions and customs: 'The good man wants the old things and that the old things shall be preserved' (*Z*, 'Of the Tree on the Mountainside'). As with morality, Nietzsche is ambivalent with respect to tradition: it provides the necessary condition for the growth of a culture, but it is also too limited for the realization of free individuality; indeed, morality and the good constitute a real obstacle to the cultivation of the noble type.

Nietzsche's concept of the morality of custom has been examined so far as the sense of community peculiar to a people and as the traditions by which morality becomes naturalized. The third aspect of Nietzsche's analysis of the morality of custom concerns its religious character, inasmuch as the sense of community and tradition are the consecration of the ways of a people into a common faith. To this extent, it is legitimate to describe Nietzsche's concept of the morality of custom as a civil religion. There are many references in his work where he characterizes this social phenomenon as a religion of a people. For example, in his analysis of Judaism in its early period of 'the Kingdom,' Nietzsche explicitly describes the intrinsic relation of a people to its traditions as a religion: 'A people which still believes in itself still also has its own God. In him it venerates the conditions through which it has prospered, its virtues – it projects its joy in itself, its feeling of power on to a being whom one can thank for them' (*AC*, 16). And even more explicitly: 'Formerly he [God] represented a people, the strength of a people, everything aggressive and thirsting for power in the soul of a people: ... There is in fact no other alternative for Gods: *either* they are the will to power – and so long as they are that they will be national Gods – *or else* the impotence for power – and then they necessarily become *good*' (*AC*, 16). Similarly, Nietzsche characterizes the Indian Law-Book of Manu as 'a religious legislation the purpose of which was to "eternalize" a grand organization of society, the supreme condition for the *prosperity* of life' (*AC*, 58); and finally he reserves high praise for the culture of Islam (*AC*, 60). Early Judaism, Hinduism, the religions of Greece and Rome, and Islam are all autochthonous religions that affirm life; and as such, they are pagan civil religions. For 'pagans are all who say Yes to life, to whom "God" is the word for the great Yes to all things' (*AC*, 55).

For Nietzsche, religion and culture are synonymous because a people is nothing but its lived common faith, its living sense of community. The coincidence of religion and culture produces a national God and thereby a civil religion that is the culture of a people (its *Sittlichkeit*). On the other hand, the dissociation of religion from culture culminates in a moralistic religion, 'the *anti-natural* castration of a God into a God of the merely good' (*AC*, 16; cf. *WP*, 146, 151). The abstraction of religion from the culture of its people through moral idealism is symptomatic of the 'denaturalization' of a people and its culture (*AC*, 25ff.).

In short, 'religion,' 'culture,' and 'a people' are all terms that are intertwined in Nietzsche's sociology of the morality of custom. If one assumes that Nietzsche does characterize the morality of custom as a kind of civil religion, what are the specific features that make it a religion? When speaking of the 'living sense of community,' Nietzsche usually elaborates this sense as a 'common faith' that arises from the sharing of habitual and undiscussable principles (*H* 1:224, 226, 227). The very coherence of the sense of community depends upon the presence of beliefs (not rational ideas, but shared habitual and indisputable principles without reasons) which are held in common, beliefs that belong uniquely to one's people. More precisely, the beliefs common to a people are able to constitute a 'universal binding force of a faith' (*GS*, 76) because they connote something lived in which one's very being is submerged and nourished, whereas an idea is something one may or may not take up and 'hold.' One pre-reflectively lives the beliefs of a common faith, but one reflectively thinks about an idea.

Beyond this, Nietzsche identifies revelation and tradition as the specific means of making the customs of a people into a civil religion. Thus, in order to 'naturalize' or 'fix and settle' the experience by which a people can live, further experimentation must be prohibited and this can only be done by making the art of culture appear as nature.

A two-fold wall is erected against this [experimentation]: firstly *revelation*, that is the assertion that the reason for these laws is *not* of human origin, was *not* sought and found slowly and with many blunders, but, being of divine origin, is whole, perfect, without history, a gift, a miracle, merely communicated ... Then *tradition*, that is, the assertion that the law has already existed from time immemorial, that it is impious, a crime against the ancestors, to call it in question. The authority of the law is established by the thesis: God *gave* it, the ancestors *lived* it. (*AC*, 57)

Over every people, there hangs 'a faith and a love' (*Z*, 'Of the New Idol'), a language of good and evil embodied in custom and law, and this faith and love is its own law-table of values, its own overcomings and will to power. By placing a table of values over itself, a people expresses its faith in itself and its love for itself; only thus does a people concede itself the right to become masterly, perfect, ambitious in the highest art of living (*AC*, 57). As Nietzsche says, 'within the bounds of such presuppositions religion is a form of gratitude' (*AC*, 16).

From the discussion of these three aspects of the morality of custom (the living sense of community, tradition, and religion), it is clear that the individual is rooted immediately in his people and customs, that gratitude for his conditions of existence as well as his overcoming of them grounds his existence. However, it is important to emphasize that this immediacy extends also to nature, the body, the passions. This is the fourth aspect of the morality of custom: gratitude to the body, the sensuous, and the Dionysian – even when they threaten the social order. Indeed, for Nietzsche, this gratitude constitutes the real paganism of a culture and religion; it is a reverence and affirmation of the natural, the sense of innocence in the natural (*WP*, 147), especially the mysteries of procreation, pregnancy, birth, and death. Real paganism not only tolerates passion but celebrates and consecrates it; it makes a festival of the passions and even the evil inclinations that threaten society; they practise a joy in the actual and active of every kind and have no desire to deny even evil altogether (*H* 2:220). This pagan celebration and affirmation of nature and the innocence of the natural defines not only the religious meaning of Dionysus, but ancient Greek culture itself:

For it is only in the Dionysian mysteries, in the psychology of the Dionysian condition, that the *fundamental fact* of the Hellenic instinct expresses itself – its 'will to live'. *What* did the Hellene guarantee to himself with these mysteries? *Eternal* life, the eternal recurrence of life; the future promised and consecrated in the past; the triumphant Yes to life beyond death and change; *true* life as collective continuation of life through procreation, through the mysteries of sexuality. It was for this reason that the *sexual* symbol was to the Greeks the symbol venerable as such, the intrinsic profound meaning of all antique piety ... The profoundest instinct of life, the instinct for the future of life, for the eternity of life, is in this word [Dionysus] experienced religiously – the actual road to life, procreation, as the *sacred road*. (*TI*, 'What I Owe to the Ancients,' 4)

For Nietzsche, the sense of innocence of the natural belongs to the sense of community, tradition, and religion that together characterize the morality of custom. This type of morality is fundamental, indeed foundational, for the development of human society and all higher forms of culture.

## Morality as the Cultivation of Types

The naturalization of a people's customary form of life constitutes one of the basic aspects of the morality of custom. And Nietzsche's ambivalence towards traditional morality has been noted particularly with reference to the necessity of the subordination of the individual to the sense of community, tradition, and religion. However, this formation and preservation of a people through the morality of custom is only a foundation and a means to something higher – to the free, autonomous, and sovereign individual with his own noble morality.

In this way, Nietzsche places this morality within a larger context and views it as a phase or a season and, to understand the significance of the seasons, it is helpful to refer to a passage that illuminates his notion of cyclical change. Speaking of an individual's 'life-year,' Nietzsche divides it into three seasons: summer, spring, and fall ('human life does not have a winter') (*WS*, 269). The summer of life (the twenties) is turbulent, thundery, voluptuous, and wearying; the spring (the thirties) is always disturbing and provoking, rich in blossoms and sap, an exuberant enjoyment of one's vigour and a present pleasure in future expectations; and, finally, the fall (the forties) is mysterious, stationary, and exudes a gentle strength – the time of harvest and cheerfulness.

While Nietzsche speaks here of the individual life, I find this metaphor appropriate to his sociology of a people and its morality. The long era before the codification of a morality of custom, the period of experimentation and fluid experience, is the summer of a people; its spring corresponds to its blossoming into a coherent and vigorous morality, a faith and a love; the fall of a people occurs when the individual ripens out of the community, when the 'the fruit of fruits hangs yellow and mellow from the tree of a people' (GS, 23). Yet the fall is also a season of decay and corruption when the fruits fall from the tree, a time of harvest and cheerfulness that is clouded by the anticipation of winter. 'The times of corruption are those when the apples fall from the tree: I mean the individuals, for they carry the seeds of the future and are the authors of the spiritual colonization and origin of new states and communities. Corruption is merely a nasty word for the autumn of a people' (GS, 23).

This image of the tree of a people and the individual as its fruit is not an isolated one in Nietzsche's work (cf. GS, 23; BGE, 258, 262; GM 2:2). Moreover, the metaphor is central and fundamental to Nietzsche's vision of grand politics because it places the customary morality of a people and the noble morality of the individual in the broader context of natural morality – of a cycle of growth and renewal. It is possible to comprehend Nietzsche's analysis of natural morality as a 'discipline [Zucht] and cultivation [Züchtung]' (BGE, 188; KGW 6.2:111) of higher individuals on the basis of a people and its morality of custom. Now one sees how the noble is related to the good type in a dissonant harmony: the fruit grows out of the tree and thereby goes far beyond it and becomes the seed of something new.[2]

In a very real sense, Nietzsche's grand politics revolves around the task of comprehending and facilitating a nurturing relationship between community and individuality. At the same time, Nietzsche, like Hegel, formulates this task in historical terms as the relationship between the classical era (Greece and Rome primarily, but also ancient India, Israel, and many others) and the modern age, as the interaction between the seasons of a people. It is not a simple question of rejecting one historical period and its social structure in favour of the other; rather, the task is one of comprehending and affirming the necessity of both through the grand politics of cultivation.

The locus of the problem is, therefore, the nature of the relationship between autonomous individuality and morality. And this problem is posed in very similar terms by Hegel and Nietzsche inasmuch as both criticize the lack of individuality in the ancient Sittlichkeit, but both also see the inadequacies of modern subjectivism or Moralität, particularly its lack of community and abstract withdrawal into pure inwardness. However, Nietzsche differs fundamentally in his manner of incorporating the 'corruption' of traditional morality through the emergence of individuality, and this divergence illuminates a great deal about his grand politics. For Hegel accepts subjective morality (Christianity) as a positive advance upon pagan culture and attempts to reconcile the two in the state; for Hegel, the individual remains a moral category and realizes himself in and through the moral saga of Christian redemption. For Nietzsche, on the other hand, subjectivity becomes truly positive only when it embraces its truth as natural immorality, as pagan 'innocence of becoming' (*TI*, 'The Four Great Errors,' 8). Contrary to Hegel, Nietzsche identifies individuality with immorality. This is the real meaning of cultivation – an ascent to nature, innocence, and sovereignty – to an autonomous innocence.

In order to understand Nietzsche's grand politics, it is essential to examine more closely this relationship between the good and the noble in the context of morality as the cultivation of the sovereign individual out of a people. Nietzsche himself defines the problem of his political philosophy in precisely these terms: 'To breed [heranzüchten] an animal *with the right to make promises* [*versprechen darf*] – is not this the paradoxical task that nature has set itself in the case of man? is it not the real problem regarding man?' (*GM* 2:1; *KGW* 6.2:307; cf. *BGE*, 126). With the inception of humanity, then, it seems as if something were promised, announced, or preparing itself; as if the human, all too human, were only a way, a bridge, a great promise and not a goal (*Z*, Prologue, 4; *GM* 2:16). For Nietzsche, if the inception of humanity corresponds to the invention of morality itself, the discovery of measuring and evaluating – that humanity is the animal that measures (*WS*, 21; *Z*, 'Of the Thousand and One Goals') – then humanity and its measuring is only a promise of something higher and completely unmeasurable: morality is the promise of something supra-moral and supra-human.

The task of cultivating an animal with the right to make promises, however, embraces a preparatory stage in which the morality of custom educates the human spirit to the sense of community. In other words, humanity is rendered regular, predictable, uniform, and thus calculable through the severity and parochialism of the morality of custom:

The task of breeding an animal with the right to make promises evidently embraces and presupposes as a preparatory task that one first *makes* men to a certain degree necessary, uniform, like among like, regular, and consequently calculable. The tremendous labour of that which I have called 'morality of mores [*Sittlichkeit der Sitte*]' (*Dawn*, sections 9, 14, 16) – the labour performed by man upon himself during the greater part of the existence of the human race, his entire *prehistoric* labour, finds in this its meaning, its great justification, notwithstanding the severity, tyranny, stupidity, and idiocy involved in it: with the aid of the morality of mores and the social straitjacket, man was actually *made* calculable. (*GM* 2:2; *KGW* 6.2:309)

The greater part of the history of humanity lies in the morality of custom and its cultivation of a type of character that is uniform, strong, and simple: the good man whose goodness reflects the strength of his sense of community (the 'herd instinct'). Thus, the long prehistoric eras of custom and the morality of custom (the summer and spring of humanity) are the seasons in which the preparatory task of cultivating a type whose identity is almost entirely social is realized. The aspects of morality (the sense of community, tradition, and civil religion) make up the principal substance of the individual's personality. The fundamental thesis that Nietzsche advances about the morality of custom is that, while its nature is obedience to the tradition and common faith that embody and preserve the sense of community, this obedience presupposes the cultivation of a being that is able to obey: that is, it assumes not merely obedience to the law but, more fundamentally, that the human animal itself becomes lawful, regular, uniform, and calculable to a large extent. In short, morality cultivates the individual to be a function of a people and to value himself as 'good' only as a function (GS, 116). Nietzsche describes the good, strong type in a number of crucial passages which deserve to be brought together because they express a fundamental dimension of grand politics.[3]

*The good, strong character.* – Narrowness of views, through habit become instinct, conducts to what is called strength of character. When someone acts from a few but always the same motives, his actions attain to a great degree of energy; if those actions are in accord with principles held by the fettered spirits they receive recognition and produce in him who does them the sensation of the good conscience. Few motives, energetic action and good conscience constitute what is called strength of character. (*H* 1:228)

A *species* comes to be, a type becomes fixed and strong through the long fight with essentially constant *unfavourable* conditions ... In this way a type with few but very strong traits, a species of severe, warlike, prudently taciturn men, close-mouthed and closely linked ... is fixed beyond the changing generations. (*BGE*, 262)

As we have seen, Nietzsche views the morality of custom as a means and not an end in itself. The tree of a people attains its highest point of fruition with the emergence of the truly autonomous individual. And the relationship between morality and the sovereign individual is the heart of Nietzsche's grand politics – the interaction between the good, strong type and the noble individual.

The relationship between the good and the noble would seem to be necessarily hostile and completely antagonistic when one considers their characteristics. The good man wants the old things and the preservation of the old ways and traditions, whereas the noble type wants to create new things and particularly new virtues (*GS*, 4; *Z*, 'Of the Tree on the Mountainside'). The good, strong type wants the old things because only the old is good; and since the new is therefore evil (*GS*, 4), the good must always find the noble type to be 'corrupt,' 'immoral,' and 'sacrilegious.' For Nietzsche, then, the good type is by his very nature antagonistic to the noble just as tradition is resistant to change and creation; this is why the good represents, for him, the greatest danger to the future of humanity.

O my brothers! With whom does the greatest danger for the whole human future lie? Is it not with the good and just? with whose who say and feel in their hearts: 'We already know what is good and just, we possess it too; woe to those who are still searching for it!' ...
O my brothers, someone who once looked into the heart of the good and just said: 'They are the Pharisees.' But he was not understood ...
But it is the truth: the good *have* to be Pharisees – they have no choice!
The good *have* to crucify him who devises his own virtue! That *is* the truth!
But the second man to discover their country, the country, heart, and soil of the good and just, was he who asked: 'Whom do they hate the most?'
They hate the *creator* most: him who breaks the law-tables and the old values, the breaker – they call him the law-breaker. (*Z*, 'Of Old and New Law-Tables,' 26)

The two noble individuals who looked into the heart of the good, Jesus and Zarathustra/Nietzsche, found that they are Pharisees (*BGE*, 135) or traditionalists and that they hate the creator of new virtues. And this is necessarily so because the 'moral' and the 'autonomous' are mutually exclusive inasmuch as autonomy implies the supra-moral standpoint (*GM* 2:2).

It seems that Nietzsche sees both continuity and discontinuity in the relationship between the good and the noble. On the one hand, he suggests that the sovereign individual (the noble) evolves out of and beyond his society and its morality of custom as the fruit grows out of the tree (*GS*, 23; *GM* 2:2); on the other hand, he characterizes them as mutually exclusive and openly hostile towards one another.

Does Nietzsche envision a less dramatic and more accommodating relationship between these two moral types? Of necessity, there must be other ways in which the two interact because, in reality, things are quite a bit more complicated. The individual can only emerge when the morality of custom is already in decline: that is, when the strong, good type is already under siege because his social conditions of existence have been corrupted. 'Corruption' is, as Nietzsche suggests, only 'a nasty word for the autumn of a people' (*GS*, 23), for that season when the life of a people relaxes, broadens, opens itself up to new and foreign influences: the culture of a people becomes pluralized, divided, and multicultural. In this way, the former traditions and sacred measures are loosened and even secularized.

Eventually, however, a day arrives when conditions become more fortunate and the tremendous tension decreases; perhaps there are no longer any enemies among one's neighbours, and the means of life, even for the enjoyment of life, are super-abundant. At one stroke the bond and constraint of the old discipline are torn: it no longer seems necessary, a condition of existence – if it persisted it would only be a form of *luxury*, an archaizing *taste*. Variation, whether as deviation (to something higher, subtler, rarer) or as degeneration and monstrosity, suddenly appears on the scene in the greatest abundance and magnificence; the individual dares to be individual and different ... The dangerous and uncanny point has been reached where the greater, more manifold, more comprehensive life transcends and *lives beyond* the old morality; the 'individual' appears, obliged to give himself laws and to develop his own arts and wiles for self-preservation, self-enhancement, self-redemption. (*BGE*, 262)

The 'old' discipline and the 'old' morality are no longer able to elicit complete obligation or command unconditional obedience. In short, as morals decay, society loses its common faith and, with it, political legitimacy collapses and a people enters that dangerous and uncanny state – illegitimacy and nihilism. At this time, there are no longer any shared customs, common understanding, or sacred authority. Even the good, strong type discovers that he is without certain foundations and, therefore, is forced to go on the defensive: that is, he has to moralize privately by consciously seeking reasons and grounds for his behaviour. Thus, the good man is himself 'corrupted' and 'illegitimate' precisely because he reflects on his behaviour privately and moralizes for the first time. As the advocate of *Moralität*, the good man, like Socrates, necessarily becomes a nihilist.[4]

Under these conditions, the strong, traditional type cannot oppose the noble man as a good man but only by moralizing as a nihilist, as someone without a common faith. Thus, there does not exist the stark and simple opposition between the two types that there seemed to be at first. Moreover, Nietzsche does indeed envision a number of ways in which individuality or 'immorality' may be accommodated within a community suffering from illegitimacy or nihilism. One form of accommodation is assimilation

(*H*, 224); another, to which Nietzsche seems to have felt more inclined, is a kind peaceful co-existence in which the noble grows beyond his people and ventures out only infrequently to find others of his ilk.

The first option is delineated in some detail in a key passage from *Human, All Too Human*. Here he puts forth the scenario of a reconciliation between the moral and the immoral types based upon a mutual need for one another. The strong, moral man embodies the sense of community and thereby almost completely subordinates himself to the common faith of his people; the free spirit is morally weaker in the sense that he has liberated himself from the traditions and faith of his people. While the moral type performs the necessary function of ensuring the duration and preservation of his community, the immoral individual makes spiritual progress possible by creating new virtues and customs.

It is the more unfettered, uncertain and morally weaker individuals upon whom *spiritual progress* depends in such communities: it is the men who attempt new things and, in general, many things ... in general, and especially when they leave posterity, they effect a loosening up and from time to time inflict an injury on the stable element of a community. It is precisely at this injured and weakened spot that the whole body is as it were *inoculated* with something new; its strength must, however, be as a whole sufficient to receive this new thing into its blood and to assimilate it ... The strongest natures *preserve* the type, the weaker help it to *evolve*. (*H* 1:224)

When cooperation spontaneously arises between the stable and stabilizing element and the creative and progressive element of a community, then the paradox occurs which Nietzsche calls 'ennoblement through degeneration' (*H* 1:224). The negative is absorbed into the body of society and made into a positive and ennobling experience through gradual assimilation. However, Nietzsche adds a note a scepticism at the end of this passage which increases in his later work. For the very strength of a people that would make such gradual progress possible without being crippled by the injury inflicted by the new also tends to resist such change: 'Only when there is securely founded and guaranteed long duration is a steady evolution and ennobling innoculation at all possible: though the dangerous companion of all duration, established authority, will, to be sure, usually resist it' (*H* 1:224).

Thus, Socrates questioned the grounds of Athenian *Sittlichkeit* and thereby severed himself from his community; eventually he was accused and convicted of corruption and immorality and sentenced to death. By rebelling against the traditions of the Pharisees, Jesus placed himself outside his people and was finally found guilty of treason and crucified. In a strictly traditional society beginning to experience its autumn of decline, this course of events is to some extent inevitable, according to Nietzsche: 'But it is the truth: the good *have* to be Pharisees – they have no choice! The good *have* to crucify him who devises his own virtue! That *is* the truth!' (*Z*, 'Of Old and New Law-Tables,' 26). And yet Socrates was succeeded by Plato and Aristotle, and the rebellion of Jesus against the priesthood was made into a church by Paul; and the same scenario seems applicable to the emergence of Buddhism and Islam. That is to say, even though Socrates and Jesus were rejected as immoral by their societies, they were still able to leave behind a posterity that was not merely preserved by a few sectarians, but able to penetrate the social body as a whole and transform it.

Here one glimpses Nietzsche's theory of change as a theory of delegitimation or nihilism through which a culture or a people suffers the denaturalization of its values. And during the turbulence of this crisis, it is offered a radical choice: either it can fight nihilism through a moral idealism ('moralization') that attempts to create a new authority grounded in an absolute Good, an abstract ideal beyond the actual world, or it can go beyond the old life and attempt a new and higher naturalization, an affirmation of the actual world.

For Nietzsche, the past is strewn with the wreckage of the first option where nihilism was confronted by idealism, by the self-deception that moralism constitutes an alternative to nihilism (*TI*, 'The Problem of Socrates,' 11). Thus Platonism and Christianity confronted the delegitimation of the old culture with only a deeper nihilism in the form of moral idealism. In these cases, the new was successfully introduced in the 'injured and weakened spot' (*H* 1:224) of the old way of life: that is, only because Athens was already so far along the road of decay that it had begun to moralize about itself could Socrates arise at all and Plato establish his school (*TI*, 'The Problem of Socrates,' 9–11; *WP*, 427ff.); only because Israel had already suffered a denaturalization of its people and a proliferation of moralists could Jesus appear and find a ready audience (*AC*, 25–7); and only because Rome was already in decline and rife with sectarian ideologies could Christianity take root there. In short, the key ingredient in each case where the new ideology flourished is not primarily corruption or delegitimation, but moralization: 'Not the "moral corruption" of antiquity, but precisely its *moralization* is the prerequisite through which alone Christianity could become master of it. Moral fanaticism (in short: Plato) destroyed paganism, by revaluing its values and poisoning its innocence' (*WP*, 438; cf. *WP*, 150,

196, 423). Corruption simply opened the old society up by providing the 'injured and weakened spot' into which the authors of moral idealism (Socrates, Plato, etc.) could step and, through their posterity, gradually gain access to the whole social body.

Nietzsche's theory of cultural change argues that the autumn of a people, the season of corruption or denaturalization, is the precondition for any fundamental social or political transformation. Two general alternatives present themselves at these historical junctures: either moral idealism ('moralization' or *Moralität*) or moral naturalism (noble morality). However, the former is not a real solution to nihilism and, in fact, merely deepens it; and yet, according to Nietzsche, naturalism is not a solution to nihilism since it also aggravates the process of decay.

In short, Nietzsche's theory of cultural change seems unable to offer any real change or improvement at all. But it is precisely this concept of change as 'improvement' that Nietzsche wishes to overcome insofar as it is idealistic. Indeed, the concept of improvement is practical nihilism itself because it negates the fundamental homogeneity of things by abstracting (idealizing) morality from life – from the natural, the 'immoral' (*WP*, 272, 299, 308). Nietzsche advocates not 'change' as reactive negation, but 'joy in the actual' that cultivates active affirmation; not the ideal, but the real as 'the *innocence* of becoming' (*TI*, 'The Four Great Errors,' 8). Furthermore, Nietzsche's conception of cultural progress lies in the paradoxical thesis that one cannot fight nihilism; in fact, to even want to combat the immoral with the moral is already a sign of nihilism. One must want the opposite: corruption, disintegration, decay, demoralization, and even '*active* nihilism' (*WP*, 22). To progress, one has no choice but to go forward '*step by step further into decadence*' (*TI*, 'Expeditions,' 43). The only way to become 'better' is to become 'more evil.'

### 'Better and More Evil'

From the preceding discussion, it is clear that Nietzsche's concept of the noble man is inseparable from both his theory of the morality of custom (*Sittlichkeit der Sitte*) and his theory of cultural progress through 'corruption,' understood as the 'autumn of a people.' Before addressing Nietzsche's second vision of the relationship between the noble and the good, we need to further elaborate this characteristic of the former: that is, his 'immorality.'

For customary morality, the good signifies unconditional and instinctive obedience to the sense of community, tradition, and the common faith, while evil is synonymous with the individual, the free spirit, the unusual or the incalculable (*D*, 9): that is, the old is the good and the new is necessarily evil (*GS*, 4). Traditional morality is therefore compelled to interpret the autonomous individual as foreign to the community and, since to be outside the people is to be outside of morality, he is also immoral. However, for Nietzsche, this free spiritedness does not happen arbitrarily but only in the late afternoon or twilight of a people. This freedom results from the growth of a strong people and morality of custom; from its very success, there follows an eventual opening up, pluralization, and fracturing of the old common faith. With the splintering of the old morality into private moralities, the individual is given much greater freedom to follow his private inclinations. In the autumn of a people, there emerges the liberation of the private person (which Nietzsche carefully distinguishes from 'the individual' (*H* 1:472) who is sovereign and autonomous). In terms of the old morality of custom, delegitimation of the old common faith and the liberation of the private person represent a corruption of legitimate society and a descent into nihilism.

For Nietzsche, however, this 'corruption' has not been understood inasmuch as the necessity of becoming has not yet been embraced as the very condition of life, happiness, and fullness. In fact, the eruption of becoming through nihilism is a kind of return of the repressed. The experience of corruption and immorality is the eruption of that which was repressed and negated by the morality of custom. By fixing and typifying experience, it sought to exclude and thereby devalue change, the new, the individual, etc. In particular, the rigidity of tradition, the ruthless assimilation of experience to the old to render life calculable, entails a devaluation of becoming.

In this sense, corruption is the eruption of a Dionysian naturalness which opens up the possibility of a genuine ascent to nature: that is, a going-up to the innocence of becoming or joy in the actual. However, the negativity of nihilism can be fully realized in the affirmation of pure becoming only if there is first of all an insight into the homogeneity of all things, the wholeness and perfection of things at every moment. With the disintegration of morality – of a Beyond, of a standard above nature by which to measure and judge – nihilism offers man the opportunity to recognize that he belongs to nature, that he grows out of the past, and therefore that no one is accountable for his or her being: 'The fatality of his nature cannot be disentangled from the fatality of all that which has been and will be' (*TI*, 'The Four Great Errors,' 8). The recognition that one is necessary, a piece of fate, because one belongs to the whole means that everyone necessarily participates in the innocence of becoming.

Nietzsche's thesis that cultural progress proceeds through active nihilism is based on this argument: that, through the delegitimation of the morality of custom, one is initially naturalized through the spread of corruption and immorality – this is the liberation of the private person. However, for Nietzsche, there is a much rarer and truly sovereign naturalization that creates the autonomous and noble individual. Thus, nihilism offers some the insight into a naturalization 'in terms of a pure, newly discovered, newly redeemed nature' (*GS*, 109). A going-up to a newly discovered and newly redeemed nature would then be an ascent to the innocence of becoming, to the knowledge that belonging to the whole implies that there is nothing outside the whole that could judge, measure, or condemn our being: '*But nothing exists apart from the whole!* – That no one is any longer made accountable, that the kind of being manifested cannot be traced back to a *causa prima*, that the world is a unity neither as sensorium nor as "spirit", *this alone is the great liberation* – thus alone is the *innocence* of becoming restored' (*TI*, 'The Four Great Errors,' 8).

Nietzsche's infamous 'immoralism' and his provocative exhortation to become 'better and more evil' must be understood as a naturalization of humanity in terms of a newly redeemed nature, an innocence of becoming. Moreover, Nietzsche's grand politics takes on a far more profound dimension when it is realized that the sovereignty of the individual signifies something supra-moral in the sense that he attains insight into this newly discovered nature to which he belongs (*WS*, 327; *GS*, 346). But even insight is not enough; one must affirm and love nature as the whole, as fate.[5] Moreover, one can naturalize oneself only through *amor fati*, the love of fate.

Indeed, for Nietzsche, the nobility of the individual derives from his naturalization through love of fate, and this means that his sovereignty is based upon a profound modesty; his freedom is paradoxically based upon a denial of free will and the pride of unconditional self-determination. Nietzschean sovereignty and nobility imply a true modesty that follows from the two dimensions of naturalization. On the one hand, modesty arises from the recognition of our complete unaccountability for our being: 'we are not the work of ourselves' (*H* I, 588) because we belong to nature. On the other hand, as insight fulfils itself in affirmation, modesty teaches gratitude for the past and the nature out of which we have grown. While morality gives man a false pride by placing him above nature through the notions of free will and responsibility, immorality teaches man modesty through recognition and affirmation of his embeddedness in nature.

Finally, since modesty is fundamentally inherent in the sovereignty and nobility of the individual who has transcended both morality and humanity (who has become supra-moral and thus supra-human), Nietzsche clearly distinguishes the evil and immorality of the noble man from the evil and immorality of free spirit who may lay claim to nobility. Unfortunately, this distinction between the noble and the free spirit in Nietzsche's work is still often misunderstood or simply neglected, an oversight which leads many to assume that, far from being modest and innocent, the sovereign spirit is simply a ruthless sociopath.[6] In his work, the distinction is constant and fundamental to his grand politics: 'The free man of the spirit, too, must still purify himself. Much of the prison and rottenness still remain within him: his eye still has to become pure' (Z, 'Of the Tree on the Mountainside'). Indeed, through his discussion of the three metamorphoses of the spirit, Nietzsche separates the spirit of the lion that is liberated from tradition and embodies the assertive will from the higher spirit of the child who represents innocence and creative affirmation (Z, 'Of the Three Metamorphoses';cf. WP, 940). Clearly, mere independence of will from the constraints of law and tradition is not enough to characterize the noble spirit. More than this, the concept of freedom as simple indulgence of one's whims, desires, or even ideas has nothing to do with the sovereignty of the higher man. However, while the noble man is still open to this danger since he also possesses the most dangerous passions,[7] Nietzsche characterizes the free spirit in terms that leave no doubt that it would constitute a degeneration of nobility:

But that is not the danger for the noble man – that he may become a good man – but that he may become an impudent one, a derider, a destroyer.

Alas, I have known noble men who lost their highest hope. And henceforth they slandered all high hopes.

Henceforth they lived impudently in brief pleasures, and they had hardly an aim beyond the day.

'Spirit is also sensual pleasure' – thus they spoke. Then the wings of their spirit broke: now it creeps around and it makes dirty what it feeds on. (Z, 'Of the Tree on the Mountainside')

Throughout his work, Nietzsche consistently condemns as weak those who equate freedom with 'letting go' because they are unable to master themselves and therefore hate all constraint, discipline, and obedience (even to themselves).[8] In short, the free spirit represents negative freedom (a liberation from old constraints), whereas the noble spirit embodies positive freedom (autonomy).

In a sense, the homogeneity of morality and immorality is the primary thesis of Nietzsche's philosophy and grand politics because it is the condition of nobility and the sovereignty of joy: 'we may set down as our chief proposition that to *make* morality one must have the unconditional will to the contrary' (*TI*, 'The 'Improvers' of Mankind,' 5). This proposition means: '"Man must grow better and more evil" – thus do *I* teach. The most evil is necessary for the Superman's best' (*Z*, 'Of the Higher Man,' 5). The homogeneity of all things signifies not only the insight that 'the greatest evil belongs with the greatest good' (Z, 'Of Self-Overcoming'), but also the affirmation of this as the condition of the innocence of becoming, of the naturalization of humanity in terms of a newly redeemed nature.

This is fundamental to Nietzsche's philosophy and grand politics: the sovereign and noble individual is immoral in the sense of being innocent and, at the same time, sovereign in being modest because he embodies a 'return' to nature and a loyalty to the earth; for to 'naturalize' man and values means to go up to the innocence of becoming and affirm life through joy in the actual.

## Noble Morality: The Virtue of the Law-Giver

Since the examination of the noble type as a law-giver will be dealt with at length in the next chapter, in this section I shall only address the question of his sovereignty by way of the relationship between the good and the noble types. Although Nietzsche appears to see the relationship between the noble individual and his society as fundamentally hostile, he does attempt to arrive at a form of peaceful coexistence in mutual misunderstanding. He generally characterizes this form of nobility as 'going alone' versus 'going ahead,' as being a sovereign as opposed to a 'shepherd' (*WP*, 901ff.). While this necessarily implies a confrontation with 'the good and the just,' it occurs in a rather oblique way because the noble does not want to change the people and its morality of custom. Indeed, nobility needs the good just as the fruit needs the tree as its foundation; moreover, since the exception needs the rule, his supreme nobility might reside in becoming 'the advocate of the rule' (*GS*, 55).

In this way, Nietzsche works out a different political relationship between the noble and the good: an 'atopian' vision that not only rejects utopian efforts to change man as such, but also views this as undesirable. To be 'a-topos' is to live without a place, dispossessed, outside the laws, morality, and common faith of one's people. However, one is never completely outside one's culture anymore than one can ever escape one's past, one's language and customs. Consequently, atopia really signifies the ambivalence and the double position of one who has liberated himself from much of his tradition and thereby feels himself to be 'outside,' but who then discovers himself to be constantly at the centre of his culture through his relentless confrontation with it. Unlike the utopian who envisions an absolute 'elsewhere' for the realization of his ideal society, the atopian individual is both outside (an individual) and at the centre of his culture (an advocate of the unchanging rule) – an out-law and law-giver at the same time.

The concept of atopia illuminates Nietzsche's view of the relationship between the exception and the rule. The sovereign individual is not engaged in the idealist and utopian venture of 'changing the world' or creating a society in which everyone could become autonomous. His atopian vision preserves the two types, the good and the noble, and thus limits the sovereignty of the individual in relation to his people.

This atopian vision can be illustrated in the way in which Nietzsche finally characterizes sovereignty itself and the nature of society. In his elaboration of the assimilation scenario, Nietzsche emphasizes that the strong and stable element of the community is an essential prerequisite for the more precarious and destabilizing activities of the creative type (*H* 1:224). In terms of the historical development of a people, there must be a long prehistoric period before the eruption of the private person and the individual in the autumn of a culture. This is the basis for Nietzsche's later concept of the people and the morality of custom as a foundation for the higher types of humanity. The lateness in the life of a people corresponds to its strength as a foundation for nobility. Thus, 'when "morals decay" those men emerge whom one calls tyrants: they are the precursors and as it were the precocious harbingers of *individuals*. Only a little while later this fruit of fruits hangs yellow and mellow from the tree of a people – and the tree existed only for the sake of these fruits' (*GS*, 23). This conception of society and the morality of custom as a means only for the cultivation of something better is expressed more explicitly in *Beyond Good and Evil*:

The essential characteristic of a good and healthy aristocracy, however, is that it experiences itself *not* as a function (whether of the monarchy or the commonwealth) but as their *meaning* and highest justification – that it therefore accepts with a good conscience the sacrifice of untold human beings who, *for its sake*, must be reduced and lowered to incomplete human beings, to slaves, to instruments. Their fundamental faith simply has to be that society must *not* exist for society's sake but only as the foundation and scaffolding on which a choice type of being is able to raise itself to its higher task and to a higher state of being ... (258)

And again in *On the Genealogy of Morals*, Nietzsche reiterates this conception of society in relation to the sovereign individual:

> If we place ourselves at the end of this tremendous process, where the tree at last brings forth fruit, where society and the morality of custom at last reveal *what* they have simply been the means to: then we discover that the ripest fruit is the *sovereign individual*, like only to himself, liberated again from morality of custom, autonomous and supramoral (for 'autonomous' and 'moral' are mutually exclusive) ... (2:2)

Clearly, Nietzsche conceives the noble individual as standing outside and above society and the morality of custom. However, this would not be enough to constitute a political philosophy, which requires a vision of the nature and interrelationships between community, individuality, and freedom as well as the legislative forms by which these realities and relations are instituted and maintained. For Nietzsche, the sovereign individual is not simply outside his people; as an atopian, he is also at the centre or the height of his culture where he acts as a law-giver and creator of new values.

Through his grand politics, Nietzsche tries to reconcile the whole and the part on a number of levels: socially as the unity of community and individuality; ethically as the relationship of the morality of custom with freedom; and historically as the reconciliation of classical antiquity and modern subjectivity. This places Nietzsche, like Hegel, in the awkward position of being a critic of modernity who is not a nostalgic conservative or reactionary. However, unlike Hegel, Nietzsche poses a solution that lies outside of morality and society. His answer is atopian and, as such, represents a complete transformation of the political questions of community and individuality, morality and freedom, and classicism and modernity. Through joy in the actual, Nietzsche envisions a new form of sovereignty that will legislate a new political and cultural order between the noble and the good.

# 4

# Hierarchy and the Overman

*Seriousness in play.* – In Genoa at the time of evening twilight I heard coming from a tower a long peal of bells: it seemed it would never stop, resounding as though it could never have enough of itself over the noise of the streets out into the evening sky and the sea breeze, so chilling and at the same time so childlike, so melancholy. Then I recalled the words of Plato and suddenly they spoke to my heart: *Nothing human is worthy of being taken very seriously; nonetheless* – (H 1:628)

With the word 'nonetheless' and the pregnant silence that follows it, the political life of the philosopher is defined as an inexorable paradox, a contradiction that determines his existence. It is the paradox that Nietzsche conjures up in his symbol of 'seriousness in play': the philosopher revolts against the seriousness of the city and man as seriousness itself; he laughs and dances high above the human things which he now looks down upon with contempt because he creates beyond himself and beyond his own seriousness. Yet in creation he rediscovers seriousness, the seriousness of the child at play. This child at play has no place in the city. Although he lives in the city, among serious men, he maintains no serious standing in their eyes. Yet through creation, the child begins to play seriously with man and the human things; without place, through placelessness, he begins to create a place, a new city, a new and higher man – and a new seriousness.

In this chapter, I shall explore the political role of Nietzsche's noble man, the philosopher-statesman, using the image of atopia. 'Seriousness in play,' with its Platonic mood of distance from the city and the noise of society, expresses the sense of atopia that characterizes Nietzsche's noble law-giver. Indeed, the Platonic Socrates represents, if not a model for Nietzsche, then at least a foretaste of this extravagance, this disruption and wandering above and outside the laws and morality of the city. Hence, the ambivalence of Socrates in relation to his people, the Athenians: he is simultaneously the founder of the true polity and yet very much the rebel and outlaw of even the most perfect city. This is the erotic extravagance of Socratic atopia: the double position whereby the philosopher is both the centre of the political world and yet outside of it. Unlike the free spirit who represents merely the liberation of the private person rather than the cultivation the noble individual, the genuine philosopher is always atopian rather than utopian: outside the city, above man, and nonetheless the foundation and law-giver for true polity.

Nietzsche's conception of the autonomous individual and the order of rank comes into its full Nietzschean focus only when the Overman is distinguished from both the good man and the free spirit. The parallels with Plato's political philosophy become even more apparent when one begins to grapple with Nietzsche's concept of hierarchy, 'the order of rank (*Rangordnung*),' that plays such a central role in his grand politics. Notwithstanding the fact that Nietzsche criticizes 'Socrates and Plato as symptoms of decay, as agents of the dissolution of Greece, as pseudo-Greek, as anti-Greek' (*TI*, 'The Problem of Socrates,' 2), he shares their view of hierarchy as the fundamental structure of any genuine political society. Hierarchy is a significant aspect of Nietzsche's work and has triggered a great deal of critical reaction that neither understands nor attempts to understand this dimension of his political philosophy. Whether Nietzsche's grand politics is viewed as continuous with his philosophy or in contradiction to it,[1] it is indisputable that, as a political value, inequality is given precedence over equality. Given this, the issue is the meaning of inequality as hierarchy in Nietzsche's work. The principle of inequality of status as expressed in his concept of hierarchy has nothing in common with the principle of inequality of power as expressed in class structure or social stratification. In an egalitarian culture, such as ours, this distinction may be all but inaccessible if not completely obscure, but it has the inestimable virtue of compelling us to examine our assumptions about the nature of society. For equality, as a moral idea, is a part of a subjectivist interpretation of society as a contract formed by abstract and asocial individuals: that is, the private person precedes and creates society in accordance with his free will. The assumptions of egalitarian political theory derive from two historical sources: the subjective morality (*Moralität*) that followed the collapse of the morality of custom (*Sittlichkeit*) and the Christian concept of freedom as the free will of the abstract subjectvity. For Nietzsche, as for Hegel, Tocqueville, and others, the concept of equality is part of a more general vision of humanity and society that is profoundly flawed by its subjective idealism. Thus, through a careful exploration of his critique of equality as the fundamental principle of social life and his view of hierarchy as a cultural order, I hope to show that the all-too-familiar criticism of Nietzsche as an advocate of 'domination,' 'exploitation,' and 'oppression' is unfounded.

When examined more closely, Nietzsche's criticism of the assumptions of modern political philosophy both incorporates and transcends these beliefs about equality and freedom, albeit within the context of his own vision of humanity and culture. In particular, Nietzsche's conception of the freedom of the sovereign individual is highly modern and yet incorporates many classical features as well. Nietzsche's Overman is neither a free spirit nor a tyrant, but is much more: a noble individual who embodies a modesty, innocence, and freedom from revenge that makes him utterly different from a merely liberated spirit; his freedom is classical but his individuality is modern. Hence, the difficulty in understanding Nietzsche's 'immoralism' and the sovereignty of the noble man: the Overman. For what specifically characterizes hierarchy also defines the sovereignty of the Overman: a relation between that which encompasses and that which is encompassed.[2] This means that, far from being a vertical relation of domination, hierarchy is a horizontal relation of encompassing in which the lesser is enclosed within the greater as a circle within a larger circle; the relation of 'encompassment' embodies a holism, whereas egalitarianism exemplifies a radical individualism in which social relations are construed as oppressive restraints that are artificial, external, and abstract.[3] The modesty, innocence, and freedom of the noble derives from a self-overcoming of morality through his immersion in the joy of becoming.

Thus the relationship between the noble individual as the law-giver and his people in grand politics reveals certain similarities to Plato's vision of political philosophy. In particular, there is a difference in kind between the noble and the good and, at the very least, a difference in degree between the noble and the free spirit.[4] This 'pathos of distance' that distinguishes the noble and his 'seriousness in play,' the political essence of the philosophic life, has its basis in the spiritual pathos that Nietzsche calls 'loving contempt.' Both Plato and Nietzsche embody a profound contempt for man and the polis in general and, accordingly, emphasize the great distance that stands between the philosopher and his political society. It follows that, since both look down upon the all-too-human as unworthy of true seriousness and yet grant to man a measure of consideration if and when he is brought under the rule of something higher than man, the political thought of Plato and Nietzsche would inevitably be pervaded by this paradoxical, atopian relationship to man and politics. What Nietzsche calls 'loving contempt' aptly characterizes the paradoxical yet essentially political nature of their philosophy: that the genuine philosopher must be political because, despite everything, the human world of polity and politics must 'nonetheless' be taken seriously; that what is worthy of contempt from the perspective of the more-than-human is also worthy of love, albeit only for the sake of something higher.

For both Plato and Nietzsche, 'loving contempt' is the fundamental precondition of the philosophic *eros* because it determines 'what can be loved in man' (Z, Prologue, 4) and thus what can be taken seriously in man – that which constitutes the measure of man and that which the philosopher as law-giver establishes as the foundation of true polity.

In this chapter, I argue that Nietzsche follows Plato in viewing the philosopher as the true statesman who, while standing and ruling above the state, legislates that which will give man his seriousness, measure, and value and thereby render him, at last, worthy of love and admiration. The very contempt and hostility that philosophy directs towards the community and that compels him to turn away from the political life of the state are also the beginning of his true statesmanship. The genuine philosopher's ascent above the human things is the first phase of his ultimate descent to man; thus 'loving contempt' is the philosophic *eros* that opens up the realm of polity within which politics can take place. For Nietzsche, philosophers are legislators of values, statesmen who practise the rare art of 'seriousness in play,' and lovers of humanity precisely because they are 'virtuosos of contempt.' Unlike Plato's statesman, however, Nietzsche's Overman is supramoral and embodies an individuality that incorporates the modern experience of subjectivity.

### 'To Love Man For God's Sake'

For both Plato and Nietzsche, the first step towards the philosophic life is explicitly and uncompromisingly anti-political: they 'remove reality from the hands of the politicians by denying the status of ultimate reality to the collective body politic on principle.'[5] Their reputation for solitude, contemplation, and quietism – in short, their apparent preference for the *furor philosophicus* over the *furor politicus* (SE, 7) – derives from the philosopher's fundamental rebellion against the city: that is, against the state, current opinions, power, or what actually prevails in the human world. Hence, the philosopher comes into being first by turning away in contempt from and rebelling against 'the blind power of the factual and the tyranny of the actual' (UDH, 8).

The philosophic life begins with a negation or a rejection of the current social understanding of reality: that is, philosophy begins with a de-legitimation of the familiar, conventional world. The emergence of philosophy is symptomatic of a culture in decline and suffering the disintegration of its old morality of custom. But the negation of this past legitimacy actually arises from a positive, new force: *eros*, will to power, the love for something higher than the human world. For both Plato and Nietzsche, it is this mysterious force that lies at the heart of philosophy. Education (*paideia*), which Nietzsche rethinks as cultivation (*Züchtung*), and the play (*paidia*) of creation presuppose the erotic passion of will to power.

The most paradoxical quality of *eros* is what Nietzsche calls, in referring to Moses, 'the love of man for God's sake' (*BGE*, 60). As the philosophic *eros* leads the spirit above its people and engenders a new love for things beyond the all-too-human, this same passion makes it possible to give the human things a certain seriousness and thus to love them. To love man for God's sake or, as Nietzsche implies, for the sake of something higher than man, the *Übermensch*, 'has so far been the noblest and most remote feeling attained among men.' 'That the love of man is just one more stupidity and brutishness if there is no ulterior intent to sanctify it; that the inclination to such love of man must receive its measure, its subtlety, its grain of salt and dash of ambergris from some higher inclination' (*BGE*, 60).

The philosophic passion establishes an order of rank through its distinction between the higher and the lower that initially drives the spirit towards the former, and yet paradoxically its desire for the higher and the most serious things compels it to return to and love man with the higher as its measure. The philosopher's contempt for the all-too-human emerges from the nature of the philosophic *eros* (the desire for the highest things), and yet this love that drives him beyond man also teaches him to love man and grant him a certain seriousness; he learns 'seriousness in play' (*H* 1:628).

It is important to avoid the temptation to interpret Nietzsche's 'contempt' as a pseudo-aristocratic affectation, a contrived pose adopted in the hope that the world will take notice and suffer from its diminished status. On the contrary, he repeatedly stresses that true contempt is 'instinctive' and 'unconscious' (*BGE*, 26, 216).[6] Rather, it is hatred or *ressentiment* that desires the recognition of its hatred and thus reveals a certain respect for the person; contempt does not partake of this pride: 'we learn to *despise* when we love, and precisely when we love best – but all of this unconsciously, without noise, without pomp, with that modesty and concealed goodness which forbids the mouth solemn words and virtue formulas' (*BGE*, 216).

The paradox of *eros* is that the philosopher who represents a contempt for, and a negation of, the human things embodies a new, transfiguring love of man: that is, a political passion intrinsic to philosophy as 'loving contempt' and 'seriousness in play.' The essential manifestation of the erotic lies in the passion for the higher things which compels him to think back to himself (cf. *UDH*, 10). To think back to the self is thus to think and cultivate a higher self, to create beyond oneself. For Nietzsche, this is the essence of love and philosophy.

Because the philosophic passion presupposes both a self-dissatisfaction and a love for the self in order to improve itself, the desire for self-knowledge (thinking back to oneself) involves both a self-rejection (contempt) and a love for a higher self, a desire to create beyond oneself. Philosophy, education, self-overcoming, and creation coincide in 'loving contempt,' in the philosophic *eros*.

For Nietzsche, it is the nature of the self to create beyond itself (cf. *Z*, Prologue, 3; 'Of the Despisers of the Body'; 'Of Marriage and Children') because it is driven by the will to power, the erotic passion of life to transcend itself and create a higher existence by negating and preserving its actuality. This self-overcoming is the nature not only of the self (will to power) but also of culture, the common life of human beings.

By coming to this resolve he places himself within the circle of *culture*; for culture is the child of each individual's self-knowledge and dissatisfaction with himself. Anyone who believes in culture is thereby saying: 'I see above me something higher and more human than I am; ...' It is hard to create in anyone this condition of intrepid self-knowledge because it is impossible to teach love; for it is love alone that can bestow on the soul, not only a clear, discriminating and self-contemptuous view of itself, but also the desire to look beyond itself and to seek with all its might for a higher self as yet still concealed from it. (*SE*, 6)

For Nietzsche, philosophy coincides with culture in the sense of self-cultivation in its erotic quest for a higher self – in the passion to create beyond itself, in self-overcoming. However, it is important to emphasize that, for Nietzsche, this does not imply a coincidence of philosophy with the state; the philosopher-statesman or the Overman is not a politician in the traditional sense of the word. Thus, this love of the higher self presupposes 'the hour of the great contempt' (*Z*, Prologue, 3); self-overcoming presupposes an intense dissatisfaction and contempt for oneself. In short, philosophy coincides with culture which, in turn, coincides with self-overcoming, a creation beyond oneself in 'loving contempt.' The paradoxical structure of *eros* pervades philosophy and culture in its strange combination of contempt and love. All self-overcoming or creative play presupposes the realization of the unity of love and contempt.

If, for Nietzsche, 'loving contempt' coincides with self-overcoming, one cannot but be struck by the similarity to Plato's depiction of the relationship of the philosopher to the city. In the *Laws*, the Athenian Stranger argues that human beings are not worthy of serious consideration; indeed, they are merely 'the puppets of the gods' created perhaps as their 'plaything, or for some serious reason' – in any case, this is beyond our knowledge. Apparently, human affairs are not to be taken very seriously because the only truly serious matter is that of God; and yet 'take them seriously is just what we are forced to do, alas.' On the one hand, Plato portrays man as a plaything, a puppet whose strings are controlled by the gods; on the other hand, man is not entirely passive because he is invited to play the supporting role of responding to the pull of the golden cord and rejecting the attractions of the baser strings. The play of human affairs, especially those of founding a just polity and legislating its laws, is therefore serious to the extent that it submits to the gentle tugs of the divine cord – man becomes 'serious play' when he lives for the sake of God.[7]

Nietzsche's formula, 'to love man for God's sake' (*BGE*, 60), mirrors Plato's conception of man as 'serious play.' Similarly, Plato reveals in his later dialogues (especially the *Statesman*, *Timaeus*, *Critias*, and the *Laws*) a significant advance beyond the *Republic* by demonstrating a new sensitivity to the realm of becoming by making becoming 'co-eternal' with the Idea/being.[8] It follows that the best order possible within the realm of history must reconcile being and becoming, and *nous* and *ananke*. Hence, there exists a permanent tension between being and becoming, and the political task is to overcome the (eternal) resistance to the Idea through *nous* and its embodiment in the laws of the city; but first the philosopher must take seriously this resistance, and therefore man's power to ignore the pull of the divine cord, and succumb to the pull of becoming (the body). The philosoher may, at first, have to turn away from becoming in contempt; but since it exercises a constant resistance to being, he must ultimately face it and, like the demiurge, attempt to use persuasion (*peitho*) in order to bring *ananke* into submission before *nous*. Plato's philosopher ascends to being through contempt for becoming and yet learns to take the latter seriously out of concern and even love for man – insofar as man becomes worthy of consideration by responding to the divine tugs of the golden cord upon his soul. Through a similar understanding of 'contempt,' both Plato and Nietzsche have placed the philosopher above his people and its morality while making him the spiritual founder and legislator for the true city: that is, they propose a long-term process of cultivation and education of man within a political community/culture over which the philosopher presides.

In order to clarify the admittedly paradoxical nature of this philosophical statesmanship, I shall borrow the distinction between le politique or 'polity' and la politique or 'politics' employed by Ricoeur.[9] By the term 'polity,' Ricoeur understands the ideal sphere of political rationality within which empirical politics can take place; the reality of political rule is this ideality, and this reality is not reducible to mere power or class domination. It is precisely with reference to this ideality that Socrates/Plato refute the sophist's identification of justice with power, the interest of the stronger. For, when one uses the word 'justice,' one does not mean 'the interest of the stronger,' even when it really does mask a real relation of power; the ideality of justice is not vitiated by the actuality of exploitation.

Here, however, polity will be distinguished from politics in the following way. The concept of polity will be used to refer to the supra-historical horizon of culture that defines a people in and through its pre-reflective customs, traditions, and values. Polity is the realization of culture, as Nietzsche understands this word. The term 'politics' refers to power politics as it takes place within the horizon of polity, including the actual struggle for the attainment and preservation of power within and around the state. In this sense, the realization of the most creative will to power in human affairs which Nietzsche calls 'grand politics' takes place, not primarily in the realm of politics, but in polity. His vision of grand politics is engaged in the struggle to create a new legitimacy for a new culture. In terms of this distinction between polity and politics, both Plato and Nietzsche attempt to achieve a relativization of the power politics of the state. They wish to demote politics (the state and its legal-military complex) to the secondary status of an instrument of polity or the principal reality of culture. For Nietzsche, culture is the creation of something beyond the human things by which humanity becomes worthy of serious consideration and real value. Thus, politics is a secondary reality, something less real, because both Plato and Nietzsche have carried out a fundamental displacement of reality beyond the political to culture, polity, and the supra-human – a displacement achieved through 'loving contempt' which grants to politics a certain seriousness by subordinating it to self-overcoming, culture, or polity, by relativizing politics to polity through 'grand politics.'

For both Plato and Nietzsche, the realm of politics and state power is not the primary focus of their philosophical statesmanship (misconceptions to the contrary notwithstanding);[10] it is an instrument, albeit a necessary, infrastructural one. Both concentrate on the dimension of legitimacy or authority that transcends power, the dimension that organizes and structures the values and discourse within which power is exercised: the polity of politics.

## The Order of Rank

How does Plato's and Nietzsche's vision of the coincidence of philosophy and polity in the cultivation of a supra-human spirit and a new order manifest itself in political activity? What form of grand politics follows from the cultivation of something higher than the human world?

First, for both Plato and Nietzsche, the philosopher is the founder of a new order of rank (*Rangordnung*) between the noble and the base souls, a spiritual hierarchy that is radically distinct from a political relation of dominance between the ruler and the ruled, as well as a social relation of subjugation between owner and worker. The philosopher-statesman founds the order of polity, the realm of legitimation that underlies and makes possible society and politics.

Second, the philosopher legislates above the whole constitutional apparatus of the state by assigning to the latter a purely subordinate, supporting status in relation to philosophy. Hence, he rules above and yet over the leaders and 'guardians' – a term which is, significantly, common to both Plato and Nietzsche – of the state. In this way, both Plato and Nietzsche clarify the manner in which philosophy and polity coincide, the manner in which philosophy rules the world. To rule, the philosopher need not become king, nor do rulers need to become philosophers. It is sufficient, as Ortega writes, 'for philosophers to be philosophers.'[11] The philosopher-statesman is sovereign because he wields the greatest power on earth, the power to create a people's 'good' and 'evil,' their 'law-table of values' (cf. Z, 'Of the Thousand and One Goals'). For Nietzsche, the philosopher rules as a creative spiritual authority through 'the stillest words': '"Do you know what it is all men most need? Him who commands great things ... It is the stillest words which bring the storm. Thoughts that come on doves' feet guide the world"' (Z, 'The Stillest Hour'). The philosopher rules, then, through the spiritual power that creates an order of rank, first, by creating a measure of value – by instituting a new order of values. Through the creation of a new 'law-table,' the philosopher founds or codifies the experience in accordance with which a people is able to live, and in this sense, he is, first and foremost, a law-giver: the founder of the constitution (*politeia*) for a people.

How does the creation of a order of rank between the noble and base souls become a political order? Before addressing this question, we need to recognize that Nietzsche's philosopher creates not an isolated noble spirit, a 'beautiful soul,' but an order of rank that includes both noble and base souls. Indeed, it reflects poorly on one's own standing in this spiritual order of rank if one is concerned only with the cultivation of 'exceptions' or superior beings: '*On spiritual order of rank.* – It ranks you far beneath him that you seek to establish the exceptions while he seeks to establish the rule' (*H* 2:362; cf. *D*, 442; *GS*, 55; *BGE*, 26).

It is significant that Plato and Nietzsche model the philosopher-statesman on the artistic demiurge because the demiurge does not create out of nothing, but on the basis of what is pre-ordered by necessity, he orders what is pre-ordered by persuading necessity with reason. Similarly, Nietzsche defines creation as the 'selection and finishing' (*WP*, 662) of something, and thus describes Zarathustra as 'walk[ing] among men as among fragments of the future' and longing 'to compose into one and bring together what is fragment and riddle and dreadful chance' (*Z*, 'Of Redemption'). Clearly, the demiurgic statesman is not omnipotent, and therefore his creation (the order of rank) is a 'selective and cultivating influence' (*BGE*, 61) which is both rooted and limited by its historical and ontological finitude. Plato and Nietzsche are not utopian idealists, but realists who transfigure and elevate reality as 'good poet[s] of the future' whose motto is: 'Only reality, but by no means every reality! – he will depict a select reality!' (*H* 2:114). Because Nietzsche conceives of the philosopher as a law-giver who ordains a political order of rank and 'not ... an individualistic morality' (*WP*, 287), it is already clear that his genuine philosopher must also be a statesman.

If the philosopher is a statesman and not a quietistic solitary, he is also not a philosopher-king who seeks to create a utopian society in which philosophy holds absolute sway.[12] Like Plato, he rejects the possibility of a human order untroubled by the dialectic of good and bad, composed purely of noble spirits freed from the contaminating influence of base souls. Even the most ideal polity is an order representing two types of spirit, both noble and base. It was precisely the recognition of becoming as a force co-eternal with being that compelled Plato, after the *Republic*, to confront the issue of the philosopher and the historical limitations of the polis in the *Statesman*, *Timaeus*, and the *Laws*. Similarly, Nietzsche neither considered nor desired the possibility of the philosopher somehow redeeming politics and human nature of its 'imperfections' because his entire philosophy rests upon the homogeneity of morality and immorality. Given this, the only solution is to aim at a spiritual hierarchy of noble and base types of men wherein the philosopher rules as a spiritual legislator rather than as a direct political leader.

The philosopher comes into being, then, by turning his back on the reality of the city (the *Sittlichkeit* of his people) and creating a higher self and, from this, a higher world beyond man; and yet without abandoning his height, the philosopher seeks to make this higher world into a basis and a measure for the human world of culture and politics. He seeks to establish not simply a noble type of man (an exception), but a relationship of authority between noble and base types. Both Nietzsche and Plato demand of the philosopher, as the spiritual power underlying a culture, that he institute, first, a hierarchical, spiritual-political order of rank between noble and common souls and thus, through his 'selective and cultivating influence,' (*BGE*, 61) create a truly good or noble type of spirit to justify or give meaning to society; second, a new law-book of values enshrined as the supreme authority; and third, a culture or people which the philosopher founds and which represents the collective unity of the order of rank, the law-book (or 'holy lie'), and the institutions of the state. In short, a people is the unity of polity and politics which the genuine philosopher initiates under the authority and legitimacy of the former.

Nietzsche explicity assigns the task of realizing his grand politics to the philosopher. Nietzsche asks of his philosopher that he found a new people through the creation of a new table of values; the philosopher's knowing is thus a creating and a legislating (*BGE*, 211) for the people in general (cf. Z, 'Of the Bestowing Virtue'; *BGE*, 126). A people or polity is defined and distinguished by the table of values that 'hangs over' it (Z, 'Of the Thousand and One Goals') because this represents its will to power, its self-overcoming, and this table of values is established by the creator or philosopher-statesman: 'It was creators who created peoples and hung a faith and a love over them: thus they served life' (Z, 'Of the New Idol'). In stark contrast to the misconception of the Nietzschean statesman as a modern Callicles or Thrasymachus, a tyrant who believes that might is right,[13] Zarathustra tells us that 'the cunning, loveless Ego, that seeks its advantage in the advantage of the many – ... is not the origin of the herd, but the herd's destruction.' Thus, the true statesman is a creative, bestowing, and loving spirit: 'It has always been creators and loving men who created good and evil. Fire of love and fire of anger glow in the names of all virtues' (Z, 'Of the Thousand and One Goals').

Therefore, the philosopher, if he is genuine and not merely a scholar, is a commander and a legislator (*BGE*, 211) who seeks to hang a new faith and love, a new law-table, over a people. Moreover, the table of values is realized in and through an order of rank (*Rangordnung*), a hierarchy. The principal features of the order of rank are the following: hierarchy is an order of precedence that involves status rather than power and is therefore not a class or social stratification based upon power or 'domination'[14]; it is not the abstract individual of the liberal imagination who embodies the same equal rights as all other subjects that is the origin of society but the relation of whole and part; moreover, the criterion that determines nobility is self-mastery or autonomy; the highest status, the noble individual, holds no public power and has no common rights except his own personal privileges. It is in terms of this concept of hierarchy that Nietzsche is entitled to call the peasant the most noble type of his time (Z, 'Conversation with the Kings,' 1).

If hierarchy is based upon an order of status rather than power or domination, how is this revealed in Nietzsche's grand politics? It is my contention that Nietzsche accomplishes this not only by separating the nobles from those who control power (the 'guardians'), but by giving them a higher status than the latter. In particular, he distinguishes first three types of man of 'divergent physiological tendency' and then three castes to correspond to the former because the '*order of castes*, the supreme, the dominating law, is only the sanctioning of a *natural order*, a natural law of the first rank' (*AC*, 57). With regard to the three types of man, he identifies: 'the predominantly spiritual type'; the 'predominantly' muscular and temperamental type; and a third and residual category, 'the mediocre type' which is neither one nor the other.

Nietzsche tells us little more than this and, in evident haste to proceed to the political consequences, outlines the corresponding castes. The highest and most important one for the destiny of humanity and culture is called '*the very few* ... the perfect caste' (*AC*, 57) which embodies the fundamental characteristics of Nietzsche's immoralism: above all, joy, beauty, modesty, and overflowing power; what he calls elsewhere *Mitfreude*, 'joying-with' (cf. *H* 1:499; *H* 2:62).[15] Furthermore, they are 'the most spiritual human beings' and yet they are also the 'rulers': however, he emphasizes that 'they rule not because they want to but because they *are*; they are not free to be second in rank' (*AC*, 57). Here Nietzsche stresses the necessity that underlies the rule of the most spiritual: they rule on the basis of something much deeper than the will and certainly not out of a subjective desire to dominate, which is the province of base spirits twisted with *ressentiment*.[16]

In a very real sense, the entire meaning of Nietzsche's order of rank is condensed into the stipulation that the highest types rule not through their will, but simply because of what they are; and what exactly they are is revealed through their differentiation from those who hold power. For the second in rank, those corresponding to the muscular and temperamental type, are called 'the guardians of the law, the keepers of order and security; the noble warriors; above all the *king* as the highest formula of warrior, judge and upholder of the law' (*AC*, 57). The 'guardians' are 'the executives of the most spiritual order' and thereby relieve the highest caste of the pettiness and coarseness of actual government. This is extremely significant and revealing of Nietzsche's conception of hierarchy and philosophic statesmanship, especially when compared to Plato's later political thought. For both, the philosopher legislates above the constitutional apparatus of the state; he thereby relativizes or subordinates politics to polity and philosophy. Moreover, while the highest caste is 'predestined to command and in whom the reason and art of a governing race [has] become incarnate,' the most spiritual type prefers 'the most subtle type of rule ... for obtaining peace from the noise and exertion of *cruder* forms of government, and purity from the *necessary* dirt of all politics.' Nietzsche illustrates this subtle form of rule through reference to the Brahmins who 'gave themselves the power of nominating the kings of the people while they themselves kept and felt apart and outside, as men of higher and supra-royal tasks' (*BGE*, 61). In short, Nietzsche's philosopher-statesman rules not on the basis of his subjective will, but because he is a creator and legislator, he is predestined to command and belongs to a governing type that rules above and over the guardians/kings by nominating them as the executives of 'the most spiritual order.' 'The highest men live beyond the rulers, freed from all bonds; and in the rulers they have their instruments.' '*Order of rank*: He who *determines* values and directs the will of millennia by giving direction to the highest natures is the *highest* man' (*WP*, 998, 999).

If the highest types rule on the basis of what they are, it becomes critical to understand how Nietzsche characterizes the noble and the philosophic beings. It suffices here to emphasize one basic feature: the Overman embodies a comprehensive wholeness. His joy in the actual grows out of the fact that he embraces and celebrates the homogeneity of all things. Therefore, Nietzsche characterizes the highest types as the most comprehensive, as the synthesizing and justifying powers: they embody 'higher, rarer, more remote, further-stretching, more comprehensive [*umfänglicherer*] states' (*BGE*, 257; *KGW* 6.2:215); they are 'the greater, more manifold, more comprehensive life [that] transcends and *lives beyond* the old morality' (*BGE*, 262); 'he constitutes the entire *single* line "man" up to and including himself' (*TI*, 'Expeditions,' 33). In short, the noble 'rule' not because they are the centre, but because they are the periphery, because they embrace and encompass the activities of those within their scope by defining the horizon and the boundary of their world. In Nietzsche's order of rank, this spacious comprehension and summary of a people constitute the atopia of the highest type: they are at the centre of a people because they represent the periphery, the encompassing horizon that defines their world.[17]

What clearly emerges from Nietzsche's conception of the political order of rank and his explicit comparison to the Indian caste order is that it is both a spiritual and a political hierarchy of noble and base souls. More important, however, is the need to elaborate the implications of Nietzsche's subordination of the 'guardians' to the philosophers for his concept of *Rangordnung*. According to sociologist Louis Dumont, the essential characteristic of the Indian caste system is the subordination of power to spiritual status.[18] Strictly speaking, while the Brahmins hold the highest status and little power, the kings possess much greater power and wealth and a secondary status. The distinguishing characteristic of the hierarchical principle (and the one which Nietzsche incorporates into his *Rangordnung*) is not simply its affirmation of inequality, but this subordination of power to spiritual status. In short, the significance of the Indian caste system for Nietzsche's order of rank is that hierarchy implies the relativatization of power to status and politics to polity. Only on the basis of the hierarchical subordination of power to spiritual status can Nietzsche's philosopher reign without having to govern. The irony remains that it is the very concept of *Rangordnung* that Nietzsche developed in order to subject power to the hegemony of philosophy that is so often mistaken for power-mongering and a lust for domination.

Another equally important aspect of Nietzsche concept of hierarchy is the association of nobility with privilege. Indeed, he specifically says: 'A right is a privilege [Ein Recht ist ein Vorrecht]' (*AC*, 57; *KGW* 6.3:241). What does this mean? Literally, Nietzsche seems to argue that a right is first of all a prerogative of a person or group, a private possession that is not a legal addition to an entity, but something that merely sanctions an already existing state of affairs: 'A right is a privilege. The privilege of each is determined by the nature of his being.' However, a 'privilege' is then not really a 'private possession,' but rather an expression of who one is: a mark of one's release into the innocence of becoming. At one level, we may interpret this in the following way: one's right is determined by one's will to power or, more precisely, is pre-determined by one's capacity to create and legislate oneself, and therefore derives from who one is. As a privilege, a right is an index of one's self-overcoming and, unlike common rights, cannot be a passive possession given by a constitution. At a deeper level, one could argue that, by making 'right' into an expression of 'privilege,' Nietzsche goes beneath not only the legal structures of a culture, but also its social stratification of power to the underlying principle of hierarchy – the order of status that is determined by one's power to legislate oneself.[19] Privilege, as *Vor-Recht*, represents the level of hierachy, the level of the encompassing innocence of becoming that circumscribes the world of rights.

How does Plato's later political theory help us understand Nietzsche's political hierarchy? In his later works, Plato considerably enlarged the field of politics 'to encompass the reality which is not ordered by the idea.'[20] After the *Republic*, the notion of the philosopher-king disappears from Plato's political philosophy although the status of the Idea remains much as it was. However, while ideality retains its standing as the highest and truest reality, its relationship with man and history (the problem of the embodiment of the Idea) becomes more and more problematic. After the *Republic*, Voegelin argues, Plato's philosopher becomes 'the bearer of the unrepresented forces' of culture – forces that no longer have a place in the people.[21] This alienation from the people compels the philosopher to reinterpret the question of politics and its position in philosophy.

While the *Republic* conjured up the vision of the polis as representative of the highest spirit, *Phaedrus* paints a picture of declining Athenian civilization, dividing into a political order devoid of spirit and a spiritual life without embodiment in the city. As a portrait of this decline, the hierarchy of souls in the *Phaedrus* (248d–e) signifies a dramatic shift from the *Republic*, for the philosopher-king is nowhere to be found. Here the philosopher along with the lover of beauty (*philokalos*), the musical and erotic soul, constitute the highest embodiment of spirit, while the soul of the law-abiding king is now separated into a second, distinct class. The first implication of this new hierarchy is that the embodiment of the Idea in the historical polis is far more unlikely and constrained by ontological factors. For another reality, one not ordered by the Idea, confronts the higher world of noetic being – the reality of becoming; moreover, this becoming is co-eternal with the reality of being, the Idea. And because of this ontolgical duality, the position of the philosopher with respect to the city, the possibility of his return to the Cave, is far more limited and problematical. As Voegelin writes, 'The understanding of this tension is the key to the understanding of Plato's work after the *Republic*.'[22]

This permanent tension at the ontological level between being and becoming (and between *nous* and *ananke*) translates into a permanent opposition at the historical level between the philosopher and the political order. In the *Republic*, Socrates declares that it is the duty of the philosopher to return to the Cave but on the condition that he becomes the philosopher-king of his people. After the *Republic*, this is no longer possible because there is an eternal, ontological resistance to the Idea and to *nous* which can never be overcome. Indeed, in the *Theaetetus*, Socrates is able to say: 'The elimination of evil is impossible, Theodorus: there must always be some force ranged against good' (176a). The philosopher, like the demiurge in *Timaeus*, can only persuade necessity with reason and, thereby, bring about as much order as is possible given the permanent tension between being and becoming.

In this new situation, the philosopher is precluded from ever becoming a philosopher-king and, at the very most, he may embody the limited power of an ordering force (*nous*) which, like the demiurge, attempts to persuade the reluctant forces of becoming and necessity to some form of order. However, the philosopher-statesman can expect little or no sympathetic response from his fellow citizens, yet in his later works, Plato still rejects the apolitical quietism of the Cynics, and in the *Statesman* and the *Laws*, he elaborates the positive, erotic force that mediates, like the demiurge, between the Idea and the historical world. Order is still possible, but it is now dependent upon the limited power of reason attainable by the human psyche and the limited effectiveness of the appeal of reason to the city and its affairs. In the *Statesman*, we see this drama of the demiurgic philosopher who has knowledge of the true art of governing, like the philosopher-king, confronted by a reality that resists the ordering force of the Idea. More important, Plato goes on to argue that the nature of the true art of ruling entails two paradoxical theses: first, true statesmanship governs beyond the institutional and constitutional framework of the laws; second, the true statesman rules above as well as over the actual rulers.

Looking at these arguments more closely, we see immediately the parallels with Nietzsche's political thought. Plato maintains that the real criterion in defining a constitution is 'the presence or absence of some science' (292c); only secondarily, and in relation to the mimetic or imitative constitutions, do criteria – such as whether few or many rule, whether by consent or not, or whether the rulers are rich or poor – enter into consideration. For Plato, the criterion of the true *politeia* is always extra-constitutional because it is the noetic power of the soul, its degree of mastery over the *logos*, that distinguishes who rules truly from who rules actually.

For according to our former argument, it is only the man possessed of the science of

kingship who must be called a king, *regardless of whether he is in power or not* ...
On this principle it is the men who possess the art of ruling and these only whom
we are to regard as rulers. It makes no difference whether their subjects be willing
or unwilling; they may rule with or without a written code of laws, they may be
poor or wealthy. (*Statesman* 293a)

Here Plato emphasizes that the true ruler is the one who possesses the art
of ruling regardless of whether he has power or not (cf. 259b). He proceeds
to clarify that the status of the statesman is above and, properly speaking,
over the governors of the city by arguing that the true legislator governs
without laws. When the Young Socrates expresses his unease at the idea of
government without laws, the Athenian Stranger declares that, while kingship certainly includes the art of legislation, 'the best thing of all is not full
authority for laws but rather full authority for a man who understands the
art of kingship and has wisdom' (294a). Since wisdom is the true criterion
of the royal art, and since it alone is capable of adapting to the individuality
of each unique situation, lawfulness is reserved for the second best constitutions. However, before the Athenian Stranger delineates the usefulness of
the law for the second best constitutions, he interjects a scathing attack on
the 'deadly paralysis of lawfulness.'[23] Disaster follows inevitably in a polis
that attempts to regulate the art of governing through strict and detailed
laws, for sooner rather than later any wisdom that deviates from and transgresses the laws will be suspect: 'For there must be no wisdom greater than
the wisdom of the laws' (299c). Indirectly, Plato indicts the lawfulness of
the city for the murder of Socrates through his critique of the rule of law.
Clearly, the creative, ordering wisdom of the philosopher must defend
itself not only from the disordering influence of becoming, but from the
lawfulness that reifies and mummifies reason while codifying it.

Having elaborated the point that the true art of ruling realizes itself
above the institutional and constitutional structure of law, Plato proceeds
to reveal a second dimension of statesmanship: that it must govern above
and over the actual rulers. The true statesman must be distinguished from
the actual rulers and executors of state power because 'it is not the province
of the real kingly science to act on its own, but rather *to control the sciences
whose natural capacity is to act*' (305d). The proper jurisdiction of the philosopher-statesman is not to act by himself, but to prevail over those who
do act: to govern the governors. It is for this reason that Plato distinguishes
the true statesman from the politicians, judges, and military leaders who
may actually wield power. The statesman 'weaves [them] all into [his] uni-
fied fabric with perfect skill' (305e).

Like Nietzsche's Brahmanic philosopher, Plato's statesman reigns above the constitution and over the actual guardians of state power; without acting himself, he makes possible the political action of the politicians. In this way, the statesman corresponds to the demiurge because he creates the order within which others may act by bringing reason to bear upon necessity. Here Plato reformulates the role of the philosopher within the historical polis as a creative mediator who brings the ordering power of the Idea down from being into the mundane world of becoming – as far as this is possible. He does not participate directly in the realm of politics but, like Nietzsche's philosopher, restricts his demiurgic creativity to the higher world of polity.

In different ways, both Plato and Nietzsche envision the philosopher's true vocation as that of the law-giver who cultivates and directs the guardians of the state through the creation of a new table of values and order of rank. Moreover, the basic concepts of Nietzsche's grand politics should be seen as flowing directly from his philosophy of will to power as an erotic force: the philosopher can reign over the guardians (i.e., subordinate power to spiritual status) only because philosophy first creates a supra-historical realm by overcoming the polis and becoming its foundation. Inasmuch as the philosopher's loving contempt for the all-too-human drives him beyond the city, it is precisely the atopia that the philosopher achieves by virtue of loving contempt that allows him to give man a higher measure of value. In short, this vision of the philosopher as statesman presupposes that, first, the philosopher rebels against the city (in contempt for its values) and ascends, through knowledge, to the supra-human realm of true being; then, he descends again to the human world and attempts to persuade the city to order itself according to the supra-human measure. This 'descent of creation,'[24] which is the problem of the philosopher's return to the Cave, is the central dilemma for the political philosophies of both Nietzsche and Plato: the philosopher must be a law-giver, but first he must persuade the people (or at least the higher types[25]) to voluntarily accept his appeal, even though the resistance is almost overwhelming. Hence the paradox of Nietzsche's grand politics: the atopia of the philosopher, which derives from his loving contempt for the human world of the polis, is the essential condition for Nietzsche's relativization of power to status and the guardians to the reign of the philosopher.

## The Overman

It is now somewhat clearer why Nietzsche ranks the spirit that attempts to establish the rule far above the spirit that seeks to establish the exceptions (*H* 2:362), and how the philosopher's knowledge is at the same time the creation of a new order of values and the legislation of a spiritual hierarchy (*Rangordnung*). It is also clearer why 'loving contempt' constitutes the fundamental experience of the philosopher-statesman, for both Nietzsche and Plato: the principle of ascent – contempt for the city and love for the higher-than-human things – eventually becomes the principle of descent whereby the philosopher (and his play of creation) brings a higher order down to the human world; his contempt for man is the condition of his love and creativity.

However, it must be emphasized again and again that neither Plato nor Nietzsche envisions a joyful, let alone a comprehending, reception for the philosopher in his legislative reincarnation among the people.[26] It is all too clear that just as Plato's demiurge is confronted by the permanent resistance of becoming and necessity to his noetic persuasion, so the statesman will never bridge the chasm dividing philosophy and the city, or polity and politics. For Nietzsche as for Plato, the statesman's legislation, like the demiurge's descent of creation, never gives birth to an eternal utopia. The sovereignty of the noble is always opposed and compromised by the enervating disintegration intrinsic to becoming and all created works, including polity. It is equally evident that the renunciation of politics is not an option; the philosopher is the law-giver for his people, and therefore his creativity, like that of the demiurge, is necessarily mediated by the political world that is not ordered by the Idea or by philosophy. In distinct contrast to the quietism of the Cynics, Plato and Nietzsche accept the necessity of this mediation because the philosopher is the one who should ordain the law-tables of his city and thus lives in a recurring descent of creation rather than in isolation. '"There is no harder misfortune in all human destiny than when the powerful of the earth are not also the first men. Then everything becomes false and awry and monstrous' (Z, 'Conversation with the Kings,' 1).

Another crucial element of Nietzsche's revaluation of the meaning of politics remains to elaborated, one which also recalls a prominent theme in Plato's political philosophy: the critique of 'the good man,' of the moderate, austere, law-abiding citizen for whom the morality of custom (*Sittlichkeit*) of his people suffices. There is a corollary of this critique: both Nietzsche and Plato see the free spirit of the tyrannic soul, with its extravagant *eros* and sacrilegious nature, as being closer to the philosophic spirit than the moderate citizen with little potency for evil or good, although both assign the highest spiritual rank to the philosopher.

This dimension of Nietzsche's grand politics must be distinguished from Plato's inasmuch as the Overman, while he represents a spirituality unknown to the tyrant, is explicitly characterized as an 'immoralist.' Although the liberation of *eros* from the restraints of the morality of custom is essential for Plato's philosopher, he is distinguished from the tyrannic spirit because his ascent is towards the Idea of the Good, whereas the Overman ascends to the supra-moral. The relationship between the free spirit of the tyrant and the philosopher is therefore more ambiguous in Nietzsche's grand politics than in Plato's thought. For Nietzsche, 'when "morals decay" those men emerge whom one calls tyrants: they are the precursors and ... the precocious harbingers of *individuals*' (*GS*, 23). Clearly, Nietzsche does not identify the free spirit of the tyrannic soul with genuine individuality or nobility; indeed, he repeatedly emphasizes the distinction: 'The free man of the spirit, too, must still purify himself. Much of the prison and rottenness still remain within him: his eye still has to become pure' (*Z*, 'Of the Tree on the Mountainside'). Nevertheless, as a result of this ambiguity between the tyrannic and the noble spirits, this aspect of Nietzsche's vision of grand politics (especially when combined with his critique of pity and the good man) has become entangled in as much misinterpretation as his concept of hierarchy, and therefore must be very carefully explicated. It is essential to distinguish the nobility of the Overman from both the good and the free-spirited because this is what leads us to an understanding of Nietzsche's conception of autonomy as supra-moral and yet highly disciplined.

Nietzsche distinguishes between the noble and the good man, and in a similar fashion, Plato contrasts the erotic soul of the genuine philosopher with the moderate soul of the good citizen. Thus both Nietzsche and Plato perceive an intimate and ineradicable bond between nobility, sacrilege, and the *eros* of the great soul: a bond that seals the relationship between 'loving contempt' and the art of political rule.

In contrast with the good citizen, the higher or noble man is, according to Nietzsche, the 'strongest and most evil spirit' (*GS*, 4), 'the man of great sacrilege' (*WP*, 845; cf. *GS*, 135), the agent of '*active sin*' (*BT*, 9), and 'the law-breaker' (*Z*, 'Of Old and New Law-Tables,' 26): the noble is the creator/legislator who wants to make man 'better and more evil' (*Z*, 'Of the Higher Man,' 5).

Nietzsche's conception of the noble man (the genuine philosopher) echoes Plato's contrast between the moderate and the erotic souls. In Plato's thought, *eros* is the *mania* that turns the soul towards the beautiful and leads it up to the purest forms of the good. In its most extreme forms, love – as the desire for the most unnecessary pleasures – can culminate in law-breaking and the pride (*hybris*) that dares everything; hence, *eros* may, as the desire for the unnecessary, realize itself as the *eros tyrannos* (cf. *Republic*, 558d, 561a, 571b, 572e, 587c). The tyrannic soul pursues not only those desires that are unnecessary, but also the unlawful, and he does so because he seeks pure pleasure, albeit confusedly and unsuccessfully – because only philosophy and its love can guarantee pure, self-sufficient pleasure. In Plato's dialogues, Socrates confronts young men inclined to the tyrannic life because the real dilemma or the ultimate choice is addressed to the most erotic souls; and the choice is either philosophy or tyranny as the best life. Even in his classification of constitutions, one can see that monarchy and tyranny hold out the possibility of achieving the greatest results because only within the most erotic souls is there reserved the potency for good or evil.

A certain Dionysian passion that does not shy away from violating even the most sacred taboos constitutes the fundamental condition for the philosophic spirit. Hence, Glaucon, Alcibiades, and even Socrates himself represent a basic Platonic theme: the philosophic life presupposes the emancipation of unnecessary and extravagant desires to be the essential condition of the good life as self-overcoming.[27]

Furthermore, Plato sees the statesman as the philosopher ruling above and beyond all institutions and regulations of the law – extra-constitutionally. It is clear that the erotic nature of the philosophic soul itself elevates him above law and morality through the pursuit of pure and unnecessary desires. In the *Statesman*, for example, moderation, as the virtue of control, gentleness, and quietness, must be married (quite literally) with courage, aggression, and vigorousness: 'Those in whom courage predominates will be treated as having the firm warplike character, as one might call it. Those who incline to moderation will be used by him for what we may ... call supple, soft, wooflike strands of the web. It then tries to combine and weave together these two groups ... (309b). How does Plato's conception of *eros* help us to understand Nietzsche's political philosophy and passages like this one: 'One would have to seek the highest type of free man where the greatest resistance is constantly being overcome: five steps from tyranny, near the threshold of the danger of servitude' (*TI*, 'Expeditions,' 38)?

Nietzsche's noble soul is explicitly driven by 'the necessity of sacrilege imposed upon the titanically striving individual' (*BT*, 9). The erotic power of the noble soul elevates him above and against the laws of the morality of custom; nobility, sacrilege, and *eros* combine in the noble spirit's drive to creation, to 'build beyond itself,' or to self-overcoming in 'loving contempt.'

Nietzsche first distinguishes the noble from the good and then shows how they are ordered in the best polity through two images. On the distinction between the noble and the good, Nietzsche writes:

The strongest and most evil spirits have so far done the most to advance humanity ... What is new, however, is always *evil*, being that which wants to conquer and overthrow the old boundary markers and the old pieties; and only what is old is good. The good men are in all ages those who dig the old thoughts, digging deep and getting them to bear fruit – the farmers of the spirit. (*GS*, 4; cf. *Z*, 'Of the Tree on the Mountainside')

The creative *eros* of the noble, even when it sublimates the will to power, acts in the form of 'active sin' (*BT*, 9), releasing the titanic and barbaric potencies of passion – emancipating the unnecessary and pure desires that the good man represses out of fear. Nobility can create beyond itself a new and more beautiful life only by unleashing the terrible and the monstrous (and being victorious over them): 'Grand style originates when the beautiful carries off the victory over the monstrous' (*WS*, 96). The free spirit with all its attendant dangers of monstrosity and tyranny is the necessary precondition of true mastery and sovereignty, but genuine individuality in all its nobility is infinitely higher than free-spiritedness. Self-overcoming builds a higher man, above morality and law, through the spiritualization of the Dionysian powers of nature: man becomes better, not through domestication and repressive taming, but when he becomes more evil, more profound, and more beautiful (cf. *BGE*, 295; *Z*, 'The Convalescent'; 'Of the Higher Man,' 5).

Just as evil belongs to the noble, the erotic passion of the tyrannic soul belongs to the spirit of the Overman as that which he has overcome; he is driven not by the passion for domination or *ressentiment*, but by the passion for creation. The cultivation of the higher spirit begins, therefore, with the celebration of the Dionysian, erotic, and 'evil' nature of man as well as with the need to transfigure or 'rechristen our evil as what is best in us' (*BGE*, 116). The *eros* for the higher things must grow out the affirmation of the 'lower' things, as Nietzsche proposes in the notion of *amor fati* and later in 'the great cultivating idea,' the eternal return of the same (*WP*, 1053, 1056).

Notwithstanding his distinction between nobility and the free spirit, Nietzsche is still criticized by some who equate his 'immoralism' with complete licence. It is alleged, for example, that the Overman is nothing more than a cruel tyrant and ruthless exploiter of the weak, a modern Thra-

symachus. Indeed, Nietzsche is believed to maintain a 'model of domination' in which the might of the 'strong' is given free rein by his
'immoralism' to do as it wishes with the 'weak.'[28]

The two issues involved here, hierarchy and the immoralism of the Overman, are intimately related and represent the very heart of Nietzsche's philosophy and grand politics. For this reason, to misunderstand the supra-
moral individual as the sovereign and noble type is to misunderstand the
very essence of Nietzsche's work. I have already dealt with the issue of
hierarchy as a critique of domination as well as the concept of immorality
as achievement of individuality. It is important to grasp the relationship
between the two issues and to accomplish this through the most provocative examples in Nietzsche's work. In short, it is not enough to emphasize
the distinction between nobility and free spirit because the continuity is
really far more important to the understanding of the Overman.

If the homogeneity of morality and immorality is fundamental to
Nietzsche's philosophy, as he suggests in his indelicate excelsior 'better and
more evil,' then one must confront this issue as the very soil out of which
the Overman is cultivated. And the best and most provocative examples of
this continuity are represented in such 'beasts of prey' as Caesar, Borgia,
and Napoleon. Why does Nietzsche eulogize these tyrannic spirits if they
do not exemplify the highest form of humanity, the noble spirit? Nietzsche
is explicit about the homogeneity of morality and immorality, the continuity of the evil with the good: 'Thus the greatest evil belongs with the greatest good: this, however, is the creative good' (Z, 'Of Self-Overcoming').
But we need to look at how this clarifies the continuity of the nobility of
the Overman with the free spirit.

Nietzsche himself describes the tyrannical spirits as 'precursors' of true
'individuals.' These tyrants emerge in the times of corruption that are 'the
autumn of a people,' when its morality of custom is disintegrating and the
legitimacy of political society is therefore collapsing. With the delegitimation of the morality of custom, morality is 'outlived,' and the private person (not the individual) is liberated from tradition – becomes 'immoral.'
The spirit is set free and the possibility of an ascent to nature is opened.
Thus two possibilities are presented in the autumn of a people: the liberation of the private person, the free spirit, and the autonomy of the individual. 'Variation, whether as deviation [*Abartung*] (to something higher,
subtler, rarer) or as degeneration [*Entartung*] and monstrosity, suddenly
appears on the scene in the greatest abundance and magnificence; the individual dares to be individual and different' (*BGE*, 262; *KGW* 6.2:225–6).
Perhaps Nietzsche wants to imply a certain common denominator to these

two variations by his use of similar words (*Abartung* and *Entartung*); one cannot help but be reminded of his early formulation of 'better and more evil' as an 'ennoblement through degeneration (*Veredelung durch Entartung*)' (*H* 1:224; *KGW* 4.2:191).

In short, Nietzsche suggests both a continuity and a discontinuity between nobility and degeneration, between ascent to the higher and descent to the lower, between the Overman and the tyrant. What is the continuity? They both live beyond the old morality and therefore without common cultural restraints or limits; indeed, as those who break and shatter the old law-tables, they are both 'law-breakers' or outlaws (*Z*, Prologue, 9; 'Of Old and New Law-Tables,' 26); what is more fundamental, they are both compelled to will their own conditions of existence, to improvise their 'good' and 'evil' in the absence of general cultural measures, just as the spirit of the lion must do (*Z*, 'Of the Three Metamorphoses of the Spirit'). The spirit of the lion says 'I will,' whereas the camel (the good, strong type) lives his 'Thou shalt.' Although the free spirit of the lion creates a freedom for itself, it lives in 'the loneliest desert' – in the cultural desert of the autumn and winter of its people. There is, then, a deep continuity between the noble individual and the free spirit. They both possess the free spirit of the lion, the beast of prey. It is in these terms that Nietzsche praises Caesar, Borgia, and Napoleon. Indeed, it is almost exclusively in the context of discussions of freedom as liberation from tradition and the strength to improvise and will one's own conditions of existence that Nietzsche praises these beasts of prey as free spirits, not as noble individuals (cf. *TI*, 'Expeditions,' 37, 38, 44).[29]

Given this basic continuity, what is the discontinuity? What is the difference between 'deviation (*Abartung*)' and 'degeneration (*Entartung*),' according to Nietzsche? In simple, crude terms, we may say that, while Nietzsche advocates a freedom of spirit, a liberation from morality, a becoming more 'evil,' he views this as a prelude to a becoming 'better,' more autonomous, and noble: a preface to the highest self-overcoming. 'And I desire beauty from no one as much as I desire it from you, you man of power: may your goodness be your ultimate self-overpowering. I believe you capable of any evil: therefore I desire of you the good.' (*Z*, 'Of the Sublime Men').

What distinguishes the noble spirit from the free spirit is simply the capacity to overcome evil and go up to a self-mastery that embodies a fundamental wholeness, a belonging to the whole. Four things in particular distinguish the two spirits. First, Nietzsche characterizes the highest type as a creative, law-giving soul: the greatest good is 'the creative good,' and it is the noble man who wants to create new things and a new virtue (Z, 'Of the Tree on the Mountainside'). Moreover, the spirit of the child transcends the freedom of the lion precisely in its capacity to create new values and a new polity for a people (Z, 'Of the Three Metamorphoses'). Second, Nietzsche insists that the will to create beyond oneself is not a free will, but a procreative will that grows out of necessity and fate: 'Where I *have to will* with all my will' (Z, 'Of Immaculate Perception'); the creator is therefore only an intermediary and 'towards every bringing forth we have essentially no other relationship than that of pregnancy and ought to blow to the winds all presumptuous talk of "willing" and "creating"' (D, 552). Higher than the 'I will' of the free spirit is the creative love of *amor fati*, love of fate; a profound modesty and awareness of one's total unaccountability for one's creations belongs to the sovereignty of the noble spirit (H 1:588). Third, unlike the 'letting go' and the liberation from tradition that characterizes the free spirit, Nietzsche describes nobility as a positive rather than a negative freedom; it therefore delights in discipline, constraint, and asceticism (cf. GS, 290; BGE, 188; AC, 57). Fourth, inasmuch as sovereignty implies a creativity that is rooted in the love of fate – in a joy in the actual – then sovereignty is something different from freedom, and autonomy is higher than free will. Clearly, the noble distinguishes himself from the free spirit because he goes far beyond mere liberation of the private person and his particular will; he aspires to wholeness and the innocence of becoming by going up to nature. For this reason, the highest type embodies a greatness of soul because it is the most encompassing, most comprehensive, and complete soul: 'Oh my soul, now there is nowhere a soul more loving and encompassing [*umfangender*] and spacious [*umfänglicher*]! Where could future and past be closer together than with you?' (Z, 'Of The Great Longing'; KGW 6.1:275; cf. BGE, 257, 262; WP, 866, 883, 933, 1027). By releasing himself back into the joy of becoming through eternal return, the Overman summarizes and justifies the history of his people: the nobility of the noble one redeems and transfigures the cultural past by encompassing the historicity of joy and suffering. Through the creative love of *amor fati*, the noble type responds to Nietzsche's challenge: 'When may we begin to "*naturalize*" humanity in terms of a pure, newly discovered, newly redeemed nature?' (GS, 109).

Nietzsche's Overman is indeed an 'immoralist.' But, for this very reason, he is not and cannot be either a free spirit or a tyrant because his immoralism guarantees his innocence, modesty, joy, and freedom from both revenge and the desire to dominate. Perhaps this is the most obscure dimension of the Overman and the one that differentiates him from Plato's philosopher-statesman: his supra-morality, the Dionysian *eros* which makes him an 'Over-man' raises him above the free spirit as well as tyranny. Thus, in contrast to both the moral idealism of Plato's philosopher and the empty freedom of the tyrant, Nietzsche's Overman grows out of an immoralism that is the ground of his sovereignty, a naturalism and innocence of becoming that is the ground of his modesty and creativity. For Nietzsche, this is what makes him a creative spirit, an embodiment of *eros*, of a creative love that affirms rather than negates, and an autonomous spirit that gives birth to a new order. As the embodiment of the sovereignty of joy, the noble spirit is a law-breaker and, above all, a law-giver.

# 5

# Nietzsche Contra Rousseau

*Progress in my sense.* – I too speak of a 'return to nature', although it is not really a going-back but a *going-up* – up into a high, free, even frightful nature and natural-ness, such as plays with great tasks, is *permitted* to play with them ... But Rousseau – where did *he* really want to return to? Rousseau, this first modern man, idealist and *canaille* in *one* person; who needed moral 'dignity' in order to endure his own aspect; sick with unbridled vanity and unbridled self-contempt. Even this abortion recumbent on the threshold of the new age wanted a 'return to nature' – where, to ask it again, did Rousseau want to return to? (*TI*, 'Expeditions of an Untimely Man,' 48)

In Rousseau, 'the mythical Rousseau' (*WS*, 216), Nietzsche finds the arche-type of 'modern man': the type who embodies the modern theology of rev-olution, that strange and exhilarating combination of 'social nihilism and political absolutism.'[1] Through his critique of Rousseau, he attempts to transcend and overcome 'modernity' itself. In Nietzsche's hands, Rousseau assumes mythical status because he is elevated to a type, a symbol of the modern 'virtue and disease' (*GS*, 337) and, in particular, of the romantic individualism of the French Revolution. Despite many similarities with Rousseau (the critique of Christianity, a deep admiration for ancient cul-ture, and a profound naturalism), Nietzsche deliberately overemphasizes their differences; he heightens the revolutionary romanticism, the Rous-seauean moralism of the French Revolution, and by reading these back into Rousseau, he broadens him into a type in order to magnify something much larger than Rousseau himself. In addressing general historical trends through Rousseau, Nietzsche follows one of his favourite models, Thucy-dides, and 'takes the most comprehensive and impartial delight in all that is typical in men and events' (*D*, 168). In this sense, one should keep in mind that Nietzsche really takes up the political implications of Rousseauism when the confronts Rousseau as a type. 'I never attack persons; I merely avail myself of the person as of a strong magnifying glass that allows one to make visible a general but creeping and elusive calamity' (*EH*, 'Why I Am So Wise,' 7). However, Rousseau is the sign of an elusive calamity that is so general that it cannot be avoided and thus infects even Nietzsche himself; and in attacking Rousseau, he is actually trying to overcome some aspect of himself.

For Nietzsche, then, Rousseau is more a polemical gesture than a person: he is a symbol of something very significant in the era following the death of God and at the height of modernity. But what exactly does Rousseau typify for Nietzsche? Why is Rousseau identified as 'this first modern man, idealist and *canaille* in *one* person'? And if Rousseau is the first modern man, what is the meaning of this primacy? More important, what is 'modernity' according to Nietzsche?

It seems that in explicating Rousseau, Nietzsche hopes to bring to light and address one of the principal dynamics of modernity itself, 'the historical sense.' And as a corollary of this historicism, Nietzsche finds in the modern world a radical withdrawal into an abstract subjectivity that grows out of Christianity and culminates in the unconditional freedom of Rousseau's and Kant's moral subjectivity. The egalitarianism of purely abstract persons, for Nietzsche, signals the disintegration of society in the classical sense of the term; the concept of equality viewed as the foundation of society represents the denaturalization of community and the dissolution of natural morality into subjective morality (*Moralität*): that is, equality represents a radical social atomism that corresponds to the historical sense and the withdrawal into private subjectivity. And insofar as modern democracy is the political consequence of egalitarianism, Nietzsche criticizes democracy as 'the *decay of the state*' (*H* 1:472; *TI*, 'Expeditions,' 39). Finally, while criticizing these qualities of modernity as nihilistic, Nietzsche also views them as an unavoidable part of himself and his culture; it is neither possible nor desirable to go back to an original Golden Age of Greece or Rome. Notwithstanding 'the enchanting and mad *semibarbarism*' of modernity, 'our great virtue of the historical sense' (*BGE*, 224) has changed us and opened new possibilities for higher culture as exemplified in Goethe. Indeed, far from wishing to simply negate modernity and return to antiquity, Nietzsche envisions a way of overcoming Rousseau by absorbing him as one would an inoculation and thereby transcending him. Hence, he holds up Goethe as an exemplary type, not because he is the antithesis of Rousseau, but because he is the self-overcoming of Rousseau.[2]

## Modernity: The Historical Sense and Ironic Existence

When Nietzsche characterizes Rousseau as 'the first modern man,' he clearly wishes to address the nature of modernity through this revolutionary figure. The political revolt of Rousseau really manifests the revolutionary character of modernity and, for Nietzsche, this springs from its historical sensibility. History, as historical consciousness, is the fundamental denaturalization of things, nihilism: if natural morality renders art into nature through the creation of an unhistorical horizon, then the historical sense reverses this process by transforming nature back into art.[3]

In his early essay, 'On the Uses and Disadvantages of History for Life,' (the second of his *Untimely Meditations*), Nietzsche explores the role of history or historical consciousness in culture. The basic thesis of this essay is that, in any form of life, health and strength depend upon forgetfulness, illusion, and narrow boundaries – 'the unhistorical.' Since every form of life is not an atom or an interiority but a perspective with a horizon, it requires the firm and obscure limits to its consciousness that natural morality (*Sittlichkeit*) provides. 'Critical history' can break up the past or old truths and thereby liberate individuals to create new truths, but it cannot by itself constitute the foundation of a new perspective or cultural horizon. For this, 'the unhistorical' is necessary.

Much of the essay is taken up with the question of what happens to culture when 'the historical sense reigns *without restraint*,' when 'it uproots the future because it destroys illusions and robs the things that exist of the atmosphere in which alone they can live' (*UDH*, 7). For my purposes here in elaborating Nietzsche's critique of modernity, the consequences of the historical sense may be summarized in three arguments.

First, when history reigns without restraint, there emerges the peculiarly modern malaise, 'the remarkable antithesis between an interior which fails to correspond to any exterior and an exterior which fails to correspond to any interior' (*UDH*, 4). Subjectivity withdraws into an inaccessible and utterly solitary interiority and the objective world becomes mere externality, *res extensa*. Through an excess of the historical sense, culture is reduced to a piece of knowledge, social identities to roles, nature to art. As first nature becomes second or third nature through historical reflection, the modern individual finds himself undressed as his identities are stripped away and revealed to be merely arbitrary forms of behaviour and irrational habits peculiar to a particular social group and particular historical period.

The celebrated alienation of the modern world resides in the unprecedented duality of form and content, social role and inner self, society and individuality – a polarity so extreme that society, as opposed to a real people, becomes a formal or legal entity, a contract negotiated by pre-existing abstract individuals. Social relations and institutions are, therefore, not only external to the individual, but they represent limitations to, rather than realizations of, individuality. In this liberal, contractualist view, the subjectivity and freedom of the individual are pre-social and essentially extrasocial, even after the advent of civil society. As Nietzsche puts it, 'the whole of modern culture is essentially subjective [*innerlich*]' (*UDH*, 4; *KGW* 3.1:270).

Second, with the antithesis of radical subjectivity and an incommensurate objectivity, the atomization of the individual brings a concomitant weakening of the personality. Paradoxically, historicism enervates as it liberates the subject by demanding objectivity, by imposing an epistemological relationship to everything (including oneself) that prizes impersonality and critical reflection above all. 'While the "free personality" has never before been commended so volubly, there are no personalities to be seen, let alone free personalities – nothing but anxiously muffled up identical people.' Having destroyed his nature by reducing it to history, having lost his 'instincts' along with his unhistorical horizon, the modern in his disinterested objectivity is simply a 'strolling spectator', a 'walking encyclopaedia', or a 'eunuch'. 'But ... this is a race of eunuchs, and to a eunuch one woman is like another, simply a woman, woman in herself, the eternally unapproachable – and it is thus a matter of indifference what they do so long as history itself is kept nice and "objective", bearing in mind that those who want to keep it so are forever incapable of making history themselves' (*UDH*, 4, 5). By radically subjectifying the being of the modern, historical consciousness leads to a denaturing of his being, an impersonality in the deepest sense.

Third, the unrestrained historical sense breeds a dangerous type of self-consciousness that culminates in what Nietzsche calls 'an ironic existence' and even cynicism. As the unhistorical horizon is stripped off and every nature is revealed to be an arbitrary art, one cultivates not only an instrumentalist relationship with one's own actions, but an enervating relativism. One is constantly plagued with the feeling that each action, with its historical goals, is already obsolete even before it is complete; a presentiment of senility and being out-of-fashion haunts every initiative. One looks backwards, over one's shoulder, as if the present and future were already dead and gone. 'Historical culture is indeed a kind of inborn grey-hairedness, and those who bear its mark from childhood must instinctively believe in the *old age of mankind*: to age, however, there pertains an appropriate senile occupation, that of looking back, of reckoning up, of closing accounts, of seeking consolation through remembering what has been, in short, historical culture' (*UDH*, 8). To live in an historicizing or 'twilight mood' (*UDH*, 9) engenders not only an ironic self-consciousness of one's historical insignificance, but a dangerous cynicism towards others and one-self. For Nietzsche, historicism entails 'a total surrender of the personality to the world-process,' as he quotes Hartmann. A blind idolatry of the actual results from this historicism, a passive resignation and even glorifica-tion of whatever horrors history throws up.

There is another aspect to this ironic and cynical form of existence: play-acting or 'artist's faith' (*GS*, 356). The modern antithesis of an interiority with no correspondence to any exterior finds expression in the opposition between the 'true self' and 'social roles.' At one time, when natural moral-ity (*Sittlichkeit*) still reigned, one's role actually became one's character as art became nature, but through the ironic self-consciousness bred by the historical sense, one adopts an instrumentalist relationship to social roles. 'The individual becomes convinced that he can do just about everything and *can manage almost any role*, and everybody experiments with himself, improvises, makes new experiments, enjoys his experiments; and all nature ceases and becomes art' (*GS*, 356). The radical subjectivism of modern, his-torical culture and its impersonality, and self-irony culminate in this 'role faith – an artist's faith.' The total alienation of his 'real self' from all social exteriority forces the modern man to play at being what he is not, to put on a social exterior that does not and cannot correspond to any interior. He must play at being himself. As historicism dissolves all nature into play-act-ing and artifice so that even the distinction between self and social role becomes historical itself, one finds that it is impossible to appeal to any standard outside of history. The modern man is an actor because he has been denatured by his historical self-consciousness. 'But what I fear, what is so palpable ... is that we modern men are even now pretty far along on the same road; and whenever a human being begins to discover how he is play-ing a role and how he *can* be an actor, he *becomes* an actor' (*GS*, 356).

## Modernity and Christianity

Modernity is characterized by historical self-consciousness, radical subjec-tivism, and an ironic existence, and Nietzsche traces this form of life to the rise of Christianity. The understanding of the relationship between Christi-anity and the modern age is especially urgent because, according to Nietzsche, there is a fundamental continuity between Rousseau and Chris-tianity. Only by addressing the Christian roots of modernity can one fully appreciate the significance of Rousseau and the French Revolution for the modern age and its withdrawal from the world into an abstract subjectivity, into subjective morality.

In this section, I shall summarize Nietzsche's analysis of Christianity as the first and most extreme form of social nihilism; and it is only as social nihilism (as anarchy) that Christianity becomes the archetype of idealism and subjective morality: idealism is simply the consequence of social nihilism. In its most basic form, nihilism arises as the denaturalization of ethical life or the customary morality (*Sittlichkeit*) of a people, and Nietzsche's analysis of this social and political disintegration begins with the emergence of Christianity out of the soil of the people and religion of Israel.

The history of Israel is invaluable as a typical history of the *denaturalizing* of natural values ... Originally, above all in the period of the Kingdom, Israel too stood in a *correct*, that is to say natural relationship to all things. Their Yaweh was the expression of their consciousness of power, of their delight in themselves [*Freude an sich*], their hopes of themselves: in him they anticipated victory and salvation, with him they trusted that nature would provide what the people [*Volk*] needed – above all rain. Yaweh is the God of Israel and *consequently* the God of justice: the logic of every nation [*Volk*] that is in power and has a good conscience about it. These two aspects of a nation's self-affirmation find expression in festival worship: it is grateful for the great destiny which has raised it on high, it is grateful towards the year's seasons and all its good fortune with livestock and husbandry. (*AC*, 25; *KGW* 6.3:191)

Here, in a world that came well before the classical world of the Greeks and especially the Romans, Nietzsche portrays the authentic and natural state of culture and morality: the self-affirmation of a people. In particular, he emphasizes the characteristics of the morality of custom which were analysed in chapter 3: the living sense of community, tradition, and civil religion. Israel and Judaism coincide in the ethical life (*Sittlichkeit*) of a people, the civil religion in and through which a nation affirms itself: 'A people which still believes in itself still also has its own God. In him it venerates the conditions through which it has prospered, its virtues – it projects its joy [*Lust*] in itself, its feeling of power on to a being whom one thanks for them ... Within the bounds of such presuppositions religion is a form of gratitude' (*AC*, 16; *KGW* 6.3:180). At this time, the concept of God is a natural concept because it is embedded and embodied in a people; here 'he represented a people, the strength of a people, everything aggressive and thirsting for power in the soul of a people'; he was, in short, 'the "God of Israel", the national God [*Volksgotte*]' (*AC*, 16, 17; *KGW* 6.3:181), and not yet a cosmopolitan God abstracted from his people and thereby reduced to an ideal, a thing-in-itself, an *'absolutum'* (*AC*, 17).

For Nietzsche, the history of Israel during the period of the Kingdom illustrates the natural morality of an authentic community, similar to that of classical antiquity and ancient India. What happens after this is 'the radical *falsification* of all nature, all naturalness, all reality, the entire inner world as well as the outer' (*AC*, 24). This falsification of all naturalness and reality means, in concrete terms, that a people begins to define itself in contradiction to its own specific conditions of life; it experiences and eventually idealizes a social nihilism.

They defined themselves *counter* to all those conditions under which a nation was previously able to live, was *permitted* to live; they made of themselves an antithesis to *natural* conditions – they inverted religion, religious worship, morality, history, psychology one after the other in an irreparable way into the *contradiction of their natural values*. (*AC*, 24)

The falsification or inversion of these five aspects of a people's conditions of life (religion, worship, morality, history, and psychology) whereby a people makes itself the antithesis to its natural conditions is, for Nietzsche, denaturalization of natural values, or social nihilism. Since Christianity is the real source of modernity's moral subjectivism and constitutes, for Nietzsche, 'the same phenomenon again and in unutterably vaster proportions' (*AC*, 24), I shall summarize briefly this history of Israel and its elaboration in Christianity in order to proceed to the analysis of Rousseau.

With this genealogy of Christianity, Nietzsche draws attention to a natural ethical life-world that is falsified through social nihilism into an abstract morality (*Moralität*), a national God falsified as a cosmopolitan moral God. Indeed, the subjectification of morality corresponds to the universalization of God.

When the prerequisites of *ascending* life, when everything strong, brave, masterful, proud is eliminated from the conception of God ...: *of what* does such a transformation speak? such a *reduction* of the divine? – To be sure: 'the kingdom of God' has thereby grown larger. Formerly he had only his people, his 'chosen' people. In the meantime, just like his people itself, he has gone abroad, gone wandering about; since then he has sat still nowhere: until at last he is at home everywhere, the great cosmopolitan – until he has got 'the great majority' and half the earth on his side. (*AC*, 17)

This point is crucial to Nietzsche's understanding of modernity: the subjectification or moralization of man is preceded by the moralization of God as the God of everyone, as the moral cosmopolitan. 'He is continually moralizing, he creeps into the cave of every private virtue, becomes a God for everybody, becomes a private man, becomes a cosmopolitan.' Whereas he formerly represented a people and its civil religion, he is now 'merely the good God'; the moral God, the *moralization* of the divine, is his denaturalization in every sense of the word: 'The *anti-natural* castration of a God into a God of the merely good would be totally undesirable here. One has as much need of the evil God as of the good God' (*AC*, 16). Through this moralization and abstraction, God is no longer a reality, but merely an ideal, a moral 'ought to be,' a purely metaphysical entity. He 'became "pure spirit", became "*absolutum*", became "thing in itself" ... *Decay of a God*: God became "thing in itself"' (*AC*, 17).

Corresponding to this denaturalization of God, there develops a denaturalization of morality. Natural morality is bound up with and embedded in a social community and, as such, it is a part of a civil religion. Therefore, the disintegration of this ethical life is really a social atomism or nihilism that entails a corresponding abstraction of social customs. '*Morality* [is] no longer the expression of the conditions under which a nation lives and grows, no longer a nation's deepest instinct of life, but [has] become abstract, become the antithesis of life – morality as the fundamental degradation of the imagination, as an "evil eye" for all things' (*AC*, 25).

This is the fundamental issue for Nietzsche's analysis of Christianity and its influence upon modernity: natural morality (*Sittlichkeit*) becomes the abstract and subjective morality (*Moralität*) of the 'ought'; and this is by no means an ideological phenomenon, but primarily a social disintegration and delegitimation that manifests itself in this ideological form. The moralization of a people follows from its denaturalization which, in turn, follows from its social atomization. Nietzsche explains this denaturalization of morality by relating it to the loss of its leading classes, its king and warriors. With the social decapitation of Israel after the period of the Kingdom comes the rise of the priesthood to the ruling position: 'The Jews tried to prevail after they had lost two of their castes, that of the warrior and that of the peasant; in this sense they are the "castrated": they have the priests – and then immediately the chandala ...' (*WP*, 184).

This denaturalization of culture, the loss of its native nobility, is a kind of sociocultural nihilism which then becomes moral nihilism: the denaturalization of morality. The hegemony of the priestly class (the loss of its own ruling class due to conquest) leads to the abstraction of the concept of God from the people of Israel: 'Yaweh is the God of Israel and *consequently* the God of justice' becomes, after the Kingdom, 'Yaweh [is] the God of "justice" – *no longer* at one with Israel, an expression of national self-confidence' (*AC*, 25). The priest becomes the only mediation between Israel and God; this 'new conception of him becomes an instrument in the hands of priestly agitators' so that 'from now on all things of life are so ordered that the priest is *everywhere indispensable*' (*AC*, 25, 26).

Christianity emerges from this background of social disintegration, ethical denaturalization, and the falsification of reality as the radical withdrawal into the private self and subjective morality (*Moralität*). 'On a soil *falsified* in this way, where all nature, all natural values, all *reality* had the profoundest instincts of the ruling class against it, there arose *Christianity*, a form of mortal hostility to reality as yet unsurpassed' (*AC*, 27). This transformation manifests itself in the evolution of Christianity and its withdrawal from not only the ancient polis, but from culture as such. And since culture constitutes human reality, Christianity represents a rebellion against reality itself, a withdrawal into an abstract subjectivity that interprets itself as sovereign over the real world.

The 'holy people' ... produced for its instinct a formula which was logical to the point of self-negation: as *Christianity* it negated the last remaining form of reality, the 'holy people', the 'chosen people', the *Jewish* reality itself. The case is of the first rank: the little rebellious movement which is baptised with the name of Jesus of Nazareth is the Jewish instinct *once more* – in other words the priestly instinct which can no longer endure the priest as a reality, the invention of an even *more abstract* form of existence, an even *more unreal* vision of the world than one conditioned by an organized Church. Christianity *negates* the Church. (*AC*, 27)

While the denaturalization of morality in Israel was precipitated by the loss of the aristocracy, leaving the priests ruling over the people, Christianity originates with the revolt against the priest – the self-redemption of the masses: 'As is only fair, a break develops among them, a revolt of the chandala: the origin of Christianity ... The Christian is the chandala who repudiates the priest – the chandala who redeems himself ... ' (*WP*, 184).

This revolt inaugurates the most radical refusal of the world. It begins the complete atomization of the individual, his abstraction from the polis and from his people (which Judaism preserved). On the one hand, there is God and, on the other, there is individual man, abstracted from his status, language, and people. Indeed, man no longer dwells in a people, a city, or even society: 'Christianity is also the abolition of society' (*WP*, 207). As

Nietzsche points out, this could only occur within a people already uprooted and depoliticized, without a culture of its own.

This was also the case with the earliest Christian community (also Jewish community), whose presupposition is the absolutely unpolitical Jewish society. Christianity could grow only in the soil of Judaism, i.e., amidst a people that had already renounced politics and lived a kind of parasitic existence within the Roman order of things. Christianity is a step further on: one is even more free to 'emasculate' oneself – circumstances permit it. (*WP*, 204)

Moreover, this apolitical ethos becomes anti-political, through the Pauline interpretation of the death of Jesus: it harbours a *ressentiment* against the Roman nobility and ruling Judaism and the Pharisees. Thus Christianity became a permanent revolution against the very principle of society – hierarchy – despite the fact that its egalitarianism cultivates a private form of community in the Church and family.

The fate of the Evangel was determined by the death – it hung on the Cross.... a disciple's love knows nothing of chance. Only now did the chasm open up: '*Who* killed him? *who* was his natural enemy?' – this question came like a flash of lightning. Answer: *ruling* Judaism, its upper class. From this moment one felt oneself in mutiny *against* the social order, one subsequently understood Jesus as having been *in mutiny against the social order* ... Precisely in the most unevangelic of feelings, *revengefulness*, again came uppermost. (*AC*, 40)

Through its subjective morality and its *ressentiment* against society Christianity not only finds itself in revolt against corrupt rule, but defines itself as the principle of mutiny against any rule and thus against polity. Indeed, the repudiation of any concrete reality is so total that the law is negated, as is the flesh: 'For from now on he [Paul] is the teacher of the *destruction of the law!* To die to evil – that means also to die to the law; to exist in the flesh – that means also to exist in the law! To become one with Christ – that means also to become with him the destroyer of the law; to have died with him – that means also to have died to the law!' (*D*, 68).

In this sense, Christianity demands that one live in the world but never become of the world, as was the case with the natural morality of the pagans. For Nietzsche, one is Christian to the extent that one views oneself abstractly, as a child of God, identical and equal to all other individuals regardless of their class, status, language, or culture. The Christian lives subjectively, abstractly, without a world, a culture, or a reality; and thereby Christianity initiates an egalitarian anarchism.

It was a revolt against 'the good and the just', against 'the saints of Israel', against the social hierarchy – *not* against a corruption of these but against caste, privilege, the order, the social form; it was *disbelief* in 'higher men', a *No* uttered towards everything that was priest and theologian ... This holy anarchist who roused up the lowly, the outcasts and 'sinners', the *Chandala* within Judaism to oppose the ruling order ... was a political criminal, in so far as political criminals were possible in an *absurdly unpolitical* society. (*AC*, 27; cf. *WP*, 209)

Nietzsche's analysis of Christianity highlights the following points: first, the disintegration of natural morality and the concomitant withdrawal into personal subjectivity; second, the universalization of God and the corresponding subjectification of being-human; third, the worldlessness of subjectivity and the hatred for actuality; and finally, the political subjectification of freedom through egalitarian anarchism: 'One may assert an absolute equivalence between *Christian* and *anarchist*: their purpose, their instinct is set only on destruction' (*AC*, 58).

*And* let us not underestimate the fatality that has crept out of Christianity even into politics! No one any longer possesses today the courage to claim special privileges or the right to rule, the courage to feel a sense of reverence towards himself and towards his equals – the courage for a *pathos of distance* ... Our politics is *morbid* from this lack of courage! – The aristocratic outlook has been undermined most deeply by the lie of equality of souls; and if the belief in the 'prerogative of the majority' makes revolutions and *will continue to make them* – it is Christianity, let there be no doubt about it, *Christian* value judgement which translates every revolution into mere blood and crime! Christianity is a revolt of everything that crawls along the ground directed against that which is *elevated:* the Gospel of the 'lowly' *makes* low. (*AC*, 43)

Nietzsche's cultural and political critique of Christianity may not have been initiated by Rousseau's work, but it is no small irony that Rousseau attained a clarity and passion in his critique that was unsurpassed until Nietzsche. While Machiavelli may have been one of the first to emphasize the negative relationship of Christianity to the political realm, Rousseau is certainly the father of the modern political attack on Christianity.[4] In the chapter on civil religion in *The Social Contract*, not only does Rousseau argue that 'the Christian law is at bottom more injurious than serviceable to a robust constitution of the state,' but he sees it as positively antithetical to society as such: 'It is said that a people of true Christians would form the most perfect society imaginable. I see but one great flaw in this hypothesis, namely that a society of true Christians would not be a society of men.'[5]

Rousseau's analysis of Christianity's basic incompatibility with the political world is strikingly similar to Nietzsche's. For Rousseau, the reason why 'a society of true Christians would not be a society of men' is that 'Christianity is a wholly spiritual religion, concerned solely with the things of heaven; the Christian's homeland is not of this world.'[6] Like Machiavelli and Nietzsche, Rousseau argues not only that Christianity removes God from the polis and degrades the concrete, lived reality of a people, but also that it thereby uproots the individual's identity from his earthly community and relocates his homeland in the other world which is yet another society (the Church). Unlike the ancient pagan identity with the polis, where the deities were the gods of a particular people and religion was a civil religion embedded in the laws and customs, Christianity separates the individual from his community by making the divine into a universal God of all humanity and by uprooting the individual from his earthly home so that the universal community of the church becomes his only 'society.' By separating religion and politics, humanity itself is divided into *bourgeois* and *citoyen*, and the once integrated society of civil religion is split into an earthly world of purely private interests and an abstract community of souls.

Finally, the otherworldliness of Christianity renders humanity indifferent to the earthly polis and even advocates docile submission to the state, whatever its constitutional disposition to freedom. 'Christianity preaches only servitude and submission. Its spirit is too favourable to tyranny for tyranny not to take advantage of it. True Christians are made to be slaves; they know it and they hardly care; this short life has too little value in their eyes.'[7] In this sense, Rousseau sees in Christianity the initiation of a profound alienation of man from himself and his community by the creation of a dual power: state and church.

In spite of the similarity of their critique of Christianity, Rousseau and Nietzsche differ in a way that becomes fundamental to their relation to modernity. Rousseau forgets how Christian he is, while Nietzsche never does. Rousseau even believes that his eulogy of freedom as the sovereign free will (the most Christian of ideas) constitutes a rebellion against Christianity. For Nietzsche, however, this Christian misunderstanding of freedom is fatally important for the character of Rousseau's political philosophy and the political nihilism of the modern age.[8]

## Rousseau: Subjective Freedom as General Will

There is, then, a fundamental continuity between Christianity and Rousseau that revolves around their subjective morality: more precisely, their
conception of freedom as subjective will – freedom as pure, infinite free
will. If Christianity abstracted the doer from the deed, Rousseau and later
Kant accentuated this radical subjectivism by interpreting freedom as the
absolute autonomy of the individual will. In this way, despite his criticism
of Christianity, Rousseau magnified this aspect of subjective morality and
thereby laid the foundations of modernity.

   This continuity may help answer Nietzsche's question: 'But Rousseau –
where did *he* really want to return to?' To avoid succumbing to the temptation to answer with the usual characterizations of Rousseau's political philosophy, we need to recall that Nietzsche is referring to 'Rousseau' as a
type that symbolizes what is peculiar to modern life. We also need to
address what this type means to Nietzsche and his analysis of modernity.
In Nietzsche's references to this image throughout his work, 'Rousseau'
signifies the romantic moralism of the French Revolution and revolution in
general.

I hate Rousseau even *in* the Revolution: it is the world-historical expression of this
duplicity of idealist and *canaille*. The bloody farce enacted by this Revolution, its
'immorality', does not concern me much: what I hate is its Rousseauesque *morality*
– the so-called 'truths' of the Revolution through which it is still an active force and
persuades everything shallow and mediocre over to its side. The doctrine of equality
[*Gleichheit*]! ... But there exists no more poisonous poison: for it *seems* to be
preached by justice itself, while it is the *end* of justice. (*TI*, 'Expeditions,' 48; *KGW*
6.3:144; cf. *D*, 163)

   In Nietzsche's political revaluation of modernity, Rousseau symbolizes
the revolutionary duplicity of 'idealist and *canaille*.' Rousseau is the source
and mouthpiece of modern idealism: the modern morality of equality, free
will and pity; and the romantic cult of feeling and conscience (*WS*, 216), the
'law of the heart'[9] as the foundation of morality. Rousseau is also the
source and mouthpiece of modern revolution and socialism, the modern
*canaille* in revolt against 'society': absolute egalitarianism; the 'abolition of
society' through a radical individualism and the attempt to reconstitute
'society' through a political absolutism of the state – through a 'social contract' arising from the 'general will' of the sovereign people (Z, 'Of the
New Idol').

For Nietzsche, 'the mythical Rousseau' represents the doctrine of equality, 'this "modern idea" *par excellence*' (*TI*, 'Expeditions,' 48), and as the archetypal modern, he is the 'echo of Christianity in morality' (*D*, 132) – and in politics. To get to the heart of the Nietzschean significance of 'the mythical Rousseau' and modernity in general, we need to grasp the unity of this 'duplicity' of 'idealism and *canaille*' in the modern political morality of equality, to understand the teaching of equality as the 'echo of Christianity' or as the echo of subjective morality.[10]

Again and again, Nietzsche illustrates the continuity between Christianity and Rousseau (as modernity) through the modern ideology of egalitarianism. The very aspect of the French Revolution that epitomizes its 'Rousseauesque *morality*' – the 'doctrine of equality [Lehre von der Gleichheit]' – is also the most Christian of teachings: 'The poison of the doctrine "*equal* rights for all" – this has been more thoroughly sowed by Christianity than by anything else' (*AC*, 43). Indeed, the political concept of equality and the related idea of society as a legal contract between abstract and equal individual wills make possible a completely historicist conception of society: equality makes revolution possible and even inevitable because society is now perceived as a social contract created by particular, historical wills: 'The aristocratic outlook has been undermined most deeply by the lie of equality of souls; and if the belief in the "prerogative of the majority" makes revolutions and *will continue to make them* – it is Christianity, let there be no doubt about it, *Christian* value judgement which translates every revolution into mere blood and crime!' (*AC*, 43).

Thus, the theory of equality and its presupposition, subjective morality (Christianity), underlie the modern (historicist) conception of society as a contract created by abstract and free wills. How does this manifest itself in Rousseau's political philosophy? Rousseau's concept of the 'general will' is at the core of his revolutionary equation of freedom and autonomy. The problem that he seeks to resolve with his theory of the 'general will' is how the law that rules over and subordinates subjective wills can be conceived as the creation of the individual will without thereby depriving the law of universality; how a particular will can become the source of a universal political order. In Rousseau's own words: '"How to find a form of association which will defend the person and goods of each member with the collective force of all, and under which each individual, while uniting himself with the others, obeys no one but himself, and remains as free as before."'[11] In short, the task Rousseau sets for himself is one of discovering a political society in which the form and legitimacy of the social contract is complete and pure autonomy, a polity where subjection to the law is at the same time the creation and institutionalization of freedom or self-legislation (autonomy), where one 'obeys no one but himself.'

To resolve this dilemma, Rousseau comes up with the idea that the will is intrinsically the law, that law and universality are internal and constitutive of the individual will as will. The true will of every individual is immediately the 'general will' itself. Moreover, the social contract creates this identity of individual and general will by means of the absolute alienation of each associate of himself and his rights to the community. For only in this way are the conditions of association the same for all – that is, universal and equal.

These articles of association ... are reducible to a single one, namely the total alienation by each associate of himself and all his rights to the whole community. Thus, in the first place, as every individual gives himself absolutely, the conditions are the same for all, and precisely because they are the same for all, it is in no one's interest to make the conditions onerous for others.[12]

If the general will is the condition of a political order where law and freedom (autonomy) are synonymous, then the condition of the general will is equality. And this equality acquires its substance in the act of 'total alienation' by everyone of their particular rights to the community (the state). The general will is general only because it rests upon the unconditional surrender of each member's individual will such that everyone gives up her or his natural independence and receives equal rights and freedoms. '"Each one of us puts into the community his person and all his powers under the supreme direction of the general will; and as a body, we incorporate every member as an indivisible part of the whole."'[13]

Thus autonomy implies equality. But, for Rousseau, equality is inseparable from political absolutism – a complete and unconditional surrender of one's natural independence for a complete dependence upon the state – and from an unconditional subjectivism that precludes all social relationships as 'sectional associations'[14] by definition since they do not embody autonomy (the immediate identity of law and will). Only the immediate relationship of polity and individual self in the general will and thereby the state remains possible and desirable. Indeed, the equality of the general will precludes all particularistic relationships (family, race, ethnicity, religion, class) to the point that the citizen becomes an abstract atom whose only moral relationship is with the state: 'each citizen shall be at the same time perfectly independent of all his fellow citizens and excessively dependent on the republic ... since it is the power of the state alone which makes the freedom of its members.'[15]

Autonomy and equality, the twin foundations of Rousseau's political theory, presuppose an unavoidable idealism and an absolute statism – a denaturalization of a people and its morality through the emergence of 'mass society.' Let us consider first idealist subjectivism: subjective freedom (free will) constitutes the moral basis of law and political society because the legitimacy of the state now becomes the predicate of individual will insofar as the latter expresses the universal or general will. This subjectivity is an abstraction that presupposes the reduction of a people and its natural morality to a contractual relationship; it is the consequence of the denaturalization of a community. More precisely, this subjectivity is an abstraction because, through the general will, it attempts to establish the moral autonomy of the subject as the standard for reality even though, by definition, the moral autonomy of the subject exists not in the world but only in the unblemished interior of the heart. In short, Rousseau sees autonomy (the immediate identity of law and will) as the moral 'ought to be' for a reality which is nevertheless defined as the opposite of moral autonomy – as the separation of law and will.

On the second point, absolute statism: Rousseau's moral autonomy implies an absolute state because, beginning with his premise of an unmediated identity of law and will, the social contract precludes all particular (mediated and conditional) relationships from political society; here again, pure autonomy and its immediacy are the only measures of the moral good of society. The very purity of this moral measure renders it a force of social atomization that leaves only the mass state as the embodiment of the general will. As the expression of moral autonomy, the general will must be unmediated by private or particularistic interests in society. The individual must stand in a direct and absolute relationship with the state.

But if groups, sectional associations are formed at the expense of the larger association, the will of each of these groups will become general in relation to its own members and private in relation to the state ... Thus, if the general will is to be clearly expressed, it is imperative that there should be no sectional associations in the state, and that every citizen should make up his own mind for himself ...[16]

The refusal of mediation which is intrinsic to the moral autonomy of the general will is therefore also a refusal of society that necessarily leads to an absolute conception of sovereignty and the state. Just as the general will is inalienable and indivisible in Rousseau's social contract, so the sovereignty of the state is equally absolute. Indeed, as the embodiment of the general will, 'the power of the state alone ... makes the freedom of its members'[17] because it atomizes the individual in such a complete fashion that the citizen and the state exist in pure immediacy: the general will combines 'social nihilism and political absolutism.'[18]

For Nietzsche, Rousseau's subjective morality is reducible to his doctrine of equality. But the political and ethical significance of this modern teaching is the denaturalization of the people through the aggrandizement of the centralized mass state. Just as Christianity is the 'abolition of society' (WP, 207) through its retreat into the moral autonomy of the abstract self, so modern egalitarianism is 'the death of peoples' (Z, 'Of the New Idol') through the state.[19]

There are still peoples and herds somewhere, but not with us, my brothers: here there are states.

The state? What is that? Well then! Now open your ears, for now I shall speak to you of the death of peoples.

The state is the coldest of all cold monsters. Coldly it lies, too; and this lie creeps from its mouth: 'I, the state, am the people.' ...

Where a people still exists, there the people do not understand the state and hate it as the evil eye and sin against custom and law.

I offer you this sign: every people speaks its own language of good and evil: its neighbour does not understand this language. It invented this language for itself in custom and law. (Z, 'Of the New Idol')

Here, one can see why culture, Nietzsche's principal concern, is fundamentally incompatible with the state and modern politics; and yet this passage also makes very clear how culture and grand politics are essentially related through the concepts of natural morality, peoples, custom and law, and tradition. For a people is defined through its unique 'language of good and evil' that evolves 'in custom and law.' Moreover, because this language arises from custom (Sitten) and law, a people is similarly defined by its customary morality (Sittlichkeit). As we have seen, Nietzsche identifies the death of a people with the disintegration of its morality of custom (Sittlichkeit der Sitte) and the emergence of an abstract and subjective morality (Moralität) – with social nihilism. Growing out of Christianity, the modern spirit finds its voice in Rousseau's eulogy of the general will and absolute equality. However, the full implications of Rousseau are elaborated and purified in the philosophy of Kant.

## Kant: Rousseau Purified

For Nietzsche, the modern spirit first emerges with Rousseau's concept of positive freedom or moral autonomy: the concept of freedom as moral autonomy[20] where one only subjects oneself to those laws that one freely wills. This entails the assumption of an absolute immediacy of subjective will and universal law that is realized in the general will. For Nietzsche, this conception of moral autonomy and its political cousin, egalitarianism, is rooted in the dissolution of customary morality and the emergence of subjective morality through Christianity.

The moral and political teaching of modern egalitarianism that emerges with Rousseau is based upon this equation of freedom and absolute autonomy, which is, for Nietzsche, completely idealistic. Underlying the theory of equality stands the concept of positive freedom of the subjective will which comes to full fruition with Kant.

For Nietzsche, Kant represents a purification of Rousseau's conception of subjective freedom. In particular, Kant argues that if positive freedom is moral autonomy, then it cannot be conceived empirically as a 'moral feeling,' but must be understood transcendentally as pure practical reason. Through this identification of the moral will with pure reason, Kant attempts to secure Rousseau's philosophy of autonomy by going beyond his cult of feeling and moral sentimentalism. In order to illuminate Nietzsche's critique of modern morality and politics, I shall explore three basic elements of Kant's argument. First, the idealism of Kant's moral autonomy entails the conception of the will as unconditionally free; this freedom is not a reality but merely 'an Idea' or 'practical postulate.' Second, this will is purified so that it is 'disinterested' and free of passion and inclination, it is purged of all actuality. Third, modern morality is the antinomy of freedom and nature which leaves only a contingent view of happiness rather than 'joy in the actual' and natural morality.

Kant takes up Rousseau's argument that the complete autonomy of the will must be the fundamental premise of morality: 'Thus *morality* lies in the relation of actions to the autonomy of the will – that is, to a possible making of universal law by means of its maxims.' However, in contrast to Rousseau, not only does he equate the moral will with pure reason, but he does so through a radical separation of reason (and thus freedom) from nature through his 'antinomy' of freedom and necessity.

Will is a kind of causality belonging to living being so far as they are rational. *Freedom* would then be the property this causality has of being able to work independently of *determination* by alien causes; just as *natural necessity* is a property characterizing the causality of all non-rational being – the property of being determined to activity by the influence of alien causes.[21]

Indeed, Kant's ethical thought, based on this conception of an unconditional freedom of will and thus a causality of freedom, is inseparable from his transcendental conception of pure reason as something above and beyond experience; the distinction between the 'ought' and the 'is' that structures Kant's moral thinking reciprocally conditions and is conditioned by his distinction between the noumenal or intelligible world of free will and the phenomenal or sensible world of mechanical determinism. Thus, Nietzsche rightly views his attack on Kant's moral autonomy as also constituting a critique of the thing-in-itself and its distinction from appearance.

It is important to recall that Kant distinguishes the realm of pure reason from experience and, in this way, makes room for faith and morality. An exhaustive account of Kant's metaphysics is not possible here, but it is necessary to briefly summarize his 'Copernican revolution' in philosophy in order to comprehend his distinctive moral theory. In his attempt to overcome the radical scepticism articulated in Hume's doubt about the correspondence of our perceptions with the objective world, Kant stood the problem on its head: instead of our mind conforming to the world, the objective world conforms to our mind.

This is the fundamental premise of transcendental idealism. Through his transcendental approach, Kant divides the world into the two realms of sensible experience (the phenomenon) and the intelligible realm (the noumenon) that precedes and conditions all experience. While sensation and understanding operate within the phenomenal world of experience, they presuppose pure reason that exists beyond experience. As pure reason, *a priori* form is not only independent of experience, but is also a condition of experience and thereby of knowledge as well. Moreover, knowledge is always only knowledge of the phenomenal world and, therefore, as the pure form of experience, pure reason is unknowable.

Kant's division of the world into the realm of phenomenal experience, which is subject to mechanical causality that is knowable, and the realm of the noumenal thing-in-itself, which possesses a causality of freedom that is unknowable, is critical for his moral philosophy. For just as the world must conform to the structures of pure reason in our experience, moral law does not reflect reality but determines moral experience: because it is beyond experience, pure reason in its practical aspect, the moral will, informs and legislates experience *a priori* rather responding to it *a posteriori*. Not only is the 'ought' separate from the 'is,' but it is primarily self-determining – autonomous. In this way, the formal world of pure reason is also the world of moral values because reason in its practical form is the absolutely free will.

This is the bedrock of Kant – and Rousseau. A space is opened up in the modern spirit for a purely subjective and absolutely unconditioned will. This freedom is secured at the cost of separating appearance and the thing-in-itself, by creating an antinomy between nature (empirical experience) and morality (practical reason and freedom). It follows from this antinomy of morality and nature that freedom is not something real but merely an 'Idea' or a 'postulate' of pure practical reason. For Kant, morality necessarily implies autonomy and the latter implies the Idea of freedom: 'As a rational being, and consequently as belonging to the intelligible world, man can never conceive the causality of his own will except under the Idea of freedom; ... To the Idea of freedom there is inseparably attached the concept of *autonomy*, and to this in turn the universal principle of morality ... ' By its very transcendence of experience and mechanical causality, freedom is both unknowable and indeterminate; it is not actual but only postulated.

We are unable to explain anything unless we can bring it under laws which can have an object given in some possible experience. Freedom, however, is a mere Idea: its objective validity can in no way be exhibited by reference to laws of nature and consequently cannot be exhibited in any possible experience. Thus the Idea of freedom can never admit of full comprehension, or indeed of insight, since it can never by any analogy have an example falling under it. It holds only as a necessary presupposition of reason in a being who believes himself to be conscious of a will ...'[22]

Kant attempts to shore up Rousseau's concept of moral autonomy through his transcendental interpretation of pure reason as both beyond experience and the transcendental condition of phenomenal experience. In this way, the thing-in-itself becomes the good will that is unconditionally good because it is pure or transcendental: it is both beyond experience and determinate of moral practice. 'It is impossible to conceive anything at all in the world, or even out of it, which can be taken as good without qualification, except a *good will*.'[23] And the good will can be unconditionally good because it is autonomous and thus free of empirical determinations.[24] Hence, the first point concerning Kantian morality is this conception of autonomy and freedom of will.

The second aspect of Kantian morality involves the purification of the moral will of all heteronomous elements – feelings, emotions, interests, etc. – by establishing the formal nature of 'duty' and the 'categorical imperative.' According to Kant, the fundamental character of morality is positive freedom or autonomy – 'namely, the Idea *of the will of every rational being as a will which makes universal law.*'[25] One is not merely subject to law but is first of all its author. In addition to this, the will which is itself a law-giver must be disinterested as a condition of its autonomy; the moral will is autonomous to the extent that it is unconditioned by alien influences, and it can be unconditional only as long as it is without interest. 'Thus the *principle* that every human will is *a will which by all its maxims enacts universal law* ... would be *well suited* to be a categorical imperative in this respect: that precisely because of the Idea of making universal law it is *based on no interest* and consequently can alone among all possible imperatives be *unconditioned.*'[26] Hence, the imperative of morality must be categorical or unconditioned in order to be autonomous and truly moral. The moral will must be good in itself, categorically, without conditions or qualification, and only in this way can it be autonomous.

However, the categorical and unconditioned nature of the moral will ensures its autonomy only by rendering it unreal; by purging morality of all heteronomous influences, Kant also leaves it purely formal. For both Rousseau and Kant, the moral content of action lies not in the action itself but in its *a priori*, in what precedes and determines it – the principle of the will. The freedom and autonomy of the will determine moral action. As Nietzsche points out, this moral *a priori* entails the abstraction of the doer from the deed in order to guarantee a noumenal or 'intelligible freedom'; it presupposes the fiction of an absolute subject with an unconditionally free will. Moreover, this conception of the moral subject and his autonomy or positive freedom involves a refusal of heteronomy and thus of nature and the very conditions of life.

The third element of Kant's morality to which Nietzsche objects brings us back to the theme that permeates the whole of Nietzsche's philosophy and grand politics: the relationship between virtue and happiness (and morality and nature). For Kant, this relationship is utterly contingent since happiness as a goal of an action cannot be the principle of the good will. To have an end outside of itself would reintroduce heteronomy into morality; as one of the 'empirical principles of heteronomy,' happiness reduces morality to a means for the attainment of an end, while morality should be an end in itself.

Happiness pertains to the phenomenal world of experience and thus conditional or sensuous motives. Moreover, concern with happiness, like concern for the result of moral action, distracts one from the purely formal, postulated character of morality and drags one down into reality – for happiness is tied to the realization of action in the world and in nature – into the realm of heteronomy. And this is hardly conceivable for Kant except in a contingent and empirical fashion; for there can be no necessary or intrinsic relationship between morality and happiness anymore than there can be between autonomy and heteronomy.

The abstraction of the doer from the deed lies at the centre of Kantian morality and constitutes its radical denaturalization. In particular, the contingent concept of happiness in Kant's morality reveals the crippling effect of the antinomy between freedom/autonomy and nature: morality is antinature in the sense that it is outside of and against reality and even its own realization in moral action. Happiness in the achievement of a moral goal is exterior to morality because reality itself is exterior to the moral will (as nature is to freedom). Morality cannot realize itself in the world without ceasing to be moral. Thus autonomy condemns morality to a refusal of happiness through a refusal of reality.[27]

A word against Kant as *moralist*. A virtue has to be *our* invention, *our* most personal defence and necessity: in any other sense it is merely a danger. What does not condition our life *harms* it: a virtue merely from a feeling of respect for the concept 'virtue', as Kant desired it, is harmful. 'Virtue', 'duty', 'good in itself', impersonal and universal – phantoms, expressions of decline ... Nothing works more profound ruin than 'impersonal' duty, any sacrifice to the Moloch of abstraction. – Kant's categorical imperative should have been felt as *mortally dangerous*! (*AC*, 11)

Moral autonomy is, therefore, an abstraction or denaturalization of life and, as such, represents a kind of nihilism that turns against nature and joy. Since reality and joy are intimately related in Nietzsche's natural morality through joy in the actual, his critique of Kant's contingent notion of happiness is central to his entire attack on modern morality. In contrast to Kant's moral autonomy, Nietzsche asserts his immoral autonomy as 'joy in the actual':

An action compelled by the instinct of life has in the joy [*Lust*] of performing it the proof it is a *right* action: and every nihilist with Christian-dogmatic bowels understands joy as an *objection* ... What destroys more quickly than to work, to think, to feel without inner necessity, without a deep personal choice, without *joy*? as an automaton of 'duty'? (*AC*, 11; *KGW* 6.3:175)

## Goethe as the Self-Overcoming of Rousseau

Nietzsche's relentless attack on modernity sometimes leaves the impression that he aspires to nothing short of a categorical negation of its most sacred virtues: subjectivity, moral autonomy (positive freedom), and the historical sense. Despite the fervour of his critique, however, the real task of Nietzsche's grand politics is the transcendence of modernity by itself, the absorption of its nihilism, decay, and barbarism as a means of naturalizing humanity in terms of a newly discovered, newly redeemed nature.

It is important to emphasize that, for Nietzsche, classicism does not belong solely to ancient cultures and nihilism is not exclusive to modernity. A genuine classicism of our own time would involve absorbing the negativity of modernity into a higher synthesis. For Nietzsche, Goethe symbolizes a type of self-redemption of modernity, a 'poetry of the future' (*H* 2:99). And whenever Nietzsche mentions Rousseau, a discussion of Goethe is sure to follow – perhaps as a means of recovery and convalescence. Goethe represents a type of nobility and sovereignty in the modern age that is not simply the opposite of Rousseau, but the self-overcoming of Rousseau.

Goethe is significant for the comprehension of Nietzsche's grand politics in two respects. First, he symbolizes the very highest achievement in Nietzsche's eyes: the power to descend into modern nihilism, drink it into oneself, and still rise above it by creating a modern classicism. Second, Goethe embodies the highest aspirations of grand politics: the power to create a post-modern and post-Christian nobility, an affirmative Dionysian spirit that no longer negates life. Power is always a will to power because it never simply is but always becomes; and this exemplifies Nietzsche's concept of sovereignty as 'something one has and does *not* have.'

The first aspect of Goethe as a type that is significant for Nietzsche's grand politics is his intrinsic relationship to Rousseau (as a type). While Goethe is almost always placed beside Rousseau as his opposite, it is clear that they are not simply polar opposites. The young Goethe was a romantic, a partisan of nature-idolatry, and sympathetic to revolutionary ideals. He was very much a part of the Rousseauean romanticism of the eighteenth century, and Nietzsche emphasizes this aspect of his character.

*Goethe* – not a German event but a European one: a grand attempt to overcome the eighteenth century through a return to nature, through a going-*up* to the naturalness of the Renaissance, a kind of self-overcoming on the part of that century. – He bore within him its strongest instincts: sentimentality, nature-idolatry, the anti-historical, the idealistic, the unreal and revolutionary ( – the last is only a form of the unreal). (*TI*, 'Expeditions,' 49)

The eighteenth century is not one of Nietzsche's favourite periods; his characterizations of it are expressed in terms that are virtually synonymous with those in his portraits of Rousseau: it is sentimental, idealist, revolutionary, anti-historical, and inclined to nature-idolatry (cf. *WP*, 95–104, 117, 119). Yet he says that Goethe carried 'its strongest instincts' within him, which is to say that Goethe was himself a Rousseauean moralist and a romantic nihilist. How, then, can Goethe represent an overcoming of Rousseau and the eighteenth century? What sources of strength did he possess that allowed him to transcend himself?[28]

From Nietzsche's admiration for the classical cultures of antiquity, one would expect that he saw in Goethe a modern reincarnation of Greek or Roman nobility. However, the virtues that he ascribes to Goethe are almost exclusively modern virtues – indeed, nineteenth century virtues: 'He called to his aid history, the natural sciences, antiquity, likewise Spinoza, above all practical activity' (*TI*, 'Expeditions,' 49). With the sole exception of 'antiquity,' Goethe employs modern and therefore nihilistic tools to overcome himself (assuming that Nietzsche is referring to modern science when he mentions 'the natural sciences'). The explicit reference to Spinoza is especially illuminating in this context because Nietzsche himself identifies Spinoza as his precursor and yet also as a supremely modern philosopher (cf.*GS*, 333, 349).

Perhaps most revealing is the allusion to history because 'the historical sense' is the peculiar 'virtue and disease' (*GS*, 337) of the modern age, its epitome. In order to be a virtue the historical sense must be something more than a force that destroys the supra-historical horizons of culture; it must offer a means of self-overcoming. Yet, surprisingly, Nietzsche seems to find the virtues of a historical consciousness precisely in its disease, in its barbarization of classical culture through the destruction of its supra-historical boundaries. For example, he sees the historical sense as the offspring of democracy and, in particular, 'the democratic mingling of classes and races' (*BGE*, 224); it is the season of a culture that is opened up to the outside world and its former integrity is loosened and delegitimized as it goes from being relatively closed and insular to becoming open and multicultural. This is Nietzsche's 'autumn of a people' where no culture or people is an island but all are swept along together in a tremendous, common current. 'The past of every form and way of life, of cultures that formerly lay right next to each other or one on top of the other, now flows into us

"modern souls," thanks to this mixture; our instincts now run back everywhere; we ourselves are a kind of chaos' (*BGE*, 224).

As a 'disease,' the historical sense expresses a social condition in which
there is not only a cultural intermingling but also a liberation of the private
person from the traditions and common faith of the morality of custom.
One no longer lives exclusively within the cultural integrity of one's own
people; one lives multiculturally. To this extent, history both undermines
traditional culture ('barbarizes') and liberates the private person ('liberal-
izes'). Nietzsche elaborates this dual effect in the following way:

Through our semi-barbarism in body and desires we have secret access in all directions, as no noble age ever did; above all, access to the labyrinths of unfinished cultures and to every semi-barbarism that ever existed on earth ... Let us finally own it
to ourselves: what we men of the 'historical sense' find most difficult to grasp, to
feel, to taste once more, to love once more, what at bottom finds us prejudiced and
almost hostile, is precisely the perfection and ultimate maturity of every culture and
art, that which is really noble in a work or human being, the moment when their sea
is smooth and they have found halcyon self-sufficiency, the golden and cold aspect
of all things that have consummated themselves. (*BGE*, 224)

This historicization or democratization of modern taste, its revolutionary free-spiritedness, is often central to Nietzsche's interpretation of
Goethe and his cultural ambiguity, his spiritual chaos (cf. *H* 1:221; *H* 2:227;
*WP*, 883). He represents a Faustian restlessness that is able to rise above
itself and discover a new classical simplicity and form (*SE*, 4). But it is precisely this 'semi-barbarism' – 'the "barbaric advantages" of our age that
Goethe urged against Schiller's objections' – that makes possible a new naturalization of culture, a self-overcoming of Rousseau.

This disease that both barbarizes and liberates is, in Nietzsche's words,
'our great virtue of the historical sense' (*BGE*, 224). The virtue of this barbaric sense is that it takes us outside morality, beyond measure and thus
above the human.

Perhaps our great virtue of the historical sense is necessarily opposed to *good*
taste, at least to the very best taste; and precisely the highest little strokes of luck and
transfigurations of human life that briefly light up here and there we can recapture
only poorly, hesitantly, by forcing ourselves – those moments and marvels when
great power voluntarily stopped this side of the immeasurable and boundless, when
an excess of subtle delight in sudden restraint and petrification, in standing firm and
taking one's measure, was enjoyed on still trembling ground. *Measure* is alien to us;

let us own it; our thrill is the thrill of the infinite, the unmeasured. Like a rider on a steed that flies forward, we drop the reins before the infinite, we modern men, like semi-barbarians – and reach *our* bliss only where we are most – *in danger*. (*BGE*, 224)

Here Nietzsche identifies himself to a large extent with the modern disease; indeed, through Goethe, Nietzsche is able to revalue and even affirm 'the mythical Rousseau,' that part of himself that is 'Rousseauesque.' This means that Nietzsche views himself as profoundly, if not completely, modern, historicist, democratic, and idealistic. Like Goethe, however, he identifies with this sense only to the extent that it naturalizes the modern spirit and represents the beginning of a new and 'marvelous growth ... that might make our old earth more agreeable to live on.' The virtue of this disease seems to be that the historical sense makes it possible for each to 'experience the history of humanity as a whole as *his own history*' and affirm it as his own; it makes possible 'a happiness that humanity has not known so far' (*GS*, 337), an affirmation unknown till now which Nietzsche calls the eternal return of the same.[29]

It seems that this is what Goethe symbolizes for Nietzsche, the self-overcoming of Rousseau or modernity. Insofar as Goethe (as a type) grows out of Rousseau (as a type), a new nobility that embodies the Dionysian affirmation of life is prepared by modernity and the historical sense: Goethe is the symbol of a new type of nobility:

a man to whom nothing is forbidden, except it be *weakness*, whether that weakness be called vice or virtue ... A spirit thus *emancipated* stands in the midst of the universe with a joyful [*freudigen*] and trusting fatalism, in the *faith* that only what is separate and individual may be rejected, that in the totality everything is redeemed and affirmed – *he no longer denies* ... But such a faith is the highest of all possible faiths: I have baptized it with the name *Dionysus*. (*TI*, 'Expeditions,' 49; *KGW* 6.3:145–6)

The second aspect of Goethe as the self-overcoming of Rousseau concerns the nature of this nobility and its will to power. Nietzsche portrays Goethe as neither classical nor romantic; rather, he is the embodiment of a Dionysian faith that no longer denies or negates – except where 'it denies with *joy*' (*D*, Preface, 4). Goethe overcomes the negative force of Rousseau, whose Faustian restlessness is the denial of joy in the actual. Nietzsche's Goethe transcends this modern negativity by encompassing and transfiguring it. Yet it is the mad semi-barbarism of the modern historical sense embodied in Faust's repudiation of the present moment that makes possible Goethe's affirmation of joy in the actual. For Nietzsche, this self-overcoming of the modern historical sense creates a new nobility that arises from the plenitude of pure becoming and from the affirmation of the eternity of each moment: the barbarism and restlessness of the modern soul make possible an unprecedented transfiguration that bestows a complete world. In this sense, Goethe represents a modern nobility that is nurtured by the dissolution of nature into pure becoming: a Dionysian ennoblement through degeneration. It seems that, for Nietzsche, Goethe embodies an unprecedented nobility that surpasses even the Greeks and the Romans in this respect (D, 199; BGE, 224).

This nobility represent a power that no longer negates except out of joy, and the self-overcoming of modernity signifies a Dionysian will to power in which the world stands complete. The affirmative power that emerges from the historical sense animates a 'concealed Yes ... that is stronger than all our No's' (WP, 405). For Nietzsche, Goethe symbolizes, not a return to a pre-modern classicism, but an unprecedented nobility that embodies a Dionysian will to power which no longer denies or, as Deleuze argues, a power in which the negative exists only as the shadow of affirmation, as the negativity of the positive.[30] In this sense, Goethe represents the nature of sovereignty itself as joy in the actual and active of every kind.

# 6

# Communion in Joy: Will to Power and Eternal Return in Grand Politics

Did you ever say Yes to one joy? O my friends, then you said Yes to *all* woe as well. All things are chained and entwined together, all things are in love;

   if ever you wanted one moment twice, if ever you said: 'You please me, happiness, instant, moment!' then you wanted *everything* to return!

   you wanted everything anew, everything eternal, everything chained, entwined together, everything in love, O that is how you *loved* the world,

   you everlasting men, loved it eternally and for all time: and you say even to woe: 'Go, but return!' *For all joy wants – eternity*! (Z, 'The Intoxicated Song,' 10)

Joy in the actual and active of every kind plays the most fundamental role in Nietzsche's philosophy because it expresses the affirmation of the homogeneity of all things, the continuous and undivided flow of the 'innocence of becoming,' in every moment. To be able to experience joy in what is presupposes a profound sense of belonging to the whole or 'being in the world'; but it also presupposes the strength to affirm what is and has been as joyful not in spite of all suffering, but *because* it includes, *all* suffering; moreover, this strength is something one has and does not have. Thus in Nietzsche's philosophy and grand politics, joy in the actual presumes that unhappiness is intrinsic to joy, 'for happiness and unhappiness are sisters and even twins that either grow up together or ... *remain small* together' (GS, 338). For Nietzsche, joy in the actual embodies a tragic rather than an optimistic or linear conception of happiness which is reached only at the end of a long process of purging away all unhappiness; for Nietzsche, one affirms the perfection of every moment not in spite of, but because of, the silent yes within suffering.

   In this sense, joy wants itself, therefore it also wants suffering; it longs for the suffering of the heart (*Herzeleid*) that is itself (cf. Z, 'The Intoxicated Song,' 11; *KGW* 6.1:399). Moreover, that joy longs (and thus suffers passionately) for itself in an other that is its 'opposite' means that it only becomes itself historically through the historicity of joy. The identity in difference of joy and pain that underlies *amor fati* and eternal return embodies, therefore, an affirmation of suffering not merely as an unfortunate reality to which one must resign oneself – a barrier to joy against which one must steel oneself; it is a joy in the actuality of suffering as desirable in itself because it belongs to the eternal joy of becoming, because suffering is itself the experience of enlargement, growth, enhancement, overflowing, and becoming.

The unity in difference of joy and pain is basic to grand politics and manifests itself in all of Nietzsche's major concepts. First, the will to power is a creative overflowing and squandering of power and joy, not the self-preservation of power: its creativity lies in its squandering of itself. Second, the gift that is given by the creative will to power is *amor fati* and eternal return whereby the will to power learns to affirm itself completely as part of the whole, to affirm unhappiness and suffering as intrinsic to joy. This means that, in *amor fati* and eternal return, a new legitimacy is established for human polity in and through a communion in joy (*Mitfreude*) that replaces the nihilism of pity or the communion in suffering (*Mitleiden*). Third, the Overman is the unity of loving and going-under because he is a prodigal and a sacrifice: 'his greatness lies in the fact that *he expends himself*' (*TI*, 'Expeditions,' 44). In this sense, joy in the actual provides the basis for sovereignty through an unprecedented communion in joy embodied in eternal return.

Finally, if natural morality embodies the most profound experience of communion of a historical people with not only its past (ancestors) and its future (children) but also with the earth and nature as a whole, then the foundation of morality must be based upon the affirmation of life: a community is born of the experience of communion and, for Nietzsche, this means not the sharing of suffering (*Mitleiden*), but the sharing of joy (*Mitfreude*). As the embodiment of creative joy, the Overman forms a community out of communion in joy through *amor fati* and eternal return. In this way, grand politics, as the sovereignty of joy, can realize itself only in communion in joy.

## Will to Power: A Giving or a Preserving?

In order to understand the sovereignty of joy through *amor fati* and eternal return, it is important first to clarify the meaning of will to power itself. On the one hand, there is a tendency to reduce the will to power, wholly or partially, to the will to dominate others and preserve one's own power. For example, by interpreting the will to power as 'the will to will,' Heidegger attempts to demonstrate that Nietzsche preserves a traditional metaphysical conception of being as willing. Through the refashioning of the object into a 'representation [*Vorstellung*],' and, for modern thinking, into a 'value,' willing presupposes a subject who constitutes the Being of beings. Objectivity thereby becomes 'world-view,' and willing is the subjective realization of the subject as the reality of the real, according to Heidegger. Fundamentally, man in his very essence changes and becomes a subject, that is, the *subjectum*.

This reduction of the Being of things to 'representation' rests upon the transformation of man into *subjectum*, 'the relational centre of that which is as such' which constitutes, for Heidegger, both humanism and nihilism. Moreover, Heidegger views Nietzsche and his philosophy as the consummation of this humanistic nihilism.

Furthermore, as the ultimate degradation of being, Nietzsche's Overman signifies less the overcoming of nihilism than its fullest manifestation in technological domination of nature and human life.[1] However, Heidegger's reading of the will to power as a value-positing will that seeks to secure and preserve its power runs up against Nietzsche's explicit characterizations of the will to power as the opposite of self-preservation. Indeed, far from seeking its own security and preservation, the will to power is, for Nietzsche, the surging forth of pure extravagance, excess, and superabundance that not only destroys all limits and measure (and thus all conditions of calculating security or technology), but wants to sacrifice itself, to squander and give itself away in its erotic extravagance. It is this very extravagance that makes life as will to power immeasurable and thus impossible to reduce to human categories of value (cf. *TI*, 'The Problem of Socrates,' 2; 'The Four Great Errors,' 8); and it is for this reason that humanity is a part of nature, fate, the will to power and can never place itself over against it: 'The whole pose of "man *against* the world," of man as a "world-negating" principle, of man as the measure of the value of things, as judge of the world who in the end places existence itself upon his scales and finds it wanting – the monstrous insipidity of this pose has finally come home to us and we are sick of it' (*GS*, 346).

Through the notions of extravagance and measurelessness, I shall elaborate Nietzsche's will to power as a giving, rather than a preserving, force by drawing attention to the coincidence of creation, love, and annihilation in his philosophy. In this way, the will to power can be seen as a revolution dethroning the metaphysics of being (as presence). Henri Birault, for example, writes: 'If Nietzsche's philosophy is not a new philosophy but a new way to philosophize, it is just because of this revolution worked in the very form or essence of desire. While the *sophia* changes its content, the *philein* changes its form.'[2] More precisely, the revolution in the very essence of desire that the will to power represents is embodied in the fullness of desire, in the unprecedented love that no longer proceeds from unhappiness, hunger, need, or lack (as in Plato and Hegel); and fulfilment or satisfaction no longer comes with the quieting or cessation of the will. On the contrary, it is only out of superabundance and happiness that Nietzsche's will to power flows: 'Thus desire now has as its father (or rather its mother) wealth, and no longer poverty; action is the child of happiness and no longer of unhappiness; beatitude is initial and no longer terminal.'[3]

But how does this extravagance in the will to power show up in Nietzsche's thought? In opposition to the desire for self-preservation, life manifests itself as will to power – as exuberance, play, sacrifice, squandering, and giving away of its over-abundance. 'The wish to preserve oneself is the symptom of a condition of distress, of a limitation of the really fundamental instinct of life which aims at *the expansion of power* and, wishing for that, frequently risks and sacrifices self-preservation' (*GS*, 349). Nietzsche then goes on to reveal how expansion of power involves risk and even the sacrifice of self-preservation: 'in nature it is not conditions of distress that are *dominant* but overflow [*Überfluss*] and squandering [*Verschwendung*], even to the point of absurdity [*Unsinnige*]' (*GS*, 349; *KGW* 5.2:267; cf. *GS*, 202). In *Thus Spoke Zarathustra*, Nietzsche makes the same point somewhat more concisely: 'I love him whose soul is lavish [*verschwendet*], who neither wants nor returns thanks: for he always gives and will not preserve himself' (Z, Prologue, 4; *KGW* 6.1:11). Moreover, those whose souls are an extravagant squandering and who will not preserve themselves are identified as 'sacrifices'; they are those who love and go under: 'Alas, my brothers, how should the first-born not be sacrifices! But our kind will have it thus; and I love those who do not wish to preserve themselves. I love with my whole love those who go down and perish: for they are going beyond' (Z, 'Of Old and New Law-Tables,' 6).

Who is the squanderer, the lavish soul, who will not preserve himself? Nietzsche seems to identify him with nature (sensuality and procreation) and 'unreason': '*A Squanderer*. – As yet he does not have the poverty of the rich who have already counted all their treasures once; he is squandering his spirit with the unreason of squandering nature' (*GS*, 202). Here the contrast between 'the poverty of the rich' who have counted their wealth and 'squandering spirit' who, like 'squandering nature,' make themselves poorer from their wealth recalls a similar dichotomy in *The Gay Science* between the noble and the common. In this case, Nietzsche characterizes the noble as 'magnanimous' and 'inexpedient.' The common type, by contrast, is possessed by the same 'poverty of the rich' who are victimized by concerns of utility and self-preservation: 'What distinguishes the common type is that it never loses sight of its advantage, and that this thought of purpose and advantage is even stronger than the strongest instincts [of nature?]; not to allow these instincts to lead one astray to perform inexpedient acts – that is their wisdom and pride' (*GS*, 3). The implication is that while the common type clings to unnatural ideas of utility and purpose, the noble type allows these instincts to lead it astray 'to perform inexpedient acts.' The noble type is thus more natural and 'more *unreasonable*, for those who are noble, magnanimous, and self-sacrificial do succumb to their instincts, and when they are at their best, their reason *pauses*' (*GS*, 3). Thus, the noble is the squandering spirit who succumbs to his squandering nature.

Nietzsche specifies the nature of this unreason; he says that the 'heart displaces the head, and one speaks of "passion".' It is precisely this unreason that Nietzsche suddenly characterizes as the 'counterreason of passion' (*GS*, 3). Why is this inexpedient, self-sacrificial magnanimity of the noble identified as passion? Because it entails 'that squandering of force which one calls passion' (*WP*, 814). Grand passion embodies the extravagant rhythm and violence of evil. As Nietzsche argues in the *The Gay Science*, the noble type is also evil because it resurrects the primal passions that the *polis* suppresses and outlaws: 'The strongest and most evil spirits have so far done the most to advance humanity: again and again they relumed the passions that were going to sleep – all ordered society puts the passions to sleep ...' (*GS* 4).

Nobility is the spirit that is squandering, unreasonable, natural, passionate, and evil, but the noble type is also a lover. All of this presupposes a luxury and wealth that allows for this profusion of extravagance. 'He [the artist] is rich enough for them: he is able to squander without becoming poor' (*WP*, 812). The wealth from which the creative spirit of the artist is able to squander is *eros*, the procreative life-will of the will to power (*Z*, 'Of Self-Overcoming'): 'the lover *is* more valuable, is stronger ... His whole economy is richer than before, more powerful, more *complete* than in those who do not love. The lover becomes a squanderer: he is rich enough for it' (*WP*, 808). Fundamentally, the noble type (as the creative/artistic type) is squandering, extravagant, passionate, and evil because he is erotic – he is intoxicated with a Dionysian *eros*. 'For art to exist...a certain physiological precondition is indispensable: *intoxication* ... All kinds of intoxication ... have the power to do this: above all, the intoxication of sexual excitement, the oldest and most most primitive form of intoxication' (*TI*, 'Expeditions of an Untimely Man,' 8).

It is important not to forget that, for Nietzsche, the intoxication of love is inseparable from the intoxication of death and going-under (cf. Z, 'Of Immaculate Perception'). For to love is to spend onself, to give away one's power, to squander one's wealth without becoming poorer: 'the degree to which one loves, spends oneself, proves the degree of individual power and personality' (*WP*, 786). Nietzsche characterizes the lover as 'more perfect,' 'more *complete*,' but he also tells us that perfection 'is the extraordinary expansion of its feeling of power, riches, necessary overflowing of all limits' (*WP*, 808, 801). And with this overflowing of all limits and measure, love begins its passionate descent into disintegration and annihilation. '"What has become perfect, everything ripe – wants to die!"' (Z, 'The Intoxicated Song,' 9). Here again, one returns inexorably to Nietzsche's unity of creativity, annihilation, and love, the unity of creation (*Schopferung*) and sacrifice (*Opfer*).

In contrast to Heidegger's interpretation, Nietzsche clearly visualizes the will to power of the Overman (and the higher types in general) as manifesting itself in sacrifice, squandering, and the giving away of power rather than its preservation. Indeed, this coincidence of love, creation, and annihilation constitutes the tragic drama of Zarathustra and his 'going-down' or 'going-under' (*Untergang*): 'Behold, I am sick of my wisdom, like a bee that has gathered too much honey; I need hands outstretched to receive it; I should like to give it away [*verschenken*] and distribute it ... (Z, Prologue, 1; *KGW* 6.1:5). Zarathustra then specifies how his giving away of wisdom must express itself: 'To that end, I must descend into the depths: as you do at evening, when you go behind the sea and bring light to the underworld too, superabundant star! Like you, I must go *down* [*untergehen*] ...' This gift-giving that Zarathustra is about to undergo is a sacrifice, a giving away of his life and power by 'going-under' as the sun does at evening when it descends into the sea so 'that the waters may flow golden' (Z, Prologue, 1).

The immersion of the sun in the sea is a central metaphor in Nietzsche's thought and one that gains significance by showing that the overflowing abundance of love, wisdom, and power not only is joy, but also entails a kind of death through sacrifice: 'the happiness of a god full of power and love, full of tears and laughter, a happiness that, like the sun in the evening, continually bestows [*wegschenkt*] its inexhaustible riches, pouring them into the sea, feeling richest, as the sun does, only when the poorest fisherman is still rowing with golden oars!' (*GS*, 337; *KGW* 5.2:245; cf. *Z*, 'Of Old and New Law-Tables,' 13).

The image of the sun's dissolution and immersion in the sea illustrates Nietzsche's contention that love and annihilation are synonymous: 'Loving and perishing [*Untergehn*] ... have gone together from eternity. Will to love: that means to be willing to die, too' (*Z*, 'Of Immaculate Perception'; *KGW* 6.1:153). It is precisely this coincidence of love and death in the creativity of the highest will to power that permits Nietzsche to call it 'lavish' or 'extravagant' rather than self-preserving. Moreover, extravagance and excess are the principal features that allow one to characterize the will to power as the will to squander rather than to preserve oneself; as the will to evil understood here as excess, overflowing, and thus 'going-under.'[4] In this sense, Nietzsche identifies play, squandering, and evil with extravagance and the excess of power and love.

The key here is the idea of excess, of overflowing abundance and play, 'the play of creation' (*Z*, 'Of the Three Metamorphoses'), the exuberance of a being passing beyond its being, beyond its own limits and thereby placing itself in question – putting its being at risk of death. Will to power is, therefore, more than a will to excess that would presuppose a traditional notion of substance as presence; it is, rather, already excess exceeding itself that makes will to power a will to more power. This has significant implications for the way in which one interprets the Overman and his sovereignty in grand politics.

## Pity as Communion in Suffering and Negation of Life

Before examining eternal return as communion in joy and its role in grand politics as the new foundation of polity, we need to understand the meaning of pity as the communion in suffering. What is Nietzsche's understanding of 'pity [*Mitleiden*]'? The conception of pity that Nietzsche attacks so forcefully is drawn from Schopenhauer's metaphysics of self-denial through renunciation of the will to live. Even in his early work, Nietzsche's relationship to Schopenhauer is ambivalent, as is evident in *The Birth of Tragedy* where Nietzsche, while accepting much of the latter's philosophy of pessimism, explicitly rejects 'a Buddhistic negation of the will' (7) as a valid response to the nature of being. Nietzsche's initial rejection of Schopenhauer's negation of the will underlies and foreshadows his ultimate break with the morality of pity.

Schopenhauer's morality of pity is intimately involved with his metaphysics of the will. Following Kant, Schopenhauer maintains the distinction between the world of phenomena or appearances and the world of the noumenon or the thing-in-itself. In contrast to Kant, he envisions the thing-in-itself as the pre-objective 'will to live' and the world of phenomena as 'representation' (*Vorstellung*) or the realm of being-object-for-a-subject. Schopenhauer characterizes the relationship between these two worlds by defining representation as the will objectified in the realm of individuation. Most important, in Schopenhauer's morality, the will to live implies endless suffering and pain inasmuch as it is born of want and perpetual dissatisfaction: 'All *willing* springs from lack, from deficiency, and thus from suffering.'[5] And since the will is also the metaphysical essence of life, it follows that life itself is interminable suffering. Moreover, the will to live objectifies itself primordially in the form of the body and particularly sexual desire, *eros*.[6] This identification of the will with *eros* has important implications for Schopenhauer's conception of morality as negation of the will to live and Nietzsche's later reaction to both.

Although representation and especially knowledge come into being as tools of the will and in general remain subservient to it, man is able to elevate himself above his will through his intellect and, in rare exceptions, purge himself of the will and its suffering. For Schopenhauer, redemption lies in the growing 'predominance of knowing over willing.' But how is this possible if the intellect is fundamentally the servant of the will? This question is really a somewhat different question: How can a profound transformation take place whereby the individuality of the individual is abolished so that he becomes a pure, 'will-less' subject of knowing? For Schopenhauer, this transformation corresponds to a fundamental change in the whole nature of the object and 'by virtue of it the subject, in so far as it knows an Idea, is no longer individual.'[7]

Knowledge that remains subservient to the will knows objects only in and through their relations and thus only in time and space – that is, subject to the principle of sufficient reason. Similarly, the subject of knowledge that serves the will remains a prisoner of these particular conditions of the principle of sufficient reason. Only among rare and exceptional human beings, however, can knowledge predominate over the will and thus free itself from suffering.

As Schopenhauer points out, this transformation can occur only through a profound change in the subject of knowledge: 'by the subject's ceasing to be merely individual, and being now a pure will-less subject of knowledge.'[8] In the pure contemplation of the eternal Ideas which stand outside the principle of sufficient reason, the subject himself is raised above himself, above his individual existence, and is freed from servitude to the will by becoming a pure, will-less subject of knowledge.

Through knowledge (the world as representation), the intellect gradually learns to free itself from the will to live (the world as will) by coming to know an objectivity that is pure and complete (the Idea) and which thereby transforms the knower into an equally pure and universal subject.[9] The rare and exceptional person who is able to transcend his individuality in this fashion Schopenhauer calls the genius, and the mode of knowledge that he practises is not science, but art.[10] Genius arises from the power of pure contemplation, 'the capacity to remain in a state of pure perception, to lose oneself in perception, to remove from the service of the will the knowledge which originally existed only for this service.' However, genius is the gift granted to one blessed with a power of intellect 'far exceeding that required for the service of an individual will'; freedom from the servitude of the will to live is thus the consequence of a 'superfluity of knowledge.'[11]

In this way, genius offers certain exceptional individuals a temporary freedom from the servility and suffering of the will through pure, disinterested contemplation of the Ideas, through the transformation of the individual into a pure, will-less subject of knowledge, 'the clear mirror of the inner nature of the world.'[12] However, the more pressing question for Schopenhauer remained that of finding a permanent emancipation from the will to live, and in justice and pity, he believed that he had discovered the path to the absolute negation of the will to live. This liberation is not accomplished all at once but via a progressive seeing through the illusions of the world of phenomena, the *principium individuationis*, or the veil of Maya. The initial stage of emancipation is identified, by Schopenhauer, as justice. Here a person sees through the illusion of individuality by placing others on the same level as himself, by recognizing his own inner being in others.[13] But he does so only to a limited degree – to the extent that he does not harm others.

The truly good man goes far beyond the just man inasmuch as he not only avoids harming others but positively loves them. Through pity (*Mitleid*), he sees through the *principium individuationis* completely by recognizing others as identical to himself and loving them as himself. Through the pure, disinterested sharing of the suffering of others (*Mitleid*), the individual negates his own individuality and his own will by seeing and treating others as identical to himself. Pity is thus the absolute negation of the will because it is pure, disinterested or will-less love for others. As Schopenhauer puts it, 'all true and pure affection is sympathy or compassion, and all love that is not sympathy is selfishness ... Selfishness is ἔρως [eros], sympathy or compassion is ἀγάπη [agape].'[14]

For Schopenhauer, then, pure love is the negation of *eros* which is both the most selfish and the most affirmative expression of the will to live. Since *eros* is the will to live, it follows that love is negative; it is the denial of the most fundamental actuality of life: the will to live. And as the negation of reality, love or pity is the will to nothingness. In this sense, pity is the original source of all true morality, of all conduct that embodies 'the denial of the will-to-live.' 'The will now turns away from life; it shudders at the pleasures in which it recognizes the affirmation of life. Man attains to the state of voluntary renunciation, resignation, true composure, and complete will-lessness.'[15] Knowledge of the inner nature of the will to live serves to silence and negate, rather than stimulate, the will; and it thereby lays the groundwork for pure, disinterested love – for pity.

For Nietzsche, the real dilemma raised by Schopenhauer's morality of pity is crystallized in the two conflicting conceptions of love: love as the affirmation of the actual (*eros*) and love as the negation of life and actuality (*agape*). The basic question lies in the value one places on life by choosing between these two loves. However, there is really only one genuine form of love inasmuch as affirmation constitutes its real substance. Thus Nietzsche attacks pity not as a form of love but as its very opposite – as self-denial. Pity is the denial of love itself, a form of hatred and revenge (*ressentiment*) against life and oneself. As the self-denial of the will to live, it is, in reality, a symptom of weakness, joylessness and a profound lack of love that is represented by the purity and disinterestedness of pity. Furthermore, although it is a desire for self-denial, pity is anything but selfless inasmuch as its desire to share its suffering is a type of egoism – the egoism of weakness. And the fundamental weakness of pity is that it expresses a flight from oneself through its negation of the will to live.

Already, in *Human, All Too Human*, Nietzsche analyses pity as the unconscious desire to hurt others by imposing one's own suffering on them, as the repressed urge for revenge spawned by impotence.

[T]he pity which these then express is a consolation for the weak and suffering, inasmuch as it shows them that, all their weakness notwithstanding, they possess at any rate *one power*: the *power to hurt* ... The thirst for pity is thus a thirst for self-enjoyment, and that at the expense of one's fellow men; it displays man in the whole ruthlessness of his own dear self. (*H* 1:50)

It is this desire to exact revenge for one's lack of power through this sole remaining power to hurt that Nietzsche isolates as the 'ruthlessness' and 'self-enjoyment' at the heart of pity. For revenge in the powerless (those unable to realize their revenge) culminates in 'a chronic illness, a poisoning of body and soul' (*H* 1:60) which Nietzsche later calls *ressentiment*. Thus pity as the sharing of suffering is in essence a form of revenge by the weak who make of their suffering a 'power to hurt' others.

Through its reactive other-directedness, pity also entails a fundamental negation of, and flight from, the self. While Schopenhauer glorifies this self-denial and selflessness as the highest expression of love, Nietzsche sees in this hatred of the self a profound sickness and lack of love. 'Pity [*Mitleiden*], insofar as it really induces suffering [*Leiden*] ... is a weakness as is any losing oneself to a *harmful* affect' (*D* 134; *KGW* 5.1:125–6). Hence, Schopenhauer's pure, disinterested love of others is not only a vengeful augmentation of suffering, but also a loss of self in a fraudulent devotion to others.

At the root of revenge, or rather the desire for revenge (*ressentiment*), that characterizes pity lies its most basic element: powerlessness, a weak will to power. To understand this notion of powerlessness, we need to return to Schopenhauer's dichotomy between pure love/pity and *eros*, for this takes us to the heart of Nietzsche's understanding of power and ultimately the will to power. Schopenhauer distinguishes pity as the manifestation of pure love from *eros* that expresses mere selfishness through his fundamental duality between freedom and slavery in relation to the will to live: pity is the active negation of *eros* and the selfishness that is intrinsic to the will.

Nietzsche agrees with Schopenhauer that pity really is the opposite of *eros*; he also concedes that *eros*, sexual intoxication and ecstasy, is selfish, and that, in contradistinction to pity, sexuality and selfishness are manifestations of the will to live or, more precisely, the will to power. However, Nietzsche views the selfishness of *eros* (the affirmative will to live) as its most positive aspect; indeed, selfishness, sexuality, and the will to power are really only different aspects of the most primal nature of life – the Dionysian experience of life.

*True* life as collective continuation of life through procreation, through the mysteries of sexuality. It was for this reason that the *sexual* symbol was to the Greeks the symbol venerable as such, the intrinsic profound meaning of all antique piety ... All this is contained in the word Dionysus ... the actual road to life, procreation, as the *sacred road*. (*TI*, 'What I Owe to the Ancients,' 4)

As the fundamental nature of life, will to power is this Dionysian '*excess* of energy' or sexuality – that is, procreation, culminating in pregnancy and birth: 'will to power, the unexhausted, procreating life-will [der Wille zur Macht – der unerschöpfte zeugende Lebens-Wille]' (Z, 'Of Self-Overcoming'; KGW 6.1:143). Furthermore, because *eros* and procreation constitute the fundamental character of will to power, the cultivation of higher forms of life must be not only a sublimation, but a continuation of this procreative force: 'Education [*Erziehung*] is a continuation of procreation [*Zeugung*], and often a kind of supplementary beautification of it' (D, 397; KGW 5.1:254). Hence, sensuality and spirit are intimately related: 'The degree and kind of a man's sexuality reach up into the ultimate pinnacle of his spirit' (*BGE*, 75). And that height of spirituality, the tragic, is animated by the erotic: 'The sense of the tragic gains and wanes with sensuality' (*BGE*, 155). According to Nietzsche, the satyr, 'the ecstatic reveler,' 'proclaims wisdom from the very heart of nature, a symbol of the sexual omnipotence of nature which the Greeks used to contemplate with reverent wonder' (*BT*, 8). And, finally, a very special continuation and cultivation of *eros* to which Nietzsche occasionally devotes particular attention is his conception of friendship:

Here and there on earth we may encounter a kind of continuation of love in which this possessive craving of two people for each other gives way to a new desire and lust for possession [*Habsucht*] – a *shared* higher thirst for an ideal above them. But who knows such love? Who has experienced it? Its right name is *friendship*. (GS, 14; KGW 5.2:61)

Procreation and pregnancy are not only the most sacred, Dionysian states of being (D, 552; TI, 'What I Owe to the Ancients,' 4, and 5), but also the most 'selfish'; and far from being accidental or mere external additions, an 'ideal selfishness' (D, 552), or an 'innocent selfishness' (GS, 99), belongs to the very essence of procreation and pregnancy: 'The prudence and providence of pregnancy is in your selfishness [*Eigennutz*]! What no one has yet seen, the fruit: that is protected and indulged and nourished by your whole love' (Z, 'Of The Higher Man,' 11; KGW 6.1:358). This 'great love of oneself,' which is procreative and a will to begetting, is precisely 'ideal selfishness'; this 'gift-giving love' is what Nietzsche calls a 'selfishness [*Selbstsucht*]' that is 'healthy and holy [*heil und heilig*]' (Z, 'Of The Gift-Giving Virtue'; KGW 6.1:94).

*Ideal Selfishness [Die idealische Selbstsucht].* – Is there a more holy condition than that of pregnancy? To do all we do in the unspoken belief that it has somehow to benefit that which is coming to be [*Werdenden*] within us! ... At the same time, a pure and purifying feeling of profound irresponsibility reigns in us almost like that of the auditor before the curtain has gone up – *it* is growing, *it* is coming to light: *we* have no right to determine either its value or the hour of its coming ... And if what is expected is an idea, a deed – towards every bringing forth [*Vollbringen*] we have essentially no other relationship than that of pregnancy and ought to blow to the winds all presumptuous talk of 'willing' and 'creating'. This is *ideal selfishness*: continually to watch over and care for and to keep our soul still, so that our fruitfulness shall *come to a happy fulfilment*! (*D*, 552; *KGW* 5.1:326–7)

This is 'the innocence of the utmost selfishness, the faith in great passion as the good in itself ... We, too, shall grow and blossom out of ourselves, free and fearless, in innocent selfishness' (*GS*, 99). In this way, Nietzsche emphasizes that his concept of grand love is not only distinct from pity, but is the very antithesis of pity. And what distinguishes grand love from pity is in its 'selfishness' (self-love), its erotic procreation, and its lavish giving away of itself to the point of squandering and even death. The first point of distinction is the concern of this section; the second and third points will be dealt with in the following sections.

Whereas pity embodies a disinterested love for another through a negation and denial of self, Nietzsche's grand love begins with an affirmation of self through an unabashed and unrestricted love of self – this is 'ideal selfishness' that is 'healthy and holy.' Furthermore, although the goal is to love beyond oneself, this is possible only if one has first learned to love and, in particular, love oneself (cf. *GS*, 334, 345; *Z*, 'Of Marriage and Children'). Indeed, this art is 'the finest, subtlest, ultimate, and most patient of all':

He calls earth and life heavy: and so *will* the Spirit of Gravity have it! But he who wants to become light and a bird must love himself – thus do *I* teach. Not with the love of the sick and diseased, to be sure: for with them even self-love stinks! One must learn to love oneself with a sound and healthy love, so that one may endure it with oneself and not go roaming about – thus do I teach. Such roaming about calls itself 'love of one's neighbour' ... (*Z*, 'Of the Spirit of Gravity,' 2)

It is important to acknowledge here that Nietzsche is not precluding 'neighbour-love' as he does pity; he is merely showing that love of the other presupposes a strong and healthy love of self: '"Always love your neighbour as yourselves – but first be such as *love themselves*"' (*Z*, 'Of the Virtue that Makes Small,' 3).

The fundamental mistake of altruism, 'neighbour-love' for example, is to ignore the selfishness of love (self-love) and to start with the other; the more fatal mistake of pity, however, is to portray subjectivity and love as mutually exclusive. Pure pity presupposes the annihilation of self in pure objectivity. In contrast to Schopenhauer's concept of pity and self-denial, Nietzsche insists on the identity of love and selfishness.

The lack of personality always takes its revenge. A weakened, thin, extinguished personality that denies itself is no longer fit for anything good – least of all for philosophy. 'Selflessness' has no value either in heaven or on earth. All great problems demand *great love* and of that only strong, round, secure spirits who have a firm grip on themselves are capable. (*GS*, 345)

Against the depersonalized love embodied in pity, Nietzsche presents the concept of 'grand love' that grows out a sound and healthy love of self. 'Great love does not *desire* love – it desires more' (Z, 'Of the Higher Man,' 16). What is the meaning of this 'more'? Does grand love eschew reciprocity in favour of solitude? Earlier Zarathustra indicates an answer that illuminates the weakness of pity: 'All great love is above pity: for it wants – to create what is loved!' (Z, 'Of The Compassionate'). Thus grand love wants to create what is loved by making its own children as the fulfillment of its *eros*. 'Once the creator sought companions and children of *his* hope: and behold, it turned out that he could not find them, except he first create them himself ... For one loves from the very heart only one's child and one's work; and where there is great love of oneself, then it is a sign of pregnancy : thus have I found' (Z, 'Of Involuntary Bliss'). Whereas pity negates life because it is suffering, joy embraces life in its most painful and dangerous aspects.

**Eternal Return as Communion in Joy**

Nietzsche's vision of a new cultural order seeks to replace the politics of pity based upon the sharing of suffering (*Mitleiden*) with eternal return as the sharing of joy – communion in joy (*Mitfreude*) – as the justification of human life and community (cf. *H* 2:62, 75; *GS*, 338). As the embodiment of the sharing of joy and real communion, *amor fati* and eternal return occupy the centre of Nietzsche's vision of grand politics: the unfolding of community out of genuine communion. This means that, through his central teachings of love of fate and eternal return, Nietzsche attempts to provide human community with a new principle of legitimacy based upon the affirmation of the whole of active life: that is, joy in the actuality of suffering insofar as it belongs to active, affirmative life.

However, the replacement of pity with eternal return entails the overcoming of the idealism of morality and its 'away from here ... away from actuality!' (*WP*, 331). For Nietzsche, the primary struggle of human culture is between morality and joy in the actual; it is 'the struggle of the theory of unconditional morality with that of unconditional unfreedom' (*H* 2:33): between the pride of free will and the modesty of fate.

If left in these terms, the choice seems to be simply between abstract freedom and an equally abstract and mechanical unfreedom. Are these really the only alternatives Nietzsche offers us in *amor fati* and eternal return? Nietzsche himself warns us against this superficial reading of his philosophy: 'Supposing someone were thus to see through the boorish simplicity of this celebrated concept of "free will" and put it out of his head altogether, I beg of him to carry his "enlightenment" a step further, and also put out of his head the contrary of this monstrous conception of "free will": I mean "unfree will," which amounts to a misuse of cause and effect' (*BGE*, 21). In rejecting free will, Nietzsche is not dismissing freedom, but trying to go beyond its traditional exclusion of necessity. Instead of interpreting freedom as absolute autonomy abstracted from the world, Nietzsche attempts to take freedom back into nature by understanding it as the act of embracing one's limitedness – one's 'unfreedom.' Thus, freedom begins only when one is able to renounce the mythology of absolute autonomy and sovereignty.[16]

This renunciation of the idealism of free will is not primarily theoretical; it is a cultural event that fulfils itself in a new *ethos*, a new form of action that takes the doer back into the deed – into the continuous and indivisible flow of becoming. As I argued in chapter 2, Nietzsche's self-overcoming of morality is realized in an action that is a creative bringing forth to fullness (*Vollbringen*) of what already is: a becoming what one is. Nietzsche symbolizes this creative action that takes the doer back into the deed in the event of pregnancy and birth; moreover, he also symbolizes it in its fulfilment: the child-spirit. For the child is the metaphor of creativity as play, affirmation, and joy: 'The child is innocence and forgetfulness, a new beginning, a sport [*Spiel*], a self-propelling wheel, a first motion, a sacred Yes' (*Z*, 'Of the Three Metamorphoses'; *KGW* 6.1:27) However, before the play of creation can begin, one must first be capable of 'a sacred Yes,' of an affirmation that will render one fertile: 'Yes, a sacred Yes is needed, my brothers, for the sport of creation [*Spiele des Schaffens*]' (*Z*, 'Of the Three Metamorphoses'; *KGW* 6.1:27).

Perhaps the play of creation occurs in and through the play of affirmation in which one takes oneself back into the deed of becoming through eternal return. I would argue that one must interpret creation and affirmation in the context of Nietzsche's critique of moral subjectivism and, therefore, through his conception of becoming that 'blow[s] to the winds all presumptuous talk of "willing" and "creating"' (*D*, 552). Thus the sport of creation is the play of bringing forth that which is coming to be; and the 'sacred Yes' of affirmation is joy in the play of becoming. Interpreted in this way, joy in the actual is itself the practice of eternal return because it is the play of bringing to fullness that which is already coming into being. The way of the creator is, therefore, the way of those who 'love the earth as creators, begetters, men joyful at entering upon a new existence [*Werdelustige*]' (*Z*, 'Of Immaculate Perception'; *KGW* 6.1:53). The creator is the one who is joyful in the play of becoming and who plays creatively as an intermediary (*D*, 552) by bringing forth what already is coming into being.

Far from being a technological dominator of nature (as Heidegger argues), Nietzsche's creative spirit – the Overman – does not stand outside of the play of becoming but is himself a part of the play; and through eternal return, he affirms the play of becoming and himself as a fellow-player (*Mitspieler*).[17]

> World game, the ruling force,
> blends false and true:
> the eternally fooling force
> blends us in too.
>   (*GS*, 'To Goethe')

> Welt-spiel, das herrische,
> Mischt Sein und Schein: –
> Das Ewig-Narrische
> Mischt *uns* – hinein!
>   (*KGW* 5.2:323)

The play of the world is the ruling and fooling force that blends us too into the play of being and appearance; and we can never step outside of the wave-play of becoming and assume the role of ruling force. If we are co-players who can never step outside of the play of becoming, what is the action or event of becoming that embraces becoming through both affirmation and creation?

Nietzsche presents the doctrine of eternal return as a re-willing of the past in which affirmation and creativity coincide. Only as a retroactive, historical act within a particular cultural milieu does eternal return realize the inner identity of the 'sacred Yes' and 'the play of creation.' As we saw in the discussion of the historicity of joy (chapter 2), Nietzsche places the problem of redemption in the context of our historical nature as human beings. For him, redemption is the recovery of the flow of becoming in history. The historicity of taking the doer back into the deed is what is at stake in interpreting the meaning of eternal return. How does one take oneself back into deeds that are in the past and therefore no longer exist?

The task is that of becoming what one is by taking possession of our past. This is the task that Goethe describes in *Faust*: 'What from your fathers you received as heir/Acquire, if you would possess it!' [Was du ererbt von deinen Vatern hast, Erwirb es, um es zu besitzen!].

For Nietzsche, too, one must acquire and take possession of the past that one has inherited in order to truly become what one is. Moreover, the history to be earned and acquired as one's own is not simply one's personal past but that of one's people, the 'tree of the people' out which one has grown, and perhaps even 'the history of humanity as a whole' (*GS*, 337). Thus the past that must be embraced, metabolized and made one's own is thousands of years old. And to take possession of this infinite past is to become a 'retroactive force'; to remember a past presupposes the recognition that we grew and continue to grow out of precisely this past. Indeed, genuine remembrance of the past presupposes a fundamental continuity with history such that the past is no longer past but an imperfect tense continuing to unfold itself in the present and future.

What is to be done to acquire as one's own that which one has inherited, and thereby truly possess it? In order to become a retroactive force that unites affirmation and creativity, one must first confront the atomistic and linear conception of time, and especially the objectification of the past as something dead and gone – with no heir to bring to harvest what was planted and rooted. Nietzsche states the problem of time and learning to will backwards, as the problem of redemption and creation itself:

To redeem the past and to transform [*umzuschaffen*] every 'It was' into an 'I wanted it thus!' – that alone do I call redemption!

Will – that is what the liberator and bringer of joy is called: thus I have taught you, my friends! But now learn this as well: The will itself is still a prisoner.

Willing liberates: but what is it that fastens in fetters even the liberator?

'It was': that is what the will's teeth-gnashing and most lonely affliction is called.

Powerless [*Ohnmächtig*] against that which has been done, the will is an angry spectator of all things past.

The will cannot will backwards; that it cannot break time and time's desire – that is the will's most lonely affliction.

Willing liberates: what does willing itself devise to free itself from its affliction and to mock at its dungeon? (Z, 'Of Redemption'; *KGW* 6.1:175–6)

One response to the will's imprisonment and powerlessness is anger and resentment; indeed, for Nietzsche, this answer to affliction and imprisonment has been decisive for the evolution of European culture for thousands of years because it has given rise to a nihilistic denial of life. 'Thus the will, the liberator, becomes a malefactor: and upon all that can suffer it takes revenge for its inability to go backwards' (Z, 'Of Redemption'). The will's revenge against time and time's 'It was' becomes the spirit of revenge (*ressentiment*), the wrath and vengefulness against our own powerlessness which has poisoned so much of culture for so long.

For Nietzsche, the will is a liberator because it is fundamentally a creator. In particular, its creativity lies in its affirmation of its powerlessness and finitude, in its belonging to the innocence of becoming. This means that the creativity of the will, its power of liberation, derives from its ability to release itself into becoming and thereby take itself 'back' into that which encompasses it now.

I led you away from these fable-songs when I taught you: 'The will is a creator.'

All 'It was' is a fragment, a riddle, a dreadful chance – until the creative will says to it: 'But I willed it thus!'

Until the creative will says to it: 'But I will it thus! Thus shall I will it!' (Z, 'Of Redemption')

The creative will surrenders to becoming by recognizing the presence of the past in itself in the present. The will itself is not something other than its own past, but merely a fragment and out-growth of it to which the will feels itself counterposed. Nietzsche does not oppose past and present as two distinct entities: 'the past continues to flow within us in a hundred waves; we ourselves are, indeed, nothing but that which at every moment we experience of this continued flowing' (*H* 2:223). To redeem the past and release the will from its prison entails a creative and affirmative releasing of the past into becoming. And for the past to yield itself to becoming, the will must first take itself back into becoming by recognizing that it is nothing but that which at every moment it experiences of this continued flowing.

Given this continuity of becoming, Nietzsche expands our sense of identity far beyond the limits of individual experience to include virtually all of human history and even its prehistory. One is not just an individual atom, but the whole chain: 'For the individual, the "single man", as people and philosophers have hitherto understood him, is an error: he does not constitute a separate entity, an atom, a "link in the chain", something merely inherited from the past – he constitutes the entire *single* line "man" up to and including himself' (*TI*, 'Expeditions,' 33). If we belong to 'the tree of the people' and if we are this continued flowing of the past in the present, then we are present and active in the whole, in both spatial and temporal terms – hence, *amor fati* and the holism of becoming that characterizes Nietzsche's entire work. 'Like trees we grow – this is hard to understand, as is all of life – not in one place only but everywhere, not in one direction [nicht an *Einer* Stelle, sondern überall, nicht in *Einer Richtung*] but equally upward and outward and inward and downward; our energy is at work simultaneously in the trunk, branches, and roots; we are no longer free to do only one particular thing, to *be* only one particular thing' (*GS*, 371; *KGW* 5.2:305).

The spatial aspect of Nietzsche's holism is represented here through the flow of becoming that takes place 'everywhere' and 'simultaneously in the trunk, branches, and roots.' However, it is the temporal dimension, the historicity of becoming, that is especially significant for understanding his critique of linear time. Just as we grow spatially in all places and directions, so we grow in all directions in time: backwards towards our ancestors and forwards towards our children; we become older and younger at the same time. Nietzsche says that, by growing (*wachsen*) and changing (*wechseln*), 'we shed our old bark, we shed our skins every spring, we keep becoming younger, fuller of future ...' (*GS*, 371; *KGW* 5.2:305). Only by taking possession of our inheritance, our roots, and the entire tree of the people, can we grow into the future, become younger, re-newed, and reborn. For Nietzsche, then, to take the doer back into the deed implies a temporal transformation and redemption of the past. The 'It was' is released into becoming and, through this redemption, one grows younger because one is released into the whole of becoming as a historicity of giving birth to new life, to new youthfulness, to the future.

The teaching of affirmation and joy in the actual contained in eternal return entails a 'sacred Yes' to an inheritance that one must make one's own in order to become what one is. This involves releasing some very unsettling and even terrifying events into becoming. Nietzsche explicitly says that, 'since we are the outcome of earlier generations, we are also the outcome of their aberrations, passions and errors, and indeed of their crimes; it is not possible wholly to free oneself from this chain' (*UDH*, 3). Since I embody 'the entire *single* line "man" up to and including [myself]' (*TI*, 'Expeditions,' 33), I grow out of its errors and even its crimes; and however much I may condemn those aberrations, that does not change the fact that I and my condemnation originate in them. But does this mean that, through eternal return, Nietzsche 'says yes to murder,' as Camus suggests? If so, then eternal return would simply constitute a continuation of the spirit of revenge rather than its overcoming. Camus argues that, while this was certainly not Nietzsche's intention, the logic of absolute affirmation lends itself to misappropriation as a pretext and justification for further crimes – 'provided they deny the spirit in favor of the letter.'[18]

Camus, however, fails to grasp the spirit of eternal return partly because he mistakes will to power for a Hobbesian will to have power by a subject twisted by revenge and *ressentiment*. Neither the logic nor the intention of eternal return legitimizes acts that proceed from the spirit of revenge; instead, they cultivate acts that grow out of joy in the actual through the redemption and transformation of the 'It was.' In other words, eternal return is both a liberation and a purification of the will such that it is freed from the dominion of *ressentiment* and cleansed of the need to harm others; far from being a simple repetition of past crimes, the affirmation, 'But I wanted it thus!' serves to transform the acts of vengeance and violence of the past and thereby to liberate oneself from the very desire to do harm. 'And if we learn better to enjoy ourselves, we best unlearn how to do harm to others and to contrive harm' (Z, 'Of the Compassionate').

Two basic tenets of Nietzsche's philosophy follow from the affirmation of eternal return. First, one can overcome the nihilism of the spirit of revenge not by disowning and condemning the past, but only by acquiring it and making this inheritance one's own. Second, one can genuinely take possession of one's inheritance only as a retroactive power that frees itself from the 'It was' by liberating the past into becoming. Thus, in re-willing the aberrations and crimes of history, one in no way opens the door to legitimizing these acts or the spirit of revenge that motivates them; quite the contrary, eternal return constitutes the retroactive power that frees itself from revenge by transforming the past. In his extraordinary essay, 'Beatitude in Nietzsche,' Henri Birault argues that, far from opening the way to unprecedented barbarism, affirmation closes the door to all actions that grow out of the spirit of revenge.

This means that, on the basis of beatitude, all desires are sanctified. He who would interpret in terms of facility this last proposition would be very mistaken. The precept is as strict as, even more strict than, those of all the old moralities; it does not open the way to all our desires – on the contrary, it closes the door to almost everything that up to now has been called love, desire, or will. All desires that proceed from unhappiness, from lack, indigence, envy, hatred are condemned.[19]

Through the total affirmation of eternal return, Nietzsche effects a revolutionary transformation of the will; and this transfiguration is so pervasive and complete that one now desires everything in and through a joy in the actual and active.[20] For Nietzsche, the affirmative will is a creative desire that takes possession of its inheritance only by creating it out of gratitude and joy for the 'tree of the people' within which one has grown. As a profound unhappiness and discontent with what is, nihilism can be overcome, not by further discontent and condemnation, but only by an immense gratitude and love for what is that makes one both creative and free of the past. 'This is why the desire that wills eternity is an essentially creative desire, the extreme, playful, and artistic form of the Will to Power. It is then that the will becomes love without ceasing to be will and Will to Power.'[21]

Nietzsche tells us that when we learn better how to enjoy ourselves – affirm ourselves through the joy in the actual of eternal return – then we best unlearn how to do harm to others (Z, 'Of the Compassionate'). Through eternal return, one overcomes the spirit of revenge that underlies the desire to harm others and oneself; one overcomes the will to commune with others out of anger at one's suffering – this is the communion in suffering that Nietzsche attacks as pity (*Mitleiden*). When one is not driven by discontent and anger towards oneself and others because one no longer stands over and against the world (abstracted and denaturalized by the desire for revenge), then the relationship towards oneself and others becomes a communion in joy (*Mitfreude*). This does not imply that the suffering that arises out of hatred and revenge in one's social and political community should be greeted with indifference or with support. Quite the contrary, eternal return teaches us to enjoy ourselves better and to build out of ourselves into the world of others through joy in the actual: to act in one's community (which necessarily includes those driven by *ressentiment* and pity) out of a communion in joy rather than a communion in suffering. The greatest danger lies in the seductive attraction of 'the religion of pity' precisely because eternal return longs to overcome the suffering that arises from the spirit of revenge:

How is it at all possible to keep to one's own way? Constantly, some clamour or other calls us aside; rarely does our eye behold anything that does not require us to drop our own preoccupation instantly to help ... I know just as certainly that I only need to expose myself to the sight of some genuine distress and I am lost ... All such arousing of pity and calling for help is secretly seductive, for our 'own way' is too hard and demanding and too remote from the love and gratitude of others, and we do not really mind escaping from it – and from our very own conscience – to flee into the conscience of the others and into the lovely temple of the 'religion of pity.' (GS, 338)

While seclusion may guarantee that one adheres to one's way, quietism is itself limited, as Zarathustra discovered when his own happiness compelled him to go down to man once more and share his joy with others. Happiness itself overflows and transcends solitude because sharing itself with others constitutes its primary dynamic. The real issue, therefore, is not whether one shares oneself with others, but how and with whom. To this, Nietzsche answers that communion in joy is the only basis of true community and should be called friendship: 'Fellow rejoicing [*Mitfreude*], not fellow suffering [*Mitleiden*], makes the friend' (H 1:499; KGW 4.2:332). The only genuine and equal relationship with another that represents true community is friendship and it is only on the basis of this sharing of joy that one can really help another:

You will also wish to help – but only those whose distress you *understand* entirely because they share with you one suffering and one hope – your friends [*Ein* Leid und *Eine* Hoffnung haben – deinen *Freunden*] – and only in the manner in which you help yourself. I want to make them bolder, more persevering, simpler, gayer. I want to teach them what is understood by so few today, least of all by these preachers of pity: *to share not suffering but joy* [*Mitfreude*]. (GS, 338; KGW 5.2:248)

Here we see the full implications of Nietzsche's revolutionary transformation of desire through eternal return: the will becomes love and creative desire while remaining will and will to power, as Birault puts it. Through communion in joy, the will to power realizes itself fully as creative love in the sense that Plato describes in *Phaedrus* as a co-creation of beauty through love as friendship (*philia*) rather than *eros*.[22] The love of the friend, as opposed to neighbour-love, is 'a festival of the earth and a foretaste of the Superman' (Z, 'Of Love of One's Neighbour') because only in love of the friend can a truly creative communion unfold itself that will bestow a complete world – a genuine community: 'I teach you the friend in whom the world stands complete, a vessel of the good – the creative friend, who always has a complete world to bestow' (Z, 'Of Love of One's Neighbour').

In the teaching of eternal return, Nietzsche seeks to bestow upon his friends a complete world – a conception of becoming that justifies life as full and complete at every moment and that will replace the notion of linear evolution in which each moment is justified only by its end or its origin. Thus Nietzsche addresses his readers as friends 'in whom the world stands complete' through *amor fati* and eternal return. However, the world stands complete at every moment only after the death of God, after the death of an absolute measure of value. The world stands complete when it is recognized that becoming is without value or meaning: when nihilism is complete. 'Becoming is of equivalent value at every moment; the sum of its values always remains the same; in other words: it has no value at all, for anything against which to measure it, and in relation to which the word "value" would have meaning, is lacking. *The total value of the world cannot be evaluated*' (WP, 708).

As the realization of eternal return, communion in joy unfolds itself only with the descent into a complete and active nihilism that affirms that nothing stands apart from the whole (cf. *TI*, 'The Four Great Errors,' 8). The impossibility of stepping outside of becoming – of standing apart from the whole as an autonomous subject – is, for Nietzsche, the ground of the fullness of becoming at every moment. This is the great liberation that restores the innocence of becoming. Through his critique of morality (free will and the autonomous subject), Nietzsche begins the revolution of grand politics and offers us a foretaste of the Overman who will bestow a complete world upon his friends. In the teaching of eternal return and its retroactive transformation of the past that takes the doer back into the deed, Nietzsche's philosophy inaugurates the grand politics of cultural renewal that attempts to realize genuine community as communion in joy.

## The Sovereignty of Joy

With this understanding of eternal return as communion in joy, Nietzsche's view of the sovereignty of the Overman in grand politics as the sovereignty of joy becomes more comprehensible. Indeed, grand politics takes on its true significance as the sovereignty of joy only after the affirmation of *amor fati* and eternal return is understood as the restoration of the innocence of becoming and communion in joy. For Nietzsche's philosophy revolves around the political task in which genuine community is redefined as communion in joy, and this redefinition presupposes the historicity of plenitude: the fullness of becoming at every moment that is affirmed in eternal return. If grand politics is the renewal of culture in which the Overman bestows a complete world through the affirmation of the plenitude of becoming, then the interrelationship of joy in the actual, genuine community, and the historicity of plenitude must be fully elaborated.

My thesis may be summarized in following way: Nietzsche's philosophy is contained in his grand politics because the task he sets himself is to redefine genuine community as communion in joy and this presupposes the restoration of the innocence of becoming (the plenitude of becoming at every moment) which, in turn, presupposes the critique of morality. In this sense, joy in the actual underlies Nietzsche's redefinition of community on the basis of the innocence and fullness of becoming.

We have seen that the critical side of Nietzsche's philosophy entails the rejection of morality as free will and the autonomous subject because it embodies an abstraction and denaturalization of the subject from 'the tree of the people.' This withdrawal into the radical solitude of pure subjectivity (free will) occurs with the collapse of natural morality (*Sittlichkeit*), the delegitimation of traditional authority, and the rise of subjective morality (*Moralität*). This is 'the dangerous and uncanny point' (*BGE*, 262) in the history of a people, its autumn, when '"morals decay [*die Sitten verfallen*]"' (*GS*, 23; *KGW* 5.2:70) and the private person is liberated from the old morality of custom. On the one hand, this state of corruption and decay represents a profound denaturalization and nihilism; on the other hand, it is also the harvest season when the 'fruit of fruits hangs yellow and mellow from the tree of a people' (*GS*, 23).

As the state of both denaturalization of a people and cultivation of individuality, nihilism is both the soil and the poison of a new tree of a people. In explicit opposition to the moral idealism that seeks to overcome nihilism by denouncing it, Nietzsche's thought pushes itself deep into this wounded and poisoned place as the opening to a new innocence of becoming. In particular, Nietzsche's cultural task of redefining community finds its habitat in the soil – the newly discovered and newly redeemed earth – that has been fertilized by the death of God. For this death is a future, an event still on its way, which will retroactively create a new past because it will restore the innocence of becoming. By destroying the myth of an absolute measure of value outside of becoming, the nihilism of the death of God creates the conditions for an understanding of becoming as valueless and therefore full and complete at every moment. As the precondition for the plenitude of becoming, nihilism opens both a wound and a new history – '"a higher history than all history hitherto."' (GS, 125).

For Nietzsche, one can overcome nihilism without regressing into another moralism only by descending further into nihilism itself and transforming it into redemption through active nihilism (cf. WP, 417). The affirmation of eternal return and *amor fati* embodies this joy in the actual and communion in joy. In this way, the fullness of becoming is discovered through the death of God and genuine community grows out of a communion in joy that presupposes the historicity of plenitude, the fullness of becoming at every moment.

This redemption (*Erlösung*) through descent into disintegration (*Auflösung*) – this 'annihilation in victory' (Z, 'Of Old and New Law-Tables,' 30) – represents the only means of overcoming nihilism and redefining community as a sharing of joy that arises from the plenitude of becoming at every moment: that is legitimizing community as a new form of communion with the past (ancestors) and future (children) as well as with the earth and nature as a whole. This means that to want redemption, one must be able to want disintegration. In saying yes to one joy, one also says yes to all suffering and pain. Joy in the actual underlies redemption, community, and communion only as a sovereign power that is strong enough to embrace its weakness, that affirms the fullness of becoming at every moment only by saying yes to the dissonance that engenders and destroys harmony – that encompasses 'annihilation in victory.'

In Nietzsche's grand politics, the Overman rules not because he wants to, but because he is. He is not free to be second in rank (AC, 57) because he is 'the friend in whom the world stands complete' (Z, 'Of Love of One's Neighbour'). And this means that the Overman is the one in whom nihilism stands complete. Becoming is restored to innocence and fullness only through active nihilism in which the measure of value is taken back into becoming so that '*the value of life cannot be estimated*' (TI, 'The Problem of Socrates,' 2). The Overman bestows and brings forth to fullness a complete world only through a joy in the complete actuality of nihilism. Thus the Overman climbs above man and measure into 'realms that are quite unmeasurable and unweighable' (WS, 21); he goes up to nature, newly discovered and newly redeemed, as communion in joy without measure and value by descending into nihilism. Only in this way of redemption through disintegration does the world stand complete and only in this way of joy encompassing suffering in communion in joy does the Overman bring forth to fullness and bestow a complete world upon his friends and his people. In the context of Nietzsche's grand politics, the Overman rules not by means of the politics of power or the domination of personal will, but only through a radical redefinition of politics that fulfils itself in the transfiguration of community and communion through the complete actuality of joy in the actual.

# The Poetry of the Future

*The poet as signpost to the future.* – That poetic power available to men of today which is not used up in the depiction of life ought to be dedicated ... to signposting the future; ... What he will do ... is emulate the artists of earlier times who imaginatively developed the existing images of the gods and *imaginatively develop* a fair image of man; he will scent out those cases in which, in the *midst* of our modern world and reality and without any artificial withdrawal from or warding off of this world, the great and beautiful soul is still possible, still able to embody itself in the harmonious and well-proportioned and thus acquire visibility, duration and the status of a model, and in so doing through the excitation of envy and emulation help to create the future. (*H* 2:99)

Through his vision of grand politics, Nietzsche offers us a poetry of the future that attempts to imaginatively develop (*fortdichten*) a higher image of being-human: an image of a great and beautiful soul. Moreover, because greatness, for Nietzsche, implies a soul that is 'loving and encompassing and spacious' (Z, 'Of the Great Longing'), it must take itself back into the innocence of becoming and embody a communion in joy that embraces and affirms what is coming to be in the past and present. In this sense, the great and beautiful soul personifies a joy in the actual and active.

The interpreter of Nietzsche's grand politics is obliged to take this image of poetry back into the flow of becoming. One is simply not free to read this poetry of the future in a subjective fashion as the creative action of a particular imagination that stands over and against the existing images of culture and manipulates them in an arbitrary and capricious manner. The imagination of Nietzsche's poet (*Dichter*) is not something separate from and outside of these images; only in communion with the world of these images is there an imagination at all by which the poet can poetize. Thus

Nietzsche's 'politics of the soul' precludes not only 'such an instrumentalist orienation' but also the autonomous solitude of heroic individualism.[1]

In this way, grand politics constitutes an interpretive signposting of what is coming to be in the existing images of humanity in our culture. More precisely, through the notion of the sovereignty of joy, I have argued not only that Nietzsche is a political philosopher, but that his vision of grand politics constitutes the core of his philosophy as a whole.

Contrary to the view that Nietzsche's politics represents a categorical rejection of modernity and a romantic attempt to recreate an aristocratic past, he specifically emphasizes the obligation of the poet/philosopher of the future to practise joy in the actual and active by developing the existing images 'in the *midst* of our modern world and reality and without any artificial withdrawal from or warding off of this world' (*H* 2:99). In contrast to political idealism and its morality of the 'ought to be,' reality is the muse of genuine poetry and especially of the art of grand politics: '*Poet and reality.* – When a poet is not *in love with* reality his muse will consequently not be reality, and she will then bear him hollow-eyed and fragile-limbed children' (*H* 2:135). Given that the reality of the modern world is nihilism and that the idealist alternative of fleeing into the moral 'ought' merely aggravates the situation, Nietzsche boldly develops the images of decay and disintegration as new sources of strength and affirmation. Far from suggesting that salvation lies in a return to the social and political structures of the past, he insists that we have crossed a cultural and historical threshold and there is no going back. Indeed, 'this is a truth for which the time has come': society, in the old sense of that word, will not and cannot be built any more (*GS*, 356), and therefore one is simply not free to be a conservative and 'dream of the crabwise *retrogression* of all things' (*TI*, 'Expeditions,' 43). At the same time, I have tried to show that, through the order of rank and the morality of cultivation, Nietzsche attempts not only a critique of political modernity (especially egalitarianism), but also a reappropriation of a radically 'aristocratic' conception of nobility: a pure, newly redeemed noble nature appropriate to the era following the death of God in which both immanence and transcendence are radically transformed. Through the sovereignty of joy, Nietzsche attempts to seek out new possibilities for an affirmative communion by those strong enough to affirm this tragic immanence without resorting to historicism.

Through a joy in the actual and active, therefore, 'the good poet of the future will depict *only reality* ... Only reality, but by no means every reality! – he will depict a select reality!' (*H* 2:114). He will seek out those cases in which a higher, more encompassing soul is still possible within existing images and within the reality itself: a self-overcoming of modernity and not a return to antiquity. Indeed, in his attack on the modern, revolutionary politics of Rousseau and Kant, Nietzsche carries out a critique, not of reality, but of a profoundly subjective idealism whose distaste for reality compels it to deny its own poetry of the future.

In this way, a 'pure, newly discovered, newly redeemed nature' (*GS*, 109) comes about through a transformation of culture and modernity that fulfils its intrinsic dynamic of disintegration and destruction. While Nietzsche's grand politics is imbued with a poetic spirit,[2] this in no way implies a serene repose in the continuous and indivisible flow of becoming; on the contrary, it announces dissonance, conflict, and even war as the very spirit of the poetry of the future. For, to imaginatively develop the existing images of humanity through the teachings of will to power, the Overman, *amor fati*, and especially the eternal return necessarily lead Nietzsche's grand politics into battle with the morality of free will and the politics of individual autonomy abstracted from nature and community. By transfiguring the intrinsic dynamic of modernity, its critique of external authority, in his metaphor of 'God is dead' (*GS*, 125), Nietzsche extends and intensifies modern nihilism into an active nihilism that also offers an image of redemption and self-overcoming. With the death of God, the absolute measure of value, Nietzsche brings forth a notion of the innocence of becoming in which becoming overflows with perfection and completion at every moment. Not only do dissonance, conflict, and even war belong to the fullness of becoming at every moment, but the passionate suffering of this dissonance is also desired and affirmed as part of the joy of each moment of becoming.

As a political vision that celebrates a tragic conception of joy, Nietzsche's poetry of the future overcomes modernity not by withdrawing from it, but by accentuating and intensifying its nihilism. Inasmuch as the very dynamic of becoming what one is entails an encompassing of 'the negative,' grand politics implies a reconception of what defines a 'great and beautiful soul' and, more important, how this spirit may be cultivated and embodied in a new order of rank as the sovereignty of a tragic affirmation – as a joy in the actual that wants itself and therefore wants all suffering and unhappiness as intrinsic to the joy of becoming.

This constitutes the atopia of grand politics: the poet of the future stands outside of the existing culture through the critique of morality and the politics of subjective freedom: hence, the ease with which it is read as an apology for tyranny or as a new form of utopianism. Yet, at the same time, by finding his way to the innocence of becoming, he also discovers a newly redeemed form of community through which polity may renew and rebuild itself: *Mitfreude*, communion in joy. The poet of grand politics thereby takes himself back into the poetry of existing images through a joy in the actual; and through the affirmation of *amor fati* and eternal return, he brings forth the dissonant becoming of what is and translates the reality of this becoming into the prose of a new politics. In this sense, Nietzsche's political vision is neither a mystical quietism nor an ideological strategy of power politics, but a prose poetry that attempts to redeem the past by releasing the existing images of our cultural life into becoming and bringing them forth into the future. In the atopia of his double position, Nietzsche's philosopher-poet does not dissolve culture in pure becoming, but gives it a complete world, a communion in joy.

Although the sovereignty of joy is certainly not the only way of finding one's way through the labyrinth of Nietzsche's work, I believe it unfolds a theme fundamental to his political vision that avoids the reductive readings (both positive and negative) that have proliferated in our time. I have tried to imaginatively develop the suggestions that Nietzsche's grand politics offers us concerning the renovation of the house of culture through the transformation of its relationship to nature. Through a newly redeemed understanding of culture and nature offered in *amor fati*, eternal return, and will to power, we are also presented with a political vocabulary of community and communion. Through this new language of joy in the actual and active of every kind, which we are only just beginning to learn, Nietzsche's vision of grand politics attempts to rebuild community on the foundation of a communion in joy.

The tragedy, however, may have begun,
Again, in the imagination's new beginning,
In the yes of the realist spoken because he must
Say yes, spoken because under every no
Lay a passion for yes that had never been broken.
   (Wallace Stevens, 'Esthétique du Mal,' 8)

# Notes

## 1: Joy, Sovereignty, and Atopia

1 The phrase 'the sovereignty of joy' comes from Georges Bataille, *Literature and Evil* (New York: Marion Boyars Publications, 1985), 163.

2 See Paul Ricoeur, 'The Political Paradox,' in *History and Truth* (Evanston: Northwestern University Press, 1965), 248–70.

3 In particular, I am employing the term 'atopia' in the sense in which Monique Canto uses it in her introductory essay to her French translation of Plato's *Gorgias* (Paris: Flammarion, 1987), 45.

4 The term 'aristocratic radicalism' is not Nietzsche's but was suggested to him by Georg Brandes and welcomed by Nietzsche as 'the shrewdest remark that I have read about myself till now.' *Selected Letters of Friedrich Nietzsche*, edited by Christopher Middleton (Chicago: University of Chicago Press, 1969), 279.

5 Walter Kaufmann, *Nietzsche: Philosopher, Psychologist, Antichrist* (Princeton: Princeton University Press, 1974).

6 Ibid., 412, 418.

7 Jean Granier, *Le problème de la Vérité dans la philosophie de Nietzsche* (Paris: Editions du Seuil, 1966), 389ff., 411ff.

8 Ibid., 589.

9 Ibid., 590.

10 In his thorough and sophisticated treatment of Nietzsche's political philosophy, *Philosophie und Politik bei Nietzsche* (Berlin: Walter de Gruyter, 1987), Henning Ottmann maintains that Kaufmann's moral interpretation is not wrong but, far from being apolitical, self-overcoming is realized in 'grand politics' (239). With regard to the role of spiritual metamorphosis in Nietzsche's utopian vision of grand politics, see Simone Goyard-Fabre, *Nietzsche et la question politique* (Paris: Editions Sirey, 1977), 127–9.

11 Raymond Polin, 'Nietzsche und der Staat oder Die Politik eines Einsamen,' in *Nietzsche, Werk und Wirkungen*, edited by Hans Steffen (Göttingen: Hans-Dieter Ullrich, Vandenhoeck, and Ruprecht, 1974), 40–2.

12 'Er [Nietzsche] hat mit dem Entwurf der 'grossen Politik' eine Art moderner Platon sein wollen, und wenn die 'Politeia' Utopie gewesen ist, dann ist es Nietzsches 'grosse Politik' auch, *Utopie* ...' Henning Ottmann, *Philosophie und Politik bei Nietzsche*, 243; cf. 237, 239, 262, 263. Granier also shares this conclusion that Nietzsche's conception of a politics that represents an immanent transcendence of history is, in the best sense, a Platonic utopia of the philosopher-king: 'Au bout du compte, c'est dans une nouvelle élite de philosophes que Nietzsche place son espoir. Le philosophe-roi de Platon, curieusement, n'est pas loin! ... la grande politique nietzschéenne n'est elle-même rien d'autre qu'une utopie ... de philosophe!' *Nietzsche* (Paris: Presses Universitaires de France, 1989), 125.

13 Tracy Strong, *Friedrich Nietzsche and the Politics of Transfiguration* (Berkeley: University of California Press, 1975), 253.

14 Ibid., 276.

15 See Jean Granier, *Le problème de la Vérité dans la philosophie de Nietzsche*, 403.

16 Michel Haar, 'Nietzsche and Metaphysical Language,' in *The New Nietzsche: Contemporary Styles of Interpretation*, edited by David B. Allison (New York: Dell Publishing, 1977), 24, 26.

17 Gilles Deleuze, 'Nomad Thought,' in *The New Nietzsche*, 149, 142.

18 Gilles Deleuze, *Nietzsche and Philosophy* (London: Athlone Press, 1983), 170. Deleuze's singular importance for an atopian interpretation of Nietzsche's grand politics is exemplary for the following reasons. First, he specifies the heterogeneous character of the Overman as a nomadic force beyond all codification and yet fundamental to all codes, that is, heterogeneity as atopia. Second, the radical alterity of the Overman resides in affirmation as the transfiguring element of transvaluation (see 54, 170, 177ff., 198). Third, the atopian sovereignty of this transfiguring joy completely eradicates the negative as an independent and autonomous power: 'The whole of the negative has become a power of affirming, it is now only *the mode of being* of affirmation as such' (179), that is, through *amor fati* and eternal return, the negative is only the negativity *of* the positive (see 180, 198).

19 Leo Strauss, *Natural Right and History* (Chicago: University of Chicago Press, 1953), 26.

20 Leo Strauss, 'Note on the Plan of Nietzsche's *Beyond Good and Evil*,' in his *Studies in Platonic Political Philosophy* (Chicago: University of Chicago Press, 1983), 188, 189, 191.

21 Werner Dannhauser, 'Friedrich Nietzsche,' in *History of Political Philosophy*,

edited by L. Strauss and J. Cropsey (Chicago: University of Chicago Press, 1987), 834, 849.

22 Laurence Lampert, *Leo Strauss and Nietzsche* (Chicago: University of Chicago Press, 1996), 15, 119, 126.

23 Bruce Detwiler, *Nietzsche and the Politics of Aristocratic Radicalism* (Chicago: University of Chicago Press, 1990), 113.

24 Ofelia Schutte, *Beyond Nihilism: Nietzsche Without Masks* (Chicago: University of Chicago Press, 1984), 58.

25 Mark Warren, *Nietzsche and Political Thought* (Cambridge: MIT Press, 1988), 211, 208, 210. In *An Introduction to Nietzsche as Political Thinker* (Cambridge: Cambridge University Press, 1994), Keith Ansell-Pearson arrives at a somewhat similar assessment of Nietzsche's grand politics as a mix of 'progressive' and 'regressive' dimensions of his political philosophy (157–62).

## 2: Joy in the Actual

1 'Und in einem weiteren Sinne ist er noch der Gefangene der Metaphysik, weil er vorwiegend das Sein als Wert interpretiert.' Eugen Fink, *Nietzsches Philosophie* (Stuttgart: Kohlhammer, 1986), 185. Fink does not mean that, for Nietzsche, values belong to life independent of human will. He recognizes that Nietzsche views life as beyond evaluation; Fink's point is that, through will to power, Nietzsche makes beings come into being only by becoming values for human subjects: 'Werthaftigkeit ist die grundsätzliche Bestimmung, die Nietzsche dem Sein des endlichen Seienden gibt, – Wertlosigkeit aber die grundsätzliche Bestimmung des Seinsganzen bzw. Werdensganzen gemäss dem Wiederkunftsgedanken. Sowohl in der vierfachen Grundgliederung seiner Problematik als in dem prinzipiellen wertphilosophischen Ansatz bleibt Nietzsche von der Metaphysik abhängig' (186).

2 'Gleichwohl bleibt die Frage *offen*, ob Nietzsche in der Grund-intention seines *Weltdenkens* nicht bereits die ontologische Probleme-Ebene der Metaphysik hinter sich lässt. Eine nicht-metaphysische Ursprünglichkeit kosmologischer Philosophie findet sich in seinem Gedanken vom "Spiel."' Eugen Fink, *Nietzsches Philosophie*, 187. Later, Fink goes further and suggests that Nietzsche had indeed freed himself from the essentialist assumptions of metaphysical thought: 'Wo Nietzsche Sein und Werden als Spiel begreift, steht er nicht mehr in der Befangenheit der Metaphysik' (188).

3 Martin Heidegger, 'The Age of the World Picture,' in *The Question Concerning Technology and Other Essays* (New York: Harper and Row, 1977), 127.

4 Ibid., 142.

5  Heidegger, 'Letter on Humanism,' in *Basic Writings*, edited by David Farrell Krell (New York: Harper and Row, 1977), 228.
6  Ibid.
7  Heidegger, 'The Age of the World Picture,' in *Basic Writings*, 128.
8  Heidegger, 'The Word of Nietzsche,' in *The Question Concerning Technology and Other Essays*, 88.
9  Heidegger, 'The Age of the World Picture,' 150.
10  Heidegger, 'The Word of Nietzsche,' 68.
11  Ibid., p.81, 78; cf. also Heidegger's *Nietzsche*, 37ff.
12  Ibid., 100.
13  Hans-Georg Gadamer, *Philosophical Hermeneutics*, edited by David E. Linge (Berkeley: University of California Press, 1977), 116.
14  Fink places particular emphasis upon Nietzsche's metaphor of play as the means of overcoming metaphysics. However, Henri Birault elaborates this more fully as 'creation,' as an action that joyously affirms the actual and active of every kind: the creative desire wills eternity (eternal return) and loves necessity (*amor fati*). Henri Birault, 'Beatitude in Nietzsche,' in *The New Nietzsche*, edited by David B. Allison (New York: Dell Publishing, 1977), 219–31. Henning Ottmann has also stressed this notion of 'creative play' as the basis of Nietzsche's post-metaphysical thinking. Henning Ottmann, *Philosophie und Politik bei Nietzsche* (Berlin: Walter de Gruyter, 1987), 378ff.
15  In his marvellous and profound essay, Henri Birault elaborates the implications of the historicity of plenitude, the fact that the joy of becoming longs for itself, but it is the longing *of* joy rather than a longing *for* joy: 'In the old perspective – that of Plato and of Hegel – desire, will, love, action, labour all proceeded from unhappiness, indigence, lack, need, hunger, appetite – in short, from negativity. Correlatively, happiness presented itself as the fulfillment, the contentment of this void, the release of this tension, the solution or the dissolution of what first presented itself as insoluble. In short, to will was fundamentally to will to will no more. Happiness was always at the end of the road ... Thus desire now has as its father (or rather its mother) wealth, and no longer poverty; action is the child of happiness and no longer of unhappiness: beatitude is initial and no longer terminal.' 'Beatitude in Nietzsche,' 228–9.

## 3: The Seasons of a People

1  There is no evidence that Nietzsche incorporated these terms into his work through the direct influence of Hegel's writings; it is more likely that Nietzsche developed the contrast between classical *Sittlichkeit* and modern, subjective *Moralität* as Hegel did – through reading Goethe and Schiller. For Hegel's dis-

cussion of the morality of custom (*Sittlichkeit*), see *The Phenomenology of Mind* (New York: Harper and Row, 1967) chapter 5, part B, 373–82, and especially chapter 6, part A, 456–82. For Hegel's critique of the moral subjectivism (*Moralität*) of Rousseau and Kant, see chapter 5, part B, 'The Law of the Heart and the Frenzy of Self-conceit' and 'Virtue and the Course of the World,' 390–412, and especially his critique of 'the moral view of the world,' 611–79. See also Hegel's *The Philosophy of History* (New York: Dover Publications, 1956), part 2, 'The Greek World,' on customary morality; and part 3, 318–36, for the relationship between Christianity and the emergence of subjectivity and subjective morality; and finally, *Hegel's Philosophy of Right*, (London: Oxford University Press, 1967).

2 Henning Ottmann presents a very thorough and insightful discussion of Nietzsche's concept of cultivation as a moral practice that is fundamental to his grand politics. See *Philosophie und Politik bei Nietzsche* (Berlin: Walter de Gruyter, 1987), 243ff. In particular, he shows that the concept of *Züchtung* may best be understood as a modern form of Platonic *paideia* (cf. 262ff.): '"Züchtung" ist wesentlich ein moralischer Begriff, steht für Bildung and Zucht ... *ein platonische Erziehung des Menschen selbst, durchgeführt mit antiplatonischen Mitteln and ausgerichtet an antiplatonischen Zielen*' (263).

3 In the following passages, Nietzsche deals with the morality of custom ('herd morality') with regard to its nature as the embodiment and preservation of the sense of community as well as its function of cultivating ('breeding') the good, strong type: *H* 1:96, 224, 226, 227, 228; *H* 2:89; *D*, 9, 10, 14, 16, 19; *GS*, 4, 23, 24, 76, 116, 290, 356; *Z*, 'Of the New Idol,' 'Of the Thousand and One Goals,' 'Of Old and New Law-Tables,' 7, 26, 27, 28; *BGE*, 126, 135, 188, 258, 262; *GM*, passim; *AC*, 16, 17, 24, 25, 26, 57, 58.

4 In *The Philosophy of History*, Hegel, like Nietzsche, characterizes Socrates as a force of corruption and decay precisely because he 'invents' subjective morality (*Moralität*): 'We have, then, now to investigate the *corruption* of the Greek world in its profounder import, and may denote the principle of that corruption as *subjectivity obtaining emancipation for itself*' (267); 'And it was in Socrates that at the beginning of the Peloponnesian War, the principle of subjectivity – of the absolute inherent independence of Thought – attained free expression. He taught that man has to discover and recognize in himself what is the Right and Good, and that this Right and Good is in its nature universal. Socrates is celebrated as a Teacher of Morality, but we should rather call him the *Inventor of Morality*' (269).

5 Laurence Lampert emphasizes this pattern of reciprocal insight and affirmation as the inseparable bond between insight into the way of nature as will to power and affirmation of eternal return in Nietzsche thought. See *Nietzsche and Mod-*

*ern Times* (New Haven: Yale University Press, 1993), 338. On the reciprocity of insight and affirmation regarding the deadly truth for grand politics, see 8–10, 278, 297–8, 301–302.

6 In *Beyond Nihilism* (Chicago: University of Chicago Press, 1984), Schutte makes a similar distinction in Nietzsche's 'immoralism' between 'the self-overcoming of morality and the overcoming of morality by the higher man' (110) thereby appropriately distinguishing the *Übermensch* from free spirit (121–2) but only by importing a distinction between 'liberating' and 'authoritarian' models of power and reducing all of Nietzsche's political thought to the latter.

7 This aspect of the noble man as 'better and more evil' where evil refers to the passions is an essential dimension of Nietzsche's grand politics which will be explored in further detail in the next chapter. For examples of Nietzsche's treatment of this theme, *TI*, 'Morality as Anti-Nature'; *WP*, 382ff., 933, 1015ff., 1025ff.

8 The theme of nobility as a product of self-mastery, discipline, and self-overcoming repeats itself throughout Nietzsche's work, along with the criticism of the concept of freedom as liberation from constraint, *laisser aller*, or self-indulgence. Some of the most relevant passages are the following: *GS*, 290; *BGE*, 188; *TI*, 'Expeditions of an Untimely Man,' 41, 47; *WP*, 122, 870, 871, 928, 933, 1025.

## 4: Hierarchy and the Overman

1 In *Nietzsche and Political Thought* (Cambridge: MIT Press, 1988), Mark Warren makes the argument that there is a radical discontinuity between Nietzsche's philosophy of power and his political philosophy in the sense that the latter is 'underdetermined' by the former and therefore requires 'unfounded assumptions to be added to his philosophy' (210). There is a fundamental continuity if grand politics is not reduced to crude domination, but the real issue at this point is the nature of inequality as a value in Nietzsche's thought.

2 In his study of hierarchy, Louis Dumont defines the relation that characterizes a genuine hierarchy (as opposed to the relationships of class structures) as '"a relation between larger and smaller, or more precisely between *that which encompasses and that which is encompassed.*"' See his *Homo Hierarchicus* (London: Paladin, 1972), 24; cf. 114–18.

3 From this perspective, 'domination' is more central to egalitarian relationships than to relationships of genuine hierarchy: 'The Dionysian hierarchy is ... the moment when the principle of individuation with its necessary correlative – power – have no need to exist, since it is in this form that the collective can be expressed. This individual, the "I think," and the monopolized state structure are just two faces of the same phenomenon. The injunction to be this or that ... is

certainly the origin of domination; it is certainly this that founds what La Boetie called "voluntary servitude."' See Michel Maffesoli, *The Shadow of Dionysus: A Contribution to the Sociology of the Orgy* (Albany: State University of New York Press, 1993), 93.

4 In *Thus Spoke Zarathustra*, the noble individual is symbolized in the spirit of the child who can create new law-tables, while the free spirit is the lion who has the power of 'an animal of prey' to create a freedom for new creation, and the good, strong type is the camel who submits to the authority of tradition. See Z, 'Of the Three Metamorphoses of the Spirit.'

5 Eric Voegelin, *Plato* (Baton Rouge: Louisiana State University Press, 1966), 140.

6 Cf. Arthur Schopenhauer, 'On Psychology,' in *Essays and Aphorisms* (Harmondsworth: Penguin Books, 1970), 170.

7 Plato, *The Laws* (Harmondsworth: Penguin Books, 1970), 644:74; 803:291–2.

8 Voegelin, *Plato*, 207–8. Voegelin contends that Plato's growing recognition of the co-existence of being and becoming was the motive that drove him beyond the *Republic* and the self-contained realm of the Idea to the question of the relationship between the Idea and the world not ordered by the Idea (cf. 135, 147, 173, 198, 206).

9 Paul Ricoeur, 'The Political Paradox,' in his *History and Truth* (Evanston: Northwestern University Press, 1965), 248ff.

10 Ignoring the 'atopia' of Nietzsche's philosopher-statesman leads to the false concretion of concepts such as the *Übermensch*, *Rangordnung*, *Züchtung*, and *Sklaverei*.

11 Jose Ortega y Gasset, *The Revolt of the Masses* (New York: W.W. Norton, 1957), 115 n.1.

12 While Henning Ottmann's *Philosophie und Politik bei Nietzsche* (Berlin: Walter de Gruyter, 1987) provides the most subtle analysis yet of Nietzsche's grand politics, I would caution that the description of Nietzsche's politics as 'utopian' (243) tends to undermine what I call his 'atopian' political position, which enlarges the very meaning of politics as Laurence Lampert admirably demonstrates in *Nietzsche's Teaching* (New Haven: Yale University Press, 1986). Others who interpret Nietzsche's grand politics as utopian include Jean Granier, *Nietzsche* (Paris: Presses Universitaires de France, 1989), 125; Simone Goyard-Fabre, *Nietzsche et la question politique* (Paris: Editions Sirey, 1977), 127–32. For an interpretation of Nietzsche's grand politics as the modern counterpart to Plato's utopian philosopher-king, see Raymond Polin, 'Nietzsche und der Staat,' in *Nietzsche, Werk und Wirkungen*, edited by Hans Steffen (Göttingen: Hans-Dieter Ullrich, Vandenhoeck, and Ruprecht, 1974), 27–44.

13 This is the interpretation of those who ignore the atopia at the centre of

Nietzsche's statesmanship and reduce grand politics to the 'petty politics' of brute domination; in particular, this is the view of those who misinterpret Nietzsche as a ruthless reactionary and proto-fascist. See, for example, Warren, *Nietzsche and Political Thought*, 211; B. Detwiler, *Nietzsche and the Politics of Aristocratic Radicalism* (Chicago: University of Chicago Press, 1990), 112–14; O. Schutte, *Beyond Nihilism* (Chicago: University of Chicago Press, 1984), especially chapters 6 and 7.

14 In *Homo Hierarchicus*, Louis Dumont makes this distinction between status ranking and social stratification central to his argument that hierarchy cannot be reduced to class structure (114–18).

15 The neglected concept of *Mitfreude* and its significance for all of Nietzsche's philosophy and particularly his grand politics is the subject of chapter 6.

16 It might be more accurate to say that whether the highest types want to rule or not is secondary to their reality as creative spirits who, reluctantly or willingly, transform the cultural horizons of their people and, in so doing, exercise sovereignty.

17 In *Homo Hierarchicus*, Dumont stresses the point that a hierarchical relationship is not that of dominator and dominated but the spiritual relation of the encompassing and the encompassed. 'We must free ourselves from familiar ideas: we tend to put the essential at the centre and the rest at the periphery. Here, by contrast, because it is a question of hierarchy ... that which encompasses is more important than that which is encompassed, just as a whole is more important than its parts, or just as a given group's place in the whole governs its own organization' (116).

18 Dumont, *Homo Hierarchicus*, particularly chapter 3, 104–32.

19 Ortega makes this point in following way: 'Contrary to what is usually thought, it is the man of excellence, and not the common man, who lives in essential servitude. Life has no savour for him unless he makes it consist in service to something transcendental ... Nobility is defined by the demands it makes on us – by obligations, not by rights. *Noblesse oblige* ... The privileges of nobility are not in their origin concessions or favours; on the contrary, they are conquests. And their maintenance supposes, in principle, that the privileged individual is capable of reconquering them, at any moment, if it were necessary, and anyone were to dispute them. Private rights or *privileges* are not, then, passive possession and mere enjoyment, but they represent the standard attained by personal effort. On the other hand, common rights, such as those "of the man and the citizen," are passive property, pure usufruct and benefit, the generous gift of fate which every man finds before him, and which answers to no effort whatever, unless it be that of breathing and avoiding insanity. I would say, then, that an impersonal right is held, a personal one is upheld.' See his *The Revolt of the Masses*, 63–4.

20  Voegelin, *Plato*, 147.
21  Ibid., 140.
22  Ibid., 147.
23  Ibid., 165.
24  Ibid., 202.
25  Nietzsche is explicit about both the necessity to descend to the human things after the ascent to autonomy and nobility and the necessity to be selective and approach only the higher types. Hence Zarathustra's change of strategy after his initial encounter with the people in the market-place: 'A light has dawned for me: Zarathustra shall not speak to the people but to companions! Zarathustra shall not be herdsman and dog to the herd! To lure many away from the herd – that is why I have come. The people and the herd shall be angry with me: the herdsmen shall call Zarathustra a robber.' (Z, Prologue, 9).
26  Indeed, the term 'people' is hardly appropriate since both Plato and Nietzsche are painfully aware that they live in a time of cultural disintegration or nihilism, and therefore a more accurate word would be 'market-place,' as Zarathustra discovers after his descent from solitude into the nearby town (Z, Prologue, 3): a descent, therefore, not so much from solitude as a solitude in descent; the terrible dilemma of philosophy in an age of nihilism where a people and a world hardly exist.
27  Allan Bloom's discussion of the erotic continuity of philosophy and the tyrannic soul in Plato's thought is especially enlightening in this regard. See his 'Interpretive Essay,' in *The Republic of Plato* (New York: Basic Books, 1968), 412, 422ff.
28  In *The Destruction of Reason* (Atlantic Highlands: Humanities Press, 1981), Lukacs devotes a chapter ('Nietzsche as Founder of Irrationalism in the Imperialist Period') to the Marxist revelation of the historical forces that spoke through Nietzsche's philosophy in the wake of the 1848 revolution and especially after the Paris Commune of 1870. According to Lukacs, a virulent and romantic irrationalism, born of the strengthened bond between the bourgeoisie and the reactionary classes, grew out of this situation and offered Nietzsche the opportunity 'to solve in mythical form – on the reactionary bourgeoisie's terms – the main problems of the subsequent period' (314–15). Thus, Nietzsche is reduced to an unwitting harbinger of a rapacious imperialist coalition of dominant classes in a new power bloc. In *Beyond Nihilism: Nietzsche Without Masks*, Schutte distinguishes two forms of 'immoralism' in Nietzsche's thought: the first, the self-overcoming of morality by the Overman, corresponds to a 'liberating' sense of continuity with life, and the second, the overcoming of morality by the higher man, implies an 'authoritarian' attempt to dominate life. For Schutte, the immoralism of the second type characterizes Nietzsche's conception of politics:

'Here he favors the subordination of the weak and the decadent to the strong' (139); 'The right of the strong to dominate the weak – the essential premise of Nietzsche's view of the overcoming of morality by the higher man – translates itself politically into a justification of highly authoritarian systems of government' (161). In *Nietzsche and Political Thought*, Warren shares the view that Nietzsche's political thought is fundamentally repressive but, unlike Lukacs and Schutte, he argues that his political philosophy of *'neoaristocratic conservatism'* (211) has no basis in his philosophy of power: 'Nietzsche's own politics ... violates the intellectual integrity of his philosophical project' (208). The underlying weakness of these interpretations resides in the tendency to ignore the homogeneity of morality and immorality ('the innocence of becoming') as the principle of an affirmative nobility whose grand politics involves, according to Michel Haar, 'a *reign* that is not at all a *domination.*' See his 'Nietzsche and Metaphysical Language,' in *The New Nietzsche*, edited by David B. Allison (New York: Dell Publishing, 1977), 26.

29  In this regard, Kaufmann's interpretation, although it errs in underestimating the role of grand politics, is far more subtle and genuine inasmuch as he appreciates the nature of Nietzsche's praise for Caesar, Borgia, and Napoleon and how it grows out of both a deep continuity and a firm distinction between the free spirit and the noble individual. Cf. Walter Kaufmann, *Nietzsche: Philosopher, Psychologist, Antichrist* (Princeton: Princeton University Press, 1974), chapters 7–11.

## 5: Nietzsche Contra Rousseau

1  Robert A. Nisbet, *Tradition and Revolt: Historical and Sociological Essays* (New York: Vintage Books, 1970), 9. The elaboration of Nisbet's interpretation of Rousseau as the interaction between social nihilism and political absolutism is contained in chapter 1, 'Rousseau and the Political Community.'

2  In *Nietzsche Contra Rousseau: A Study of Nietzsche's Moral and Political Thought* (Cambridge: Cambridge University Press, 1991), Keith Ansell-Pearson appreciates the advantages as well as the disadvantages of Nietzsche's strategy of rendering Rousseau into a broad rhetorical type: 'In describing himself as "contra Rousseau" it is clear that Nietzsche is compelled to exaggerate and distort certain aspects of Rousseau's moral and political thought in order to highlight, in a rhetorical manner, his challenge to the Christian-moral tradition and its secular successors. Nietzsche constructs an image of the Rousseauian man and ends up depicting a caricature of Rousseau' (49; see also 34).

Nietzsche first compares 'the man of Rousseau' and 'the man of Goethe' as 'images' of modern existence in 'Schopenhauer as Educator.' He already highlights an infinite Faustian longing as characteristic of these modern types: 'In his youth Goethe was himself a devotee of the gospel of nature with his whole loving heart; his Faust was the highest and boldest reproduction of the man of Rousseau, at any rate so far as concerns his ravenous hunger for life, his discontent and longing, his traffic with the demons of the heart' (*SE*, 4).

3 Beginning with Kant, interpreters have often characterized Rousseau's accomplishment as a revolution in moral and political philosophy. In *The Question of Jean-Jacques Rousseau* (Bloomington: Indiana University Press, 1963), Ernst Cassirer presents this case by emphasizing that Rousseau understands civil society, not as an empirical collection of individuals bound together in a purely external fashion, but in a transcendental sense as 'the form in which the will, as ethical will, really exists' (63). As the autonomous freedom of the general will, polity is neither given in nature nor imposed from without upon individuals; rather, it is 'the constituent principle of these wills, the element that confirms and justifies them spiritually' (63). For Cassirer, 'It was by assigning this ethical task to politics, by subordinating politics to this ethical imperative, that Rousseau accomplished his truly revolutionary act' (66). In *From Rousseau to Lenin: Studies in Ideology and Society* (New York: Monthly Review Press, 1972), Lucio Colletti puts the revolutionary impact of Rousseau in even stronger terms. Rousseau is the first to assert the primacy of politics: 'Morality ... is therefore resolved for Rousseau into politics' (147). In *Nietzsche Contra Rousseau*, Keith Ansell-Pearson argues that Rousseau's originality resides in his attempt to legitimize the social order in a radically modern fashion 'on the basis of the primacy of the will of the autonomous individual' (22). In this way, Rousseau places the question of legitimacy – and free will – at the very centre of politics (34). The primacy of politics in the cultivation of the ethical will, along his rejection of the notion of original sin, would seem to confirm the radical incompatibility of Rousseau and Christianity, and assure his revolutionary originality. However, Nietzsche's emphasis upon both Rousseau's revolutionary uniqueness and his continuity with Christianity revolves around the profound debt Rousseau owes to the Christian notion of free will. Hannah Arendt criticizes both the Christian equation of freedom and free will which arose after the disintegration of the classical world and the role that free will assumes in modern political theory through Rousseau. See 'What Is Freedom?' in her *Between Past and Future: Eight Exercises in Political Thought* (Harmondsworth: Penguin Books, 1977), especially 156–65.

4 Machiavelli's critique of the subjectivism of Christianity anticipates both Rousseau and Nietzsche insofar as he argues that real *virtù* and love of freedom are enervated and undermined by Christianity. For Machiavelli's argument, see *The*

*Prince* and *The Discourses* (New York: Random House, 1950); see especially *The Discourses*, Book 1, chapter 11; Book 2, chapter 2.

5 Jean-Jacques Rousseau, *The Social Contract* (Harmondsworth: Penguin Books, 1968), 180, 182.

6 Ibid., 183.

7 Ibid., 184.

8 In *Natural Right and History* (Chicago: University of Chicago Press, 1953), Leo Strauss sees a strong similarity in the way that Rousseau and Nietzsche criticize modernity. First, he argues that there is a fundamental ambivalence in Rousseau's critique of modernity: it entails a return to the classical ideals of the city and virtue and yet it legitimates these ideals through a modern return to the independence of the state of nature. The tension between the return to the classical city and the return to the state of nature constitutes 'the substance of Rousseau's thought' (254). Strauss concludes that Rousseau's return to the city and classical virtue constitutes a radical advance of modernity: as the natural good, natural freedom remains the positive and legitimating measure that transcends the positive freedom of civil society (see 281–2, 290). Second, Strauss suggests that Nietzsche's critique of modernity is intimately related to the terms established by Rousseau and the 'first crisis of modernity' (252–3). However, I would argue that, while Rousseau 'abandoned himself to modernity' (252) by making free will the essence of freedom itself, Nietzsche surpassed modernity and Rousseau through a going-up to nature in *amor fati* and eternal return.

9 'The law of the heart' is the expression Hegel uses in *The Phenomenology of Mind*, (New York: Harper and Row, 1967) to characterize the moral sentimentalism of the Romantics influenced by Rousseau (390–400). Hegel also grounds the moral subjectivism (*Moralität*) of modernity and its revolutionary political consequences (e.g., egalitarianism) in Christianity. For Hegel's discussion of Christianity and the emergence of subjectivity, see *The Philosophy of History*, (New York: Dover Publications, 1954), 318–36; for his analysis of the French Revolution in relation to the principle of subjectivity, see *The Philosophy of History*, 438–57, and *The Phenomenology of Mind*, 599–610.

10 In *Nietzsche Contra Rousseau*, Keith Ansell-Pearson argues that Nietzsche addresses the modern ideology of revolution 'as a mere episode in the history of Christian-moral culture,' as 'secularizations of Christian teaching,' and 'buries the text of the Revolution under the weight of his interpretation' (34). This objection reflects that fact that Nietzsche criticizes Rousseau as a type, symbolic of modern conceptions of freedom as free will and equality.

11 Rousseau, *The Social Contract*, Book 1, chapter 6, 60.

12 Ibid.

13 Ibid., 61.

14  Ibid., Book 2, chapter 3, 73.
15  Ibid., Book 2, chapter 12, 99.
16  Ibid., Book 2, chapter 3, 73.
17  Ibid., Book 2, chapter 12, 99.
18  Robert Nisbet, *Tradition and Revolt*, 9. It is interesting to note how much Nietzsche's analysis of egalitarianism corresponds to de Tocqueville's in this regard: that equality and egalitarian democracy imply both an atomization of society and a concentration of power in the modern state. The radical novelty of egalitarianism that de Tocqueville, like Nietzsche, is concerned to emphasize is its inclination to both independence and servitude particularly because the latter is less apparent (Democracy in America, vol. 2: 304–5, 306, 312, 336, 337). Indeed, the very enthusiasm for individualism and equality brings with it a concentration and centralization of all power in the state: 'The notion of secondary powers [sectional associations] placed between the sovereign and his subjects occurred naturally to the imagination of aristocratic nations ... This same notion is naturally wanting in the minds of men in democratic ages ... whereas they conceive ... the notion of a single and central power which governs the whole community by its direct influence' (306). The Rousseauean passion to reduce society to a contract of abstract and equal individuals engenders the creation of an absolute and indivisible power: 'This never dying, ever kindling hatred which sets a democratic people against the smallest privileges is peculiarly favourable to the gradual concentration of all political rights in the hands of the representative of the state alone. The sovereign, being necessarily and incontestably above all the citizens, does not excite their envy, and each of them thinks that he strips his equals of the prerogative that he concedes to the crown' (312). Thus, the social atomism of egalitarianism gives rise to a tendency towards the centralization of all political power in the state and thereby facilitates an unprecedented form of despotism, which is so new that 'the old words *despotism* and *tyranny* are inappropriate' (336), because it combines the two tendencies of egalitarianism: independence and servitude. 'They devise a sole, tutelary, and all-powerful form of government , but elected by the people. They combine the principle of centralization and that of popular sovereignty; this gives them a respite: they console themselves for being in tutelage by the reflection that they have chosen their own guardians. Every man allows himself to be put in leading-strings, because he sees that it is not a person or a class of persons, but the people at large who hold the end of his chain' (337).
19  In *The Rebel: An Essay on Man in Revolt* (New York: Vintage Books, 1956), Albert Camus argues that Rousseau legitimizes an unprecedented form of political absolutism by deifying the general will as a principle of legitimacy, distinct from the will of all: the 'political entity, proclaimed sovereign, is also defined as

a divine entity' (115). There are many objections to this interpretation. Insofar as the identity of law and the individual free will is interpreted in a transcendental fashion, then one may argue, as Cassirer does in *The Question of Jean-Jacques Rousseau*, that Rousseau's general will is 'the form in which the will, as ethical will, really exists' (63), and its 'law is of such a nature that we must assent to it freely when we assimilate its meaning and can absorb this meaning into our own will' (62). Yet Cassirer concedes that the 'law as such possesses not limited but absolute power' (97). In *Nietzsche Contra Rousseau*, Ansell-Pearson suggests that the formalism of the general will testifies to its relevance as a principle of legitimacy in the absence of the regulative role custom in modern political life (92–3) and to its dangers inasmuch as the historical cultivation of the general will is 'forced to fall back on notions of coercion and constraint in order to save its argument on the moral transfiguration of humanity from total collapse' (94). The argument put forward by Strauss, in *Natural Right and History*, seems more compelling here; that is, for Rousseau, 'the novel understanding of moral freedom originated in the notion that the primary moral phenomenon is the freedom of the state of nature' (282). Natural freedom remains the positive standard of moral and political freedom, and Rousseau always maintains the possibility of transcendence of any given historical society by means of natural freedom as the positive standard (290). However, this means that Rousseau remains a victim of the basic antinomy of modern political philosophy – the struggle between natural freedom of the individual and ethical freedom of the citizen.

20 Nietzsche, on the other hand, emphasizes that morality and autonomy are mutually exclusive (cf. *GM* 2:2). See the discussion of this aspect of grand politics in chapter 3.

21 Immanuel Kant, *Groundwork of the Metaphysic of Morals* (New York: Harper and Row, 1964), 107, 114.

22 Ibid., 120, 127; cf. the discussion of freedom as a 'practical postulate' in Kant's *Critique of Practical Reason* (Indianapolis: Bobbs-Merrill, 1956), Book II.

23 Kant, *Groundwork*, 61.

24 Cf. *Groundwork*, 98, 108, 114; and *Critique of Practical Reason*, Theorem 3, 26–33, and Theorem 4, 33–42.

25 Kant, *Groundwork*, 98.

26 Ibid., 99.

27 Nietzsche's critique of Kant's radical separation of freedom and nature, and its crippling consequences for the realization of actions in happiness, corresponds in many respects to Hegel's critique of Kant's moral view of the world. In particular, Hegel emphasizes the unavoidable contradiction of *Moralität*: on the one hand, morality and nature are utterly antithetical realities that are completely indifferent to one another; on the other hand, in order to act and actual-

ize itself, the moral will must subordinate nature to itself in some postulated synthesis of morality and happiness. Cf. *The Phenomenology of Mind*, 616ff.

28 The intrinsic relationship between Goethe and Rousseau as modern types is emphasized in Nietzsche's claim that 'Faust was the highest and boldest reproduction of the man of Rousseau' (*SE*, 4). The modern ambivalence between classical form and romanticism's restless striving of the alienated individual, which preoccupied Rousseau, is embodied in Goethe's life and art. In *Conversations of Goethe with Eckermann* (London: J.M. Dent, 1930), Goethe characterizes the classical as 'strong, fresh, joyous, and healthy' and the romantic as 'weak, morbid, and sickly' (305). At the same time, the classical and the romantic forms are viewed as 'equally good' (335). More revealing of Goethe's attempt to integrate the two as forms of art and ways of life can be seen in the following passage in his *Criticisms, Reflections, and Maxims of Goethe* (London: Walter Scott Publishing, 1897): 'The so-called Nature-poets are fresh and newly-created talents, repelled by an over-cultured and stagnant art-period abounding in affectation. They cannot themselves evade the insipid and commonplace, and may thus be regarded as retrograde. Yet they are regenerative and open out the way for a further advance' (159). This insight anticipates Nietzsche's own form of overcoming modernity: 'ennoblement through degeneration' (*H* 1:224).

29 Faust ('the man of Rousseau') exemplifies the romantic sensibility which despises the affirmation of the moment as 'a bed of ease.' From *Faust* (1:87):

> If to the fleeting hour I say
> 'Remain, so fair thou art, remain!'
> Then bind me with your fatal chain,
> For I will perish in that day.

In contrast to the romantic flight from the present, Goethe, like Zarathustra, embodies a joy in the actual that affirms the eternity of moment, not as the negation of time, but as the plenitude of becoming at every moment. In 'Testament,' Goethe wrote:

> No thing on earth to nought can fall,
> The Eternal onward moves in all;
> Rejoice, by being be sustained.
> Being is deathless: living wealth,
> With which the All adorns itself,
> By laws abides and is maintained.
> ...
> Then bygone time gives permanence,
> The future lives, and in advance:
> Eternity the moment is.

30 'To the famous positivity of the negative Nietzsche opposes his own discovery: the negativity of the positive.' See Gilles Deleuze, *Nietzsche and Philosophy* (London: Athlone Press, 1983), 180.

## 6: Communion in Joy

1 For Heidegger's reduction of will to power to the will to will, see 'The Word of Nietzsche,' in his *The Question Concerning Technology and Other Essays* (New York: Harper and Row, 1977).
2 Henri Birault, 'Beatitude in Nietzsche,' in *The New Nietzsche*, edited by David B. Allison (New York: Dell Publishing, 1977), 229.
3 Ibid.
4 My interpretation of Nietzsche's will to power as *eros* which unites creativity, annihilation, and love in the will to squander and spend oneself has been strongly influenced by Georges Bataille's reading of will to power in *Sur Nietzsche* (Paris: Editions Gallimard, 1970), where he characterizes it as a 'love of evil' (166) or a 'will to evil' (169) because, in opposition to the good which values preservation and utility, Nietzsche's will to power is 'the will to spend, to play' (169) and 'the power to give' (190). Bataille argues that one cannot understand Nietzsche at all unless one has experienced this 'annihilation in victory': 'on n'a pas entendu un mot de l'oeuvre de Nietzsche avant d'avoir *vecu* cette dissolution éclatante dans la totalité.' (22).
5 Arthur Schopenhauer, *The World as Will and Representation*, 2 volumes (New York: Dover Publications, 1969), 1:38, 196.
6 Cf. Schopenhauer, *The World as Will and Representation*, 1:60.
7 Ibid., 1:38, 197; 1:33, 176.
8 Ibid., 1:34, 178.
9 Cf. Ibid., 1:34, 179.
10 Cf. Ibid., 1:36.
11 Ibid., 1:36, 185; 1:36, 186; cf. 2, chapter 31, 376–98.
12 Ibid., 1:36, 186.
13 Cf. Ibid., 1:66.
14 Ibid., 1:67, 376.
15 Ibid., 1:68, 378; 1:68, 379.
16 Hannah Arendt makes this point in her essay on the concept of freedom: 'Politically, this identification of freedom with sovereignty is perhaps the most pernicious and dangerous consequence of the philosophical equation of freedom and free will ... Under human conditions, which are determined by the fact that not

man but men live on the earth, freedom and sovereignty are so little identical that they cannot even exist simultaneously ... If men wish to be free, it is precisely sovereignty they must renounce.' See 'What is Freedom?,' in her *Between Past and Future* (Harmondsworth: Penguin Books, 1977), 164–5.

17 In contrast to Heidegger, Fink has specifically emphasized this aspect of Nietzsche's philosophy: 'Das Halkyonische im Bild des Übermenschen weist auf den *Spieler*, nicht auf den Gewalttater oder den technischen Giganten ... Aber der spielende Mensch ... lebt nicht in einer schweifenden Willkur der unbedingten Freiheit; er ist Mitspieler im Spiel der Welt and will zutiefst das Notwendige.' See Fink, *Nietzsches Philosophie* (Stuttgart: Kohlhammer, 1986), 189. See also Henning Ottmann, *Philosophie und Polilik bei Nietzsche* (Berlin: Walter de Gruyter, 1987), 378–80, 391–4.

18 Albert Camus, *The Rebel: An Essay on Man in Revolt* (New York: Vintage Books, 1956), 76.

19 Birault, 'Beatitude in Nietzsche,' 228–9.

20 In her book, *Nietzsche et la question politique* (Paris: Editions Sirey, 1977), Simone Goyard-Fabre describes this transfiguration through eternal return as physiological metamorphosis: 'L'antipodéité nietzschéenne est métaphysique avant que d'être politique. Elle n'invite pas à une évasion, mais à une conversion. La 'difference' politique n'a pas pour première condition un dépaysement géographique, mais une métamorphose physiologique qui est une transfiguration messianique' (129).

21 Birault, 'Beatitude in Nietzsche,' 230.

22 Plato, *Phaedrus* (Harmondsworth: Penguin Books, 1973), 57–66.

## 7: The Poetry of the Future

1 In *Friedrich Nietzsche and the Politics of the Soul: A Study in Heroic Individualism* (Princeton: Princeton University Press, 1990), Leslie Paul Thiele reveals the inadequacy of such an instrumentalist interpretation and its reduction of Nietzsche's 'spiritual politics' to a crude 'social politics' (220). However, his emphasis upon the 'heroic individualism' of Nietzsche's vision of politics tends to obscure the primacy of communion through joy in the actual – although Thiele does present the 'over-hero' as a joyful, albeit momentary, transcendence of the hero (cf. 185–94).

2 For an eloquent and insightful elaboration of Nietzsche's poetic spirit, see Barker Fairley's essay, 'Nietzsche and the Poetic Impulse,' in *Bulletin of the John Rylands Library*: 19, no. 2 (July 1935): 344–61. Similarly, in explicating

Nietzsche's critique of the correspondence theory of truth, Henri Birault also emphasizes the poetic character of his philosophy: 'Sur un texte de Nietzsche: "En quoi, nous aussi, nous sommes encore pieux,"' in *Revue de Metaphysique et de Morale* 67 (1962): 25–64.

# Works Cited

Allison, David B., ed. *The New Nietzsche: Contemporary Styles of Interpretation.* New York: Dell Publishing, 1977.

Ansell-Pearson, Keith. *An Introduction to Nietzsche as Political Thinker.* Cambridge: Cambridge University Press, 1994.

– *Nietzsche Contra Rousseau: A Study of Nietzsche's Moral and Political Thought.* Cambridge: Cambridge University Press, 1991.

Arendt, Hannah. *Between Past and Future: Eight Exercises in Political Thought.* Harmondsworth: Penguin Books, 1977.

Bataille, Georges. *Literature and Evil.* Translated by Alistair Hamilton. New York: Marion Boyars Publications, 1985.

– *Sur Nietzsche.* In his *Oeuvres complètes*, vol.6. Paris: Editions Gallimard, 1970.

Birault, Henri. 'Beatitude in Nietzsche.' In *The New Nietzsche*, edited by David B. Allison.

– 'Sur un texte de Nietzsche: "En quoi, nous aussi, nous sommes encore pieux."' *Revue de Metaphysique et de Morale* 67 (1962): 25–64.

Bloom, Allan. 'Interpretive Essay.' In *The Republic of Plato*, translated by Allan Bloom. New York: Basic Books, 1968.

Camus, Albert. *The Rebel: An Essay on Man in Revolt.* Translated by Anthony Cowers. New York: Vintage Books, 1956.

Canto, Monique. Introduction to Plato's *Gorgias*, translated by Monique Canto. Paris: Flammarion, 1987.

Cassirer, Ernst. *The Question of Jean-Jacques Rousseau.* Translated and edited by Peter Gay. Bloomington: Indiana University Press, 1963.

Colletti, Lucio. *From Rousseau to Lenin: Studies in Ideology and Society.* Translated by John Merrington and Judith White. New York: Monthly Review Press, 1972.

Dannhauser, Werner. 'Friedrich Nietzsche.' In *History of Political Philosophy*, edited by Leo Strauss and Joseph Cropsey. Chicago: University of Chicago Press, 1987.

Deleuze, Gilles. *Nietzsche and Philosophy*. Translated by Hugh Tomlinson. London: Athlone Press, 1983.

- 'Nomad Thought.' In *The New Nietzsche*, edited by David B. Allison, 142–9.

Detwiler, Bruce. *Nietzsche and the Politics of Aristocratic Radicalism*. Chicago: University of Chicago Press, 1990.

Dumont, Louis. *Homo Hierarchicus*. London: Paladin, 1972.

Fairley, Barker. 'Nietzsche and the Poetic Impulse.' *Bulletin of the John Rylands Library* 29 (1935): 344–61.

Fink, Eugen. *Nietzsches Philosophie*. Stuttgart: Kohlhammer, 1986.

Gadamer, Hans-Georg. *Philosophical Hermeneutics*. Translated and edited by David E. Linge. Berkeley: University of California Press, 1977.

Goethe, J.W. *Conversations of Goethe with Eckermann*. Translated by John Oxenford, edited by J.K. Moorhead, with an introduction by Havelock Ellis. London: J.M. Dent, 1930.

- *Criticisms, Reflections, and Maxims of Goethe*. Translated by W.B. Ronnfeldt. London: Walter Scott Publishing, 1897.

- *Faust*. Translated by Philip Wayne. 2 volumes. Harmondsworth: Penguin Books, 1949.

- 'Testament.' In *Johann Wolfgang von Goethe, Selected Poems*. Edited by Christopher Middleton. Boston: Suhrkamp/Insel Publishers, 1983.

Goyard-Fabre, Simone. *Nietzsche et la question politique*. Paris: Editions Sirey, 1977.

Granier, Jean. *Nietzsche*. Paris: Presses Universitaires de France, 1989.

- *Le problème de la Vérité dans la philosophie de Nietzsche*. Paris: Editions du Seuil, 1966.

Haar, Michel. 'Nietzsche and Metaphysical Language.' In *The New Nietzsche*, edited by David B. Allison, 5–36.

Hegel, G.W.F. *Hegel's Philosophy of Right*. Translated by T.M. Know. London: Oxford University Press, 1967.

- *The Phenomenology of Mind*. Translated by J.B. Baillie. New York: Harper and Row, 1967.

- *The Philosophy of History*. Translated by J. Sibree. New York: Dover Publications, 1956.

Heidegger, Martin. *Basic Writings*. Edited by David Farrell Krell. New York: Harper and Row, 1977.

- *Nietzsche*. 2 vols. Translated by David Farrell Krell. San Francisco: HarperCollins, 1991.

– *The Question Concerning Technology and Other Essays*. Translated by William Lovitt. New York: Harper and Row, 1977.

Hobbes, Thomas. *Leviathan*. New York: Collier Books, 1962.

Kant, Immanuel. *Critique of Practical Reason*. Translated with an introduction by Lewis White Beck. Indianapolis: Bobbs-Merrill, 1956.

– *Groundwork of the Metaphysic of Morals*. Translated by H.J. Paton. New York: Harper and Row, 1964.

Kaufmann, Walter. *Hegel: A Reinterpretation*. Garden City: Doubleday, 1966.

– *Nietzsche: Philosopher, Psychologist, Antichrist*. Princeton: Princeton University Press, 1974.

Lampert, Laurence. *Leo Strauss and Nietzsche*. Chicago: University of Chicago, 1996.

– *Nietzsche and Modern Times: A Study of Bacon, Descartes, and Nietzsche*. New Haven: Yale University Press, 1993.

– *Nietzsche's Teaching: An Interpretation of 'Thus Spoke Zarathustra.'* New Haven: Yale University Press, 1986.

Lukacs, Georg. *The Destruction of Reason*. Translated by Peter Palmer. Atlantic Highlands: Humanities Press, 1981.

Machiavelli, Niccolò. *The Prince* and *The Discourses*. New York: Random House, 1950.

Maffesoli, Michel. *The Shadow of Dionysus: A Contribution to the Sociology of the Orgy*. Translated by Cindy Linse and Mary Kristina Palmquist. Albany: State University of New York Press, 1993.

Nietzsche, Friedrich. *Selected Letters of Friedrich Nietzsche*. Edited and translated by Christopher Middleton. Chicago: University of Chicago Press, 1969.

Nisbet, Robert A. *Tradition and Revolt: Historical and Sociological Essays*. New York: Vintage Books, 1970.

Ortega y Gassett, José. *The Revolt of the Masses*. New York: W.W. Norton, 1957.

Ottmann, Henning. *Philosophie und Politik bei Nietzsche*. Berlin: Walter de Gruyter, 1987.

Plato. *The Laws*. Translated by Trevor J. Saunders. Harmondsworth: Penguin Books, 1970.

– *Phaedrus* and the *Seventh and Eighth Letters*. Translated by Walter Hamilton. Harmondsworth: Penguin Books, 1973.

– *Statesman*. Translated by J.B. Skemp. Indianapolis: Bobbs-Merrill, 1957.

– *Theatetus*. Translated by Robin A. H. Waterfield. Middlesex: Penguin Books, 1987.

– *Timaeus* and *Critias*. Translated by Desmond Lee. Middlesex: Penguin Books, 1971.

Polin, Raymond. 'Nietzsche und der Staat oder Die Politik eines Einsamen.' In *Nietzsche, Werk und Wirkungen*, edited by Hans Steffen. Göttingen: Hans-Dieter Ullrich, Vandenhoeck, and Ruprecht, 1974.

Ricoeur, Paul. *History and Truth*. Translated by Charles A. Kelbley. Evanston: Northwestern University Press, 1965.

Rousseau, Jean-Jacques. *The Social Contract*. Translated by Maurice Cranston. Harmondsworth: Penguin Books, 1968.

Schopenhauer, Arthur. *Essays and Aphorisms*. Translated by R.J. Hollingdale. Middlesex: Penguin Books, 1970.

- *The World as Will and Representation*. Translated by E.F.J. Payne. 2 volumes. New York: Dover Publications, 1969.

Schutte, Ofelia. *Beyond Nihilism: Nietzsche Without Masks*. Chicago: University of Chicago Press, 1984.

Stevens, Wallace. *The Collected Poems of Wallace Stevens*. New York: Vintage Books, 1990.

Strauss, Leo. *Natural Right and History*. Chicago: University of Chicago Press, 1953.

- 'Note on the Plan of Nietzsche's *Beyond Good and Evil*.' In his *Studies in Platonic Political Philosophy*. Chicago: University of Chicago Press, 1983.

Strong, Tracy B. *Friedrich Nietzsche and the Politics of Transfiguration*. Berkeley: University of California Press, 1975.

Thiele, Leslie Paul. *Friedrich Nietzsche and the Politics of the Soul: A Study of Heroic Individualism*. Princeton: Princeton University Press, 1990.

Tocqueville, Alexis de. *Democracy in America*. 2 volumes. Translated by Phillips Bradley. New York: Vintage Books, 1945.

Voegelin, Eric. *Plato*. Baton Rouge: Louisiana State University Press, 1966.

Warren, Mark. *Nietzsche and Political Thought*. Cambridge: MIT Press, 1988.

# Index

affirmation: as the play of creation 141–3; as releasing past into becoming 40–7, 144, 145, 146; as retroactive 41, 42, 44, 45, 143, 146, 150. *See also* creation; eternal return; redemption

affirmative *ethos* 5, 6. *See also ethos*

Alcibiades 94

alienation: and Christianity 111; and modernity 102–4; and social contract (Rousseau) 114

*amor fati* 3, 8, 50, 69; and creativity 98; and eternal return 37, 95, 145, 149–52, 156; and joy in the actual 8, 9, 98, 140, 145, 150–2; and will to power 8

*ananke* 80, 88

Ansell-Pearson, Keith 159n25, 166–7n2, 167n3, 168n10, 169–70n19

Arendt, Hannah 167n3, 172–3n16

aristocratic radicalism 12, 157n4

Aristotle 66

'artist's faith' 104. *See also* historical sense

atomism: Nietzsche's critique of 27, 29, 30, 145; social 101

atopia: and distinction of politics and polity 11; and genuine philosopher 75, 76, 87, 91; and grand politics 10, 11, 12, 14, 47, 71–3, 74, 75, 76, 91, 155, 156; and problem of interpretation 15–18, 20, 21, 158n18, 163n10, 163–4n13; vs utopia 11, 15, 71, 72, 75, 155, 163n12

authority: and transformation of custom into morality 54–6

autonomous individual 49, 50, 59–62; as child-spirit 70, 98, 163n4; as noble 62–3, 67–73, 75–6, 93, 98–9. *See also* immoralism; noble type

autonomy 53; and equality 112–15, 117; and immorality 50, 61, 63–73, 93, 98, 99, 121; and legitimacy 113, 115; moral (Kant) 117–21; moral (Rousseau) 113–16. *See also* immoralism; innocence of becoming

Bataille, Georges 157n1, 172n4

becoming: joy of 36, 42, 44

Birault, Henri 130, 146, 148, 160n14, 160n15, 173–4n2

Bismark 10

Bloom, Allan 165n27

Borgia 96, 97, 166n29